SAKI:
A Life of Hector Hugh Munro

With Six Short Stories Never Before Collected

A. J. LANGGUTH

Simon and Schuster/New York

Library of Congress Cataloging in Publication Data

Langguth, A. J., date.
  Saki, a life of Hector Hugh Munro.

   Bibliography: p.
   Includes index.
   1. Munro, H. H. (Hector Hugh), 1870–1916.   2. Authors,
English—20th century—Biography.   I. Munro, H. H.
(Hector Hugh), 1870–1916.   II. Title.
PR6025.U675Z76   823'.912 [B]   81-5607
                                      AACR2

ISBN 0-671-24715-8

Contents

1

The Background
(1870-1887)

Had the victim been anyone but his mother, the irony to the story might have made Saki smile:

It was the winter of 1872, and Mary Frances Munro, who had borne three children in less than three years, was pregnant again. Despite the primitive conditions of northwest Burma, where her husband was an officer in the British military police, each of the earlier births had been successful. But when she was found to be carrying yet another baby, her husband took Mary back to his family's home in Devonshire so that her fourth delivery might be less hazardous than the others.

There, in the safeness of western England, she was struck down by the kind of fate that her youngest child grew up to respect and celebrate. On a quiet country lane, a runaway cow charged Mary Munro. The shock caused a miscarriage that took the new life and her own. Left suddenly motherless were Ethel Mary, born in April 1868; Charles Arthur, born fifteen months later; and another boy, a frail child who had been born in Akyab, Burma, on December 18, 1870. It was this son, named by his parents Hector Hugh Munro, who would take the pen name Saki.

Their father, Charles Augustus Munro, would soon be due back at his post. For him to look after three small children in Burma seemed impracticable. His wife had been a rear admiral's daughter, a Mercer, and although Charles Munro enjoyed good and affectionate relations with her family, he decided to entrust his charges to his own widowed mother and his two spinster sisters. The Munro clan had been innovative in neither namings nor careers. Charles Augustus' father had also been a military man, Colonel Charles Adolphus Munro, and the Colonel had christened his daughters with the feminine versions of their brother's name—Charlotte and Augusta. Besides these sisters, the new widower had two brothers, Wellesley and Hector Bruce Munro. But the household that was to raise his three children was exclusively female.

Before he returned to duty, Charles Augustus took a large villa for his six dependents in Pilton, not far from the town of Barnstaple. George Orwell, whose early life would duplicate aspects of Hector's, called the station of the Munros "lower-upper-middle class." Its members were unlikely to own land but they kept up their aristocratic pretensions by going into the professions or the military service instead of into trade. With four hundred pounds a year, Orwell wrote, one's gentility was somewhat abstract. "Theoretically, you knew how to shoot and ride, although you had no horse to ride and not an inch of ground to shoot over." Nonetheless, Charlie and Hector were brought up to be gentlemen, and throughout their lives their claim to the title was not challenged.

Except for an unyielding strictness in observing the Sabbath, Lucy Jones Munro, the children's grandmother, was gentle with them. Left to herself, she might have provided Hector and the others with a calm and loving home. But power in the new household lay with her bustling and willful daughters. Ethel called them "turbulent," but she waited until after their death to do so. Writers may remember the good times of their childhood but they make use of the bad. Few grandmothers figure in Hector's work; instead, his stories abound with aunts, whose emotions range from unfeeling to diabolic.

One mark of the Victorian Age that had come from the Queen herself was a dislike for children, and her advisers at court had fretted over her evident hostility toward Edward, her son and heir. The same imperialism that had assumed the burden of ruling over ungrateful peoples across the world found it distasteful to confront the small savages on their own hearths. The culture responded by encouraging a wholehearted repression of children for their own good, a task to which Aunt Charlotte and Aunt Augusta brought an awesome vigor. Charlotte Maria was the elder by fifteen years, but that distinction regularly surprised their acquaintances. Since Augusta Georgina was even more headstrong and domineering, people assumed that she had been practicing at it longer. Augusta had a talent for being able to work herself into a passion over the most trivial annoyance. The look in her eye, the rage in her voice, could make Ethel shiver. When the children came to live with her, she was not even middle-aged, only about thirty. But already her fury was elemental.

Charlotte was always called "Tom." According to a family story, which the children found impossible to credit, she had been a tomboy in her youth. For whatever high spirits or rebelliousness she had once displayed, she was now spending her life in atonement. By the time the children entered her domain, she was a model maiden lady of a certain age and more certain opinion.

If the sisters had ever negotiated a truce to their own bickering, the children's life might have been still worse. As it was, they watched the daily skirmishes and scored the victories. Early in his life, Hector developed a gift for mimicry, and he could recreate a battle to its final salvo. Aunt Tom won whenever Augusta took to her bed for the day with a sick headache. As Hector wrote later, "Aunts who have never known a day's illness are very rare; in fact I don't personally know of any." Augusta's triumphs were more subtle, marked by a faintly amused smile that the children came early to recognize and hate.

"The meaning smile" they called it, and it played over Augusta's face whenever she caught one of them in a display of emotion. The smile was warning enough for the children to make themselves invulnerable by tamping down any demonstration of feeling.

The ill will between the aunts was rumored to have sprung from jealousy. As a young woman, Aunt Tom had sojourned in Scotland for an extended period, and when she returned to Devon she found Augusta growing up pretty and petted. In response, she launched the hostilities that persisted through their lifetime together. At least that was the story from family members troubled enough by the feud to invent a reason for it.

Perhaps the true explanation for the aunts' ferocity was that both of them had inherited the Munro martial temperament in an age when women found few acceptable outlets for it. Male or female, the Munros were proud of the antiquity and the courage of their clan. The line could be traced to the reign of Alexander II in the thirteenth century, and by the eighteenth century the Munros were known for their invariable support of the established government. By the end of that century, Munros were going to India to build the empire, not always without sacrifice. In 1792, the only son of General Hector Munro was slain during a hunting expedition; one of his companions reported that he "heard a roar, like thunder, and saw an immense royal tiger spring on the unfortunate Munro, who was sitting down. In a moment his head was in the beast's mouth, and he rushed into the jungle with him with as much ease as I could lift a kitten, tearing him through the thickset bushes and trees, everything yielding to his monstrous strength." That catastrophe sufficiently caught the public imagination to be commemorated with a Staffordshire ornament titled "The Death of Munrow." It showed the victim with his head deep in the tiger's mouth, and for several decades it sold briskly.

But women could not hope to tame India or be mauled there. Nor did an unmarried woman of the period usually make her way to Bristol or London to find employment and a room of her own. She stayed at home, and, in the case of the Munro sisters, made the worst of it. Ethel

Munro grew up wondering why her aunts had not been consumed by their hatred. At the least, she decided, all that passion was worthy of a grander cause—a crusade, an *auto da fé,* a world war. Whatever its origin, by the time the children arrived, the women's hostility ran so deep that no gesture could escape an imputation of malice. Should Aunt Tom return from Barnstaple with a hen that she had bought for two shillings and sixpence, Augusta could not rest until she had located a plumper chicken priced twopence cheaper.

"There was something alike terrifying and piteous in the spectacle of these frail old morsels of humanity consecrating their last flickering energies to the task of making each other wretched." Hector was describing here the evils that could lie beneath the calm of an English countryside. He was writing of witches, not aunts, and, writing as an adult, he could tell the difference.

Broadgate Villa, forty-five years old when the Munros came to it, was a part of the estate of Broadgate House across the road. The villa was fronted with brick and set off by ten-foot pillars to shield French windows that would otherwise have looked out on the yard. Shut off from the sun, the interior seemed to the children a murky and stagnant tomb. At the top of the house there was one enchanted room but, the source of its enchantment, it was always kept locked. Outside, the house was flanked front and rear by walled gardens, but the children were permitted to play only on grassy slopes at the front, where rooks, which Hector detested, perched in the two towering elms. The children were forbidden to enter the kitchen garden at the back with its apple and quince trees and patches of gooseberries and raspberries. The aunts might be as stern as Jehovah but they were considerably less trusting, and they had no faith that the children could resist the fruit. Years later, Hector wrote, "People talk vaguely about the innocence of a little child but they take mighty good care not to let it out of their sight for twenty minutes."

The countryside as the children grew up was an expanse of green fields and copses made for romping, but that too was disallowed. Aunt Augusta led her charges only down the narrow road to the village of Pilton, where she collected a few purchases and the day's petty gossip. On these excursions, they never cut through a pasture. Augusta was afraid of cows, given the misfortune that had befallen her sister-in-law.

The house always seemed fetid because Augusta also harbored a deep misgiving about fresh air; particularly in winter she barred every window against it. Any conflicting theories of hygiene or health she rejected with a word she had made up when the dictionary had nothing strong enough to convey her contempt. "Choc rot," Augusta said. But again she may have been operating less on whim, as Ethel believed, than from a misguided concern. The family doctor in Barnstaple, whose opinions were never to be contested, had pronounced that all three children were too frail and high-strung to survive. Hector was the most doomed of the lot. His spirit of excitement and daring rattled his slender rib cage and by the end of each day had drained his limited store of energy.

In one regard this extreme delicacy proved a boon. The aunts punished him less than they did either Charlie or Ethel, and they treated him on occasion to unwonted endearments. As a boy, his skin was flawless, his eyes were a cool gray, his hair blonder than could have been suspected in his later years, after a dark Celtic strain had asserted itself. The aunts called him "Chickie" and fussed over him as though he were indeed a little bird. Ethel, being a girl, was also spared the birch. It was Charles, older, stronger, and unmistakably male, who got whatever beatings were left over.

As an adult, Hector could take a sanguine attitude toward the punishments he had escaped. "Now, my mother never bothered about bringing me up," one of his characters announced. "She just saw to it that I got whacked at decent intervals and was taught the difference between right and wrong; there is some difference, you know, but I've forgotten what it is."

Charlie could hardly afford to be so blithe, and, to console him, his uncles let him understand that he had been singled out for Augusta's wrath because he reminded her of a former beau who had, in the parlance of the day, led her on before marrying elsewhere. Or it may have been simply that, aged four and red-haired, Charlie was already too much the rooster for the Broadgate henhouse.

His immunity from whippings spurred Hector to greater exploits and led Ethel and Charlie, despite their seniority, to acknowledge him as master of their revels. Even when they had not misbehaved, the children were sent to bed early each night, but such quivering natures in so staid a surrounding had to find an outlet, and theirs came after hours. The aunts knew that one board in the boys' bedroom squeaked, and they counted on it to alert them to any unseemly play upstairs. But the children incorporated the loose plank into their games and skipped across it as they crept about in their nightly amusements.

During the day, fun could be a bit more overt. Ethel's first memory of Hector in the Broadgate nursery was of him plunging a long-handled hearth brush into the open fire and then, brandishing it as a sword, chasing her and Charlie around a small table shouting, "I'm God! I'm going to destroy the world!" Round and round the table they went, the older children too afraid of the flames to break away and dash to the door. Hector's face was alight with glee as he tried to fulfill the gospel as it was preached at Broadgate. The clamor at last brought to the scene Aunt Augusta, who scolded all three children impartially.

The vengeful side to religion probably had been Augusta's contribution in the first place. Aunt Tom had that dreaded vitality and indifference to the sensibilities of others that allowed her to trample over every opponent but her sister. To Aunt Tom's credit, at least in Ethel's eyes, she adored Hector so long as he didn't invade the flower beds or tear up the kitchen garden. And her piety was suspect. For years, the children had believed that Aunt Tom knew the Psalm Book by heart, until one day when Ethel discovered she was only muttering in her throat while she used the time to inspect through long-distance spectacles the wardrobe of her fellow worshipers. Augusta's faith was more demanding. Not for her Sunday mornings at the modest Pilton chapel, which was distinguished only for having had its tower knocked down by Cromwell in 1649. Augusta traveled instead to Barnstaple on Sunday evenings for the High Church ceremony at St. Anne's, two centuries older than the chapel and the place where John Gay had once studied.

Augusta's punctiliousness did not, however, betoken an awe for either the clergy or their institution. "She was one of those people who regard the Church of England with patronizing affection, as if it were something that had grown up in their kitchen garden," wrote Hector of a duchess, who, with her unearned authority, often served in his early stories as a surrogate aunt.

Augusta did her best to impress the children with her intimacy with the Almighty. When a thunderstorm broke, she let them understand that it was a divine warning about their past excesses. But because she had invested all terror in herself, the tactic did not work, at least with Hector. He did not grow up fearing God or, on the evidence, believing in Him.

Although the aunts each favored rigid discipline, they differed on specific taboos. If Augusta told the children, "Don't play on the grass," Aunt Tom felt compelled to say, "Children, you're not to play on the gravel." In a story about an aunt traveling by train with her three young wards, Hector noted, "Most of the aunt's remarks seemed to begin with 'Don't' and nearly all of the children's remarks began with 'Why?' " In his own life, he found it safer to ask Aunt Tom "Why?" and to heed Aunt Augusta's "Don't."

A quarter of a century after Augusta's death, Ethel Munro produced an epitaph for her that was untempered by time or charity: "A woman of ungovernable temper, of fierce likes and dislikes, imperious, a moral coward, possessing no brains worth speaking of, and a primitive disposition. Naturally the last person who should have been in charge of children."

Compared to that, Ethel's summation of Aunt Tom was almost loving—"a colossal humbug, and never knew it."

As a writer of fiction, Hector could revenge himself even more gratifyingly, although he too waited until Augusta was securely buried. "It was her habit," Hector wrote of a similar tyrant, "whenever one of the children fell from grace, to improvise something of a festival nature from which the offender would be rigorously debarred; if all the children sinned collectively they were suddenly informed of a circus in a neighbouring town, a circus of unrivalled merit and uncounted elephants, to which, but for their depravity, they would have been taken that very day."

That story, "The Lumber-Room," ends with the aunt richly humiliated. She has fallen into a rain-water tank in the gooseberry garden, and young Nicholas, who has been kept home because of naughtiness, refuses to come to her help. " 'I was told I wasn't to go into the gooseberry garden,' said Nicholas promptly.

" 'I told you not to, and now I tell you that you may,' came the voice from the rain-water tank, rather impatiently.

" 'Your voice doesn't sound like aunt's,' objected Nicholas; 'you may be the Evil One tempting me to be disobedient. Aunt often tells me that the Evil One tempts me and that I always yield. This time I'm not going to yield.'

" 'Don't talk nonsense,' said the prisoner in the tank; 'go and fetch the ladder.'

" 'Will there be strawberry jam for tea?' asked Nicholas innocently.

" 'Certainly there will be,' said the aunt, privately resolving that Nicholas should have none of it.

" 'Now I know that you are the Evil One and not aunt,' shouted Nicholas gleefully; 'when we asked aunt for strawberry jam yesterday she said there wasn't any. I know there are four jars of it in the store cupboard, because I looked, and of course you know it's there, but she doesn't, because she said there wasn't any. Oh, Devil, you *have* sold yourself!'

"There was an unusual sense of luxury in being able to talk to an aunt as though one was talking to the Evil One, but Nicholas knew, with childish discernment, that such luxuries were not to be overindulged in. He walked noisily away, and it was a kitchen-maid, in search of parsley, who eventually rescued the aunt from the rain-water tank."

In that incarnation, Aunt Augusta was only embarrassed. Charlie and Ethel both recognized her again in "Sredni Vashtar." There, when Hector called up his childhood fury, she did not survive the result.

Although the doctor was proved wrong in all three cases and the Munro children were surviving if not exactly thriving, they were held to their tedious isolation. They even came to appreciate the Sunday church services in Pilton with their granny and Aunt Tom. At least the outing gave them a glimpse of other children. The rest of the week their confinement was so total that Charlie grew up wondering whether it had been a tactic to prevent them from having a standard of comparison that would show them how badly they were being treated. Once a year their isolation ended for one afternoon when the young Munros were permitted to attend a Christmas party. Before the event, pledges were extracted that they would not eat any of the delicacies. When the children asked why, they were told "for fear of consequences." Even so, on their return their Grandma Lucy gave them hot brandy in water in case the party had in some way contaminated them.

To the aunts, food was not only the staff of life but also another rod of punishment. Later in life Hector acquired a reputation for his appreciation of *haute cuisine,* but his was an acquired taste and not acquired from the aunts. "Hors d'oeuvres have always had a pathetic interest for me," said one of Hector's earliest creations. "They remind me of one's childhood that one goes through wondering what the next course is going to be like—and during the rest of the menu one wishes one had eaten more of the hors d'oeuvres."

Their single taste of high life came on the children's birthdays, when they were served roast duck, a favorite with all three. Duck was also on the menu when guests who had come from afar were asked to stay on for lunch; local visitors were expected to get home and feed themselves. One day the mere aroma of roast duck got Charlie again into Aunt Augusta's bad graces. It had been drilled into the children that although the choice for guests would include duck and cold beef, when they were asked their preference, they were to choose the beef, which was cheaper. On this occasion, Augusta was carving two ducks and the children's grandmother was tending the beef. When all of the adults had been served, Augusta began the charade of asking the children for their choice.

"Cold beef," said Ethel.

"Cold beef," said Hector, already a fatalist. The art of life, he later wrote, was the avoidance of the unattainable.

But Charlie, who never learned to dissemble as effectively, voted his appetite. "Roast duck, please."

The wrath of Augusta turned on him. "What did you say?" She punctuated the question with a sharp kick under the table.

"Oh, cold beef, please."

"What extraordinary children, to prefer cold beef to duck!" The visitor was either unobservant or quietly twitting Augusta. But the judgment was correct. They were extraordinary children, living in the refuge of their own company, given to fanciful dreams and shared stories and so appalled by the constant battling of the aunts that among themselves they never gave vent to a curse or a quarrel. Because she loved beetles in all their forms, the boys called Ethel "Scarabee." Much later, when she came to be a trial to her brother Charlie, he betrayed the strain on his patience only by addressing her as Ethel rather than by her name from the nursery.

Since a favorite punishment was to take away the children's toys, it was lucky for the young Munros that they shared a daring and fertile inventiveness. The boys loved to penetrate the forbidden garden at the rear and to ravage a storeroom where the canned fruits were stored. Once they smuggled into their sleeping quarters a jar of tamarinds, the juicy pods used in chutney, and hid the jar deep in one of Augusta's trunks amid the folds of a black silk dress. For a time the sticky jar was safe there, until the day Augusta went hunting for her dress. Forty years later, Ethel could remember the way Augusta's bellow had resounded throughout the villa, and she decided that in an earlier life Augusta must have been a dragon. It was a jaundiced view of reincarnation that Hector shared. As one of his characters put it, "How frightfully embarrassing to meet a whole shoal of whitebait you had last known at Prince's! I'm sure in my nervousness I should talk about nothing but lemons."

Aunt Tom gave the children one gift: by reading aloud to them, she bred a love of books that lasted throughout their lives. A favorite was *Robinson Crusoe,* the tale of a man barely more isolated than they were. *Johnnykin and the Goblins,* by Charles G. Leland, fascinated Hector at age seven. Ethel assumed it was his Celtic blood that predisposed him to goblins and woodland sprites. Major Munro had a lifetime habit of giving books as presents: at the age of fifteen he had given his older sister, Tom, *The Lay of the Last Minstrel.* Now he sent Ethel a copy of Lewis Carroll's *Through the Looking Glass,* inscribed "Ethel M. Munro. From Papa." All three children loved the Alice books, and Hector's first publishing success was to come with one of the few skillful parodies of her adventures.

The children closed their ears, however, to such stories of moral uplift as *Sanford and Merton.* And when the aunts taught them a maxim that ran, "I will not number in my list of friends the man who needlessly sets foot upon a worm," all they seem to have succeeded in doing was raise speculation among the children over the word "needlessly." As he was growing, Hector was becoming more mischievous and developing a slyness to shield him from the consequences. One summer, friends of the aunts came to visit, bringing along a child named Claud. "So good a boy," the aunts said, preparing the young Munros for their companion. "He always does what he is bid." Hector could have had Claud in mind when, in one of his best stories, he described a young girl as being "horribly good."

Claud and his mother arrived, and Hector contrived to rush the good but malleable boy from naughtiness to naughtiness until, when at last the visitors left, Aunt Tom pronounced a perfect benediction on the day: "Claud is not the good child I imagined him to be."

By now Hector was fighting at the annual Christmas parties, rough-and-tumbling with other little boys. Once he was roused to battle, even Augusta's warnings could not hold him in check. Ethel, who would have found excuses for Hector if he had killed the Queen, explained years later that he was a sweet child and not at all pugnacious but that after the long rustication at Broadgate Villa his native ebullience demanded an outlet.

At one Christmas party, a play was staged, the first that Hector had ever seen, and it launched a love affair that proved durable but one-sided. When the play's villain appeared, Hector tried to climb onto the stage to throw his frail force on the side of righteousness. Later, when right and wrong were less clearly delineated, Hector usually found justice in the positions of the political conservatives. It was a tendency Ethel traced back to the age of seven. The children had been taken to Barnstaple for the announcement of parliamentary elections, and they were installed in seats at a window across the street from the venerable Golden Lion Inn and Public House. The contest had been hard fought, but the winner was a lord's son who was suspected of being radical. Hector, feverish from the crowds and the oratory, was inconsolably irate at the outcome. From then on, he would be enthralled with politics, indignant at its practitioners and alert to its potential for ridicule. "The art of public life," he concluded later, "consists to a great extent of knowing exactly where to stop and going a bit farther."

When time came for their schooling, Charlie and Ethel were taken to a dame's school on Ebberley Lawn in Barnstaple, where they were taught to read and write. Sickly Hector was kept at home, and throughout his youth he spent very little time in formal schooling, which may explain why, except for one grim chapter in his first novel, he set none of his scenes in a school. He had a character explain, "Anything that is worth knowing one practically teaches oneself, and the rest obtrudes itself sooner or later."

If Ethel had guessed that her eight-year-old brother was destined to have a career in the arts, she would have predicted that it would be as a painter. Hector did write a bit for "The Broadgate Paper," which the children produced.

But he loved to draw animals, preferably animals getting the better of a human being. Since the aunts did not care for pets, the young Munros came to care for them passionately, and their first enthusiasm was for a fine retriever that Augusta had acquired and then kept chained for years to an outbuilding in the back yard. The dog was taken for a walk only twice a year, and Ethel was sure he was eating his heart out. She looked on the animal and concluded that, after all, life for her and her brothers could be worse. The dog's salvation came, as did the children's, whenever Major Munro came home on a six-week leave. He took the dog, delirious with happiness, for exercise, and he unleashed his children for picnics in the open air and excursions to the neighboring farms, where there were pigs for the boys to ride and haystacks to slide down. Aunt Augusta might be a despot but she was a woman; the children had nothing to fear from her when the Major was in residence. The boys' only other male companionship came from the annual visits of their bachelor uncle, Wellesley, a civil servant in the India Office at Whitehall. He took Hector around the countryside to fish and to sketch. Although Wellesley had heard from his maiden sisters all about the shocking behavior of the Munro children, his impression was much different. After one visit, he wrote to his mother that "the children are never naughty with me because I take the trouble to amuse them."

And by encouraging Hector to draw, Wellesley was abetting an artistic impulse that the aunts chose to ignore. On one dreary afternoon that Ethel never forgot, the children resolved to pass the time by painting pictures and then holding an exhibition. They let their granny and the aunts know about the grand showing. But when the moment came, some of the late inspirations still wet on the walls, no one from downstairs came up to see them. It was a disappointment but hardly the first. The children appointed themselves judges and patrons, and Hector, eight years old, won the only prize he would ever be awarded—Ethel's worn copy of Aesop's *Fables*.

Besides art and politics, Hector was developing a taste for history. By now, Charlie had been dispatched to a preparatory school at Exmouth; it was no mark of favor. For Ethel and Hector, a young woman came each day to read one page from a history book. When they reached the English Civil War, one of those rare disagreements arose between sister and brother, and it was resolved as simply as they always would be. "You must take the Roundheads' part," Hector informed Ethel. He was eight years old; she was eleven.

Ethel protested. "But I would rather be a Royalist."

"We can't both be Royalists, so you must be a Roundhead."

Hector had chosen the romantic side, the Cavaliers, partisans of Charles I, as opposed to Cromwell's Roundheads who showed their support for Parliament by wearing their hair close cropped. Ethel wondered afterward how it happened that, having been coerced into it, she should have remained a Roundhead all her life. The children began to take their allegiances seriously. Hector would denounce a Roundhead victory until Ethel rose up to abuse the Royalists. Finally their governess put a stop to the game. But after she had left for the day, Hector and Ethel hauled down the history book and fought again each bloody battle.

They had hit upon a primitive version of what Hector was later to name "The Schartz-Metterklume Method." In his story, Lady Carlotta, who has missed her train at a country station, is mistaken for a governess, a Miss Hope, by an imposing local matron who seizes her up and takes her home to tutor her four children. Throughout Hector's fiction, autocrats seldom proved a match for aristocrats, and Lady Carlotta decides to play along. " 'I shall talk French four days of the week,' she tells her astonished hostess, 'and Russian in the remaining three.'

" 'Russian? My dear Miss Hope, no one in the house speaks or understands Russian.'

" 'That will not embarrass me in the least,' said Lady Carlotta coldly."

Once installed in the house, she teaches history by a method of her impromptu invention. Just before she is sacked, Lady Carlotta sends the two older sons to carry away the small daughters of a nearby lodge keeper. Hearing the resulting row, the boys' mother storms on the scene. " 'Wilfred! Claude! Let those children go at once. Miss Hope, what is the meaning of this scene?'

" 'Early Roman history; the Sabine women, don't you know. It's the Schartz-Metterklume method to make children understand history by acting it themselves; fixes it in their memory, you know. Of course, if, thanks to your interference, your boys go through life thinking that the Sabine women ultimately escaped, I really cannot be held responsible.' "

It took thirty years, but at last Hector had provided Ethel and himself with a governess worthy of them.

At the age of nine, Hector suffered an illness that was diagnosed as brain fever. Later the family assumed that he had contracted meningitis, an inflammation of the membranes of the brain. During his sickness, Ethel observed again what she had noticed during lesser ailments: whenever a child fell ill, the scoldings stopped and the aunts were transformed into solicitous nurses.

A year later, when Hector was taken to Barnstaple to sit for a formal photograph, there were no visible traces of the ailment. He had not contracted "spotted fever," the worst form his illness could have taken, which left the body darkly discolored. He was instead a beautiful child with fine features and large clear eyes. Everything about him was neat and precise. Only the cast of his mouth looked slightly twisted, as though it took effort to preserve its solemn thin line.

Spending so much of his time in their company, Hector had become adept at making himself agreeable to old ladies. One afternoon Aunt Tom took him and Ethel to call upon a very old woman with a daughter who was, in Ethel's phrase, not a chicken. At a lull in the conversation, Hector approached the hostess and, at his most courtly, remarked, "And so I hear, Mrs. Simpson, that Miss Janet is away in Scotland, enjoying all kinds of debauchery."

All other conversation stopped. As the nervous laughter died away, Aunt Tom stepped in to apologize. "That dreadful Roman history! That's where he picks up these extraordinary expressions!"

Major Munro had been home on another quadrennial leave when his mother began to fail, and, possibly to compensate the children for the inevitable loss, he selected a real governess for Ethel, not a neighbor woman with a smattering of history. This woman was also expected to teach Hector until he was strong enough for the preparatory school at Bedford, and the coming of this stranger to their home had both children agog. "After all," said Hector, "we have only the grownups' word for it that she is a *real* governess, but how are we to know? We must put a pea under her mattress and see how she sleeps."

Ethel had also read Hans Christian Andersen, and she fell in with the plan. Before the new governess arrived, the children inserted a dried pea under her mattress.

The next morning they asked how she had slept.

The young woman seemed both surprised and pleased by their concern. "Very well indeed, thank you."

"Ah, then you can't be a *real* governess," said Hector. His sister reported afterward that he had been "greatly disappointed." But he was now twelve years old, and his response sounds more like the straight-faced teasing of the child who has seen through St. Nicholas. In any case, after they confessed what they had done, the children found the governess a fresh and amusing friend. But it was a short-lived friendship. Aunt Augusta was convinced that the governess was using her dark eyes to hypnotize her, and she persuaded her dying mother to dismiss the woman.

When the children's grandmother succumbed at the age of seventy-four, the one soothing female presence in the house was gone. Lucy Munro left an estate valued at twelve hundred pounds; it was to be held in trust, with the interest to support Aunt Tom and Augusta. A tactful mother, Lucy even made provision for disposal of the fund should either daughter marry. The sobriety that attended her grandmother's death made Ethel, now fourteen, the more aware of how little time they had ever spent in Kent with their mother's family, the Mercers. Grandfather Mercer, the retired admiral, was jovial and fun-loving, and he had passed on those qualities to his daughters. He also indulged in practical jokes, which all three young Munros loved, and which Hector first emulated and then made the foundation for much of his best work. Really, Ethel decided, the Mercers were more their sort than doughty Aunt Tom and impossible Aunt Augusta.

With governess and granny both departed, the children were left to themselves for a few months, which Ethel remembered as a sad time. Then a new governess, chosen by Augusta, put in a term with them, and when it was over Hector was pronounced enough recovered to follow his brother to the Pencarwick school in Exmouth. By that time Charlie had gone on to Charterhouse, the distinguished public school that had moved a decade earlier from its quarters in a former Carthusian monastery to a new site in Surrey. From India their father sent a regular allowance for Charlie's keep, but the aunts resolutely refused to forward it to the school. To his adolescent chagrin, Charlie was one of two boys in the entire institution who did not have a "home bill" for tuck and treats.

It was a deprivation Hector was soon to share. For a minor infraction over the holidays, Aunt Augusta sent him back to Exmouth with no pocket money, and Hector was forced to admit to the masters that he was to have no allowance for the entire term. But at home he had resourceful allies. Charlie had not yet returned to Charterhouse, and he and Ethel sold the books they had been given for Christmas to a second-hand dealer. Secretly they mailed the proceeds by postal money order to Hector. Then Charlie wrote to their father, who in turn sent a message taking Augusta to task.

When Hector was ready to enroll at a public school, the aunts would not permit it to be Charterhouse. Charlie was convinced that they wanted to keep the boys, now adolescents, separated. Together they might scheme against their elders; united they might even carry off their rebellion. At fourteen, Hector went instead to Bedford Grammar School, where he stayed four terms. Bedford at that time had become stagnant over the three hundred years since its licensing by Edward VI. A period of growth began several years after Hector left it in 1886, but during his time he had the company of fewer than two hundred boys, many of them the sons of Anglo-Indian officers. Because the school had long recruited among young men who intended to follow their fathers into the military, it was called a nursery of the Empire. Ethel, who recorded that Hector had been happy at Exmouth, gave no such testimonial to Bedford. She noted only that his school reports read: Plenty of ability but little application.

In his stories a public school education is assumed, not depicted, and whatever letters Hector wrote to Ethel during that period she destroyed, first to stop the family from prying and later to thwart posterity from doing the same. We are told often and properly that no writer should be mistaken for one of his fictional characters. But in what Hector wrote of Comus Bassington there seems to have been an element of self-description: "Gaiety and good looks had carried Comus successfully and, on the whole, pleasantly, through schooldays and a recurring succession of holidays." Since Hector left Bedford early, if he took part in the traditional punishments at the school, he was more caned against than caning. More likely he was spared that particular initiation but not others. When he did touch on school years in his fiction, he was flippant and sly: "You can't expect a boy to be vicious till he's been to a good school."

On his Easter holiday at home, Hector went bird-nesting with some of the Pilton neighbors and began a collection of eggs that survived—fragile, dusty, and not attributed to their collector—in small museums around the nearby town of Bideford for eighty years. Collecting gave Hector an excuse at last to ramble through the Devonshire countryside, and its celebrated beauty, combined with his own maturing feelings, gave an erotic charge to the landscape whenever he recalled it. "There was a charm, too, even for a tired man, in the eerie stillness of the lone twilight land through which he was passing, a grey shadow-hung land which seemed to have been emptied of all things that belonged to the daytime, and filled with a lurking, moving life of which one knew nothing beyond the sense that it was there. There, and very near. If there had been wood-gods and wicked-eyed fauns in the sunlit groves and hillsides of old Hellas, surely there were watchful, living things of kindred mould in this dusk-hidden wilderness of field and hedge and coppice."

When she was well past eighty, Ethel Munro took as her duty the correcting of facts about Hector's early life, which, she believed, were being misstated. The offender was Graham Greene, whose essay on Saki, she believed, had confused his own unhappy childhood with her brother's. By this time Miss Munro was not at all robust and she had begun to suspect that men with umbrellas were lurking behind doors, ready to smite her. Yet her letter to the *Spectator* was entirely cogent and assured. What is this extraordinary delusion, she asked, on the part of some writers that Saki's childhood was miserable? She and her brothers had most definitely enjoyed growing up in their grandmother's house. All three of them "being blessed with amazing vitality and love of mischief rode over all storms with an appetite for the next! When forbidden visits were paid to the lumber-room, with knowledge of the punishment that would follow if found out, those visits were naturally intensely exciting, and exciting events were continually happening in that house. I should say that the stern discipline he had in early life, far from causing a 'cruel element' in him, was enough to make him detest cruelty in any form but not enough to stop him from writing about it. He once said to me that, in spite of our strict upbringing and having no other children to play with, he was glad of it, as otherwise we should never have been original."

Graham Greene rose to this unequal combat with a letter to argue that if there was a delusion on the matter, it was based on Ethel Munro's own writing. He then cited from Ethel's memoir instances of the psychic harm that had befallen the children. Ethel was not a woman to suffer contradiction. A week later, she was back in the *Spectator*'s letters column. Saki, she insisted, was a Puck to the end of his life. "I cannot imagine a miserable Puck.

"Aunt Augusta being such an unlovable character we extended only a lukewarm sort of liking to her. But a miserable boy would have had no liking at all for her."

Belatedly Greene saw the folly in prolonging this exchange, and there was no further correspondence. Both had, in their different ways, been right. Emotionally, those early years were sufficiently withering to deserve being called miserable. And, equally surely, Hector did not complain about that period to his sister or to anyone else. He learned instead to humiliate his oppressors in a dozen ingenious ways on the printed page. At the times when his rage returned and rose past the level of mere bile, he could send Augusta forth to be devoured by beasts. With those weapons at his command, he hardly needed to seek relief in a sigh or a reproach.

2

The Forbidden Buzzards
(1887-1893)

Hector's age and his enrollment at school had extended his vistas, and then his father returned to England and effectively ended the aunts' sway over Hector's life. Charles Augustus Munro had risen to the rank of colonel; he seems to have retired in his mid-forties primarily to see at last to his motherless children. As a first treat in their new life together, he took Hector and Ethel to the beach at Etretat in Normandy. There they met amusing French and Russian young people of their own age, "playmates" Ethel called them, although she was nineteen at the time and Hector two years younger. At Charterhouse, Charlie was being exposed to a doctrine that valued maturity, but at Broadgate Villa there had been no incentive to grow up and Hector was betraying no intention of doing so. In France, he launched upon an unimpeded frolic that lasted, with one dire interruption, for the next ten years.

Ethel was never direct in discussing any of Hector's

lapses from propriety, but when she wrote that the bathing at Etretat would certainly have shocked the aunts, she had found a way to suggest that she, Hector, and their young companions were swimming in less than full Victorian rig. It also seems certain that the Russians among their new friends inspired a taste for that country that led Hector to learn its language and later find a way to see it for himself. The Munros' next trip abroad was designed to be educational; the colonel took his high-spirited children to Dresden, where Charlie joined them on his school holiday.

The family settled into a *pension* filled with American guests and run by a German woman. From landlady and fellow tourists, Hector formed opinions of the two countries that he carried through his life. That he should be contemptuous, resentful, and more than a little afraid of Germany was one more mark of the Late Victorian Age. Throughout Hector's childhood the Prince of Wales had shown his distrust of Bismarck; by 1888, when the Prince's nephew ascended to the German throne as Kaiser Wilhelm, the entire British royal family had come to see him as a potential enemy.

Hector's patronizing attitude toward Americans was also typical of his time. Ethel said that his complaint was the distressing materialism among Americans, but more often his target was their pretension to culture. At one point he wrote of a village vicar's daughter that she was generally conceded to be an intellectual because "she had been twice to Fécamp to pick up a good French accent from the Americans staying there." In another story, an aunt and her nephew speak of launching a protégé into society: " 'One is so dreadfully under everybody's eyes at Homburg. At least you might give him a preliminary trial at Etretat.'

" 'And be surrounded by Americans trying to talk French? No, thank you. I love Americans, but not when they try to talk French. What a blessing it is that they never try to talk English.' "

In Germany, the uproarious nature of his children, their rebellion against their upbringing, became fully revealed to Colonel Munro, along with a previously suppressed taste for practical jokes. Ethel boasted that well into his twenties Hector looked like a boy, and his predisposition to boyish jokes survived even longer than that. Hector discovered in Dresden that the floor below their rooms was occupied by a girls' school. Ethel pronounced all the girls ugly. Either she had a keenly developed esthetic sense or an equally keen determination to keep her father and her favorite brother to herself. With Hector, that jealousy would prove to be misplaced. But on the one occasion that Colonel Munro considered marrying again, Ethel was so horrid to the prospective bride that the match came to nothing.

Hector once announced that there were only two classes that could not help taking life seriously—schoolgirls of thirteen and Hohenzollerns. Now, in the hope of outraging one and possibly both groups, he and Charlie waited for the Colonel to go out and then fashioned out of his decorous bathing costume a dummy stuffed with paper and clothes. For a face, they took a sponge and topped it with a jaunty hat. Their intent was to alarm the girls. But when they lowered the figure to the balcony below, the schoolmistress was entertaining a minister, and it was they who saw the apparition. Immediately from downstairs came a note of complaint. The German landlady, even when exposed to the dummy's attractions, had not been moved to laugh. All that saved the situation was a burst of convulsive laughter from a stiff American woman staying at the hotel who had never before betrayed a sign of humor. That, along with a note of apology from the Munros, closed the affair.

During those months, Hector began to spend more time by himself. He walked in Dresden's parks scouting for birds, and, despite his limited command of the language, he made acquaintances. One method was to stop a German and draw in the gravel an outline of the bird he was pursuing. The German would then furnish the bird's name and suggest where it might be found. Certainly Hector's interest in birds was a genuine one; it had begun in Devonshire and it endured through the last article he was to write. It is also true that a handsome foreigner, young for his years, would find in a park congenial responses from those men he chose to approach.

Charlie left Dresden for the crammer's classes that might get him into the army, and Colonel Munro took Ethel and Hector throughout Germany and into eastern Europe. They trooped through many galleries, where Hector developed a sharp but tolerant eye for the Philistine. Of an English couple he later wrote, "They leaned toward the honest and explicit in art, a picture, for instance, that told its own story, with generous assistance from its title. A riderless warhorse with harness in obvious disarray, staggering into a courtyard full of pale swooning women, and marginally noted 'Bad News,' suggested to their minds a distinct interpretation of some military catastrophe. They could see what it was meant to convey, and explain it to friends of duller intelligence."

Long before this grand tour, Hector had been alert to cruelty, and when he noted the appeal that St. Sebastian held for German artists he and Ethel began a count to establish which city showed him skewered most often in its museums. Berlin won with eighteen. Otherwise it was the old towns—Nuremberg, Pskoff, Prague—that pleased Hector best and spoke to a developing taste for the medieval. In Potsdam, Hector and Ethel refused to inspect the Palace of Sans Souci until they found a custodian who could point out the graves of Frederick the Great's chargers and palace dogs, and at Wallenstein's castle in Prague, they each leaned out from a window, held fast by their father, that they might know how opposition councilors felt when they were thrown from that window. Hector recalled the sensation when he wrote a melodramatic playlet: "The bravest man's courage might be turned to water, looking down at death from that horrid window. It makes one's breath go even to look down in safety; one can see the stones of the courtyard fathoms and fathoms below. I assure you the glimpse down from that window has haunted me ever since I looked."

The last leg of their tour took them to Innsbruck and across the border to the village of Davos, where they stayed for several months. Davos had two distinctions: its clean mountain air, regarded as healthful for tuberculars; and John Addington Symonds, the British man of letters. On alighting in Davos when Hector was still a child, Symonds had written an essay on the town that made its reputation among English travelers. In choosing Davos, Colonel Munro may have considered its benefits to Hector's health. Certainly both he and Ethel had been exhausted by their travels, and they spent their first week at the Hotel Belvedere resting, drinking quantities of fresh milk, and evaluating their fellow guests. Once they had recovered, they did not again interrupt their round of tennis, horseback riding, dancing, and paper chases. They climbed the mountains and tracked marmots to the peaks. Only an avalanche, Ethel said proudly, could have stopped the whirl of two young people drunk on Swiss air and liberty.

After the rigors of the East, hotel life in a modest resort agreed with Colonel Munro. An affable and courtly man, adept at social pleasantries and the kissing of ladies' hands, he was equipped to win hearts and he had certainly won over his children. Hector came to love this man who represented benign deliverance, and Ethel, sharp in her other summations, doted on him. One of the regulars at Davos called Colonel Munro "the Hen that hatched out ducklings," but there is no sign that he was ever anything but proud of his spirited offspring.

When middle-aged men sometimes sought out the young Munros, Ethel preferred to think that they wanted to become extra fathers for her and for Hector. She seems to have been unaware that she had become a striking young woman with a brisk and military carriage, a trim figure, and the Munros' finely etched features. Combined with her sense of fun, boisterous and inappropriate as it may sometimes have seemed, there were ample reasons, none of them avuncular, for men to draw around her. Hector, who would have been emanating a different sort of appeal, became a regular visitor at the Symonds' house. There he played chess, discussed heraldry, and put to use those light conversational skills he had acquired in the company of spinsters. Symonds was the first literary man

Hector had come to know; his translation of Benvenuto Cellini's autobiography had been much admired, and he had recently finished a seven-volume appraisal of the Italian Renaissance. Symonds had decided views on literature, and Hector was accustomed to informal tutoring. The older man railed against slovenly workmanship and those writers ignorant of their duty to seek always the right phrase. He deplored the influence of the German language, "that great curse," and admired satire. His enthusiasms were for the Greeks, Cervantes, Swift, Dryden, and Pope.

Symonds was also openly homosexual, and his honesty could make him a trial to men unwilling to join the ranks of his crusade. It was to deter Symonds from his persistent rummaging for homoerotic imagery in his poems that Walt Whitman bragged in a letter of having six illegitimate children and, should that not end the matter, a bastard grandchild. Symonds was no less skeptical than Whitman's subsequent biographers, but despite his inconvenient candor he charmed most visitors with moods that swung between the heartiness of an alpine scout and an introspection that bordered on the morbid. Robert Louis Stevenson, something of an authority on riven personalities, was a great admirer of Symonds, and since he returned gladly to the cottage, Hector shared the fascination.

Colonel Munro saw to more formal instruction— learned lectures from neighboring scholars and painting lessons from a Professor Meyer, whose specialty endeared him to his two English students. Meyer painted only birds of prey, and under that congenial influence Hector drew an eagle, life size, bringing a seagull to her young. In lesson days, Meyer often became prey himself. Ethel and Hector would creep into his bedroom and ambush him with pillows until the assault turned into a romp through his studio. Always practical and not a little ingenuous, Ethel gave him high marks for these indulgences. He understood the needs of the young Munros, she said. They simply had to burn off their excessive vitality before they could settle down to a calm session of sketching.

When winter fell across Switzerland, snow and sleighs and picnics beneath the noontime sun made Davos even more attractive than it had been in summer. Wellesley

Munro brought Charlie for a holiday, and after weeks of fancy dress and masked balls, theatricals and tea dances, the Colonel's children could agree that they had never spent a happier winter together. Ethel dressed in sheet and pillow case for one of the impromptu dances and decided that no girl had ever had a better coming-out. Through it all, though mannerly to a fault, Hector was of the party and apart from it. With the trace of a smile, he observed those women whose complexions he described later as nomadic but punctual and the young men who smoothed their hair dubiously, as though it might strike back. He was on his way to formulating the credo that youth should suggest innocence but never act on the suggestion.

The following spring, when the family returned at last from Davos, Colonel Munro took a house at Heanton, only four miles from Barnstaple and the aunts but far removed from the tyranny of Broadgate. The Colonel, whose one lapse from fitness was his devotion to cheroots, nailed open the windows of his bedroom, and his children were finally breathing fresh air in Devon. When the aunts came to visit now, one at a time and unmistakably on sufferance, they got a better reception than Ethel thought they deserved. But the horrors of Broadgate seemed far away, and there was time now to notice that Tom and Augusta were, after all, loyal to their friends and generous to the poor.

Possibly it was that latter virtue, blooming in such otherwise inhospitable soil, that made so deep an impression on Hector and led him to abhor miserliness. He became adroit at detecting any sign of meanness and at mocking it in his stories: "Mrs. Jallatt didn't study cheapness, but somehow she generally attained it," and Louisa Mebbin "adopted a protective elder-sister attitude towards money in general, irrespective of nationality or denomination. Her energetic intervention had saved many a rouble from dissipating itself in tips in some Moscow hotel, and francs and centimes clung to her instinctively under circumstances which would have driven them headlong from less sympathetic hands."

For Charlie, life beyond the family was again beckoning. Bad eyesight had kept him from the army but he was accepted for the Burma police and soon after his twenty-second birthday he left for Asia. As Ethel told it, any sense of loss at Heanton seems to have been well compensated by the addition to the household of Gillie, a fox terrier, the first dog the younger Munros had ever been permitted as their own. Hector drew the dog baying and again standing vigilant and foursquare, and in the second sketch Victorian prudery did not deter him from rendering the sex of his male dog. But it was a rare acknowledgment of nature's plan and one he did not carry over into his fiction.

If there was to Charlie something of a dog's open and loyal nature and if Ethel's attachment to cats would later suggest a thorough identification with them, there was developing in Hector a fondness for skulking animals capable, should the need arise, of inflicting rough justice. Better even than polecats, ferrets and tigers was that most feline of the dog family, the wolf, slinking with yellow-eyed cunning toward its prey.

There were no wolves for him near Heanton, but in the two years Hector spent there he picked up a knowledge of the occult mysteries that had lived on among the old women. Only thirty years before his birth and well within Aunt Tom's lifetime, ancient Nanny Oram, the last known witch in Barnstaple, was still casting her spells. And there were even greater mysteries to rural life that intrigued Hector. One of his first stories concerned an actual Devon feud: One farm woman had thrown clods of earth at a hen from a neighboring farm that was scratching up her onions. Although they were isolated from other neighbors, the two families did not speak for many years, and the feud outlived its protagonists. Elegiacally, Hector drew the moral that "other onions have arisen, have flourished, have gone their way, and the offending hen has long since expiated her misdeeds and lain with trussed feet and look of ineffable peace under the arched roof of Barnstaple market."

Late in life, Hector could sound almost Elizabethan as he sang the glories of England's verdant countryside. More often, when he recalled Devon he sided with his character who found the country scene charming enough but went on to protest, "Those cherry orchards and green meadows, and the river winding along the valley, and the church tower, peeping out among the elms, they all make a most effective picture. There's something dreadfully sleepy and languorous about it, though; stagnation seems to be the dominant note. Nothing ever happens here; seed-time and harvest, an occasional outbreak of measles or a mildly destructive thunderstorm, and a little election excitement about once every five years, that is all we have to modify the monotony of our existence. Rather dreadful, isn't it?"

After two years of that languor, with studies overseen by the Colonel, the Munros left Heanton and, after a season in London, went again to Davos for the winter. Hector was twenty-two, but before he was faced with considerations of a career there would be one last burst of spirited indulgence. Not surprisingly given their ages, Hector and Ethel's sport took on a new tone, and their pranks became more ambitious. One target was the Hôtel des Iles, the swankest spot in Davos, and to assail it Hector organized a group of other bored young people into what was called a "Push." One night Ethel and five others from the Push stood guard while Hector painted drunken devils across the walls of the hotel in enamel of red and blue.

When Hector made literature from these pranks, daubing a hotel must have struck him as too literally child's play and he made no use of the episode. Instead, he invented a young man avenging himself for being trapped at a dull house party:

"I've been carefully brought up, and I don't like to play games of skill for milk-chocolate, so I invented a headache and retired from the scene. I had been preceded a few minutes earlier by Miss Langshan-Smith, a rather formidable lady, who always got up at some uncomfortable hour in the morning, and gave you the impression that she had been in communication with most of the European Governments before breakfast. There was a paper pinned on her door with a signed request that she might be called particularly early on the morrow. Such an opportunity does not come twice in a lifetime. I covered up everything except the signature with another notice, to the effect that before these words should meet the eye she would have ended a misspent life, was sorry for the trouble she was giving, and would like a military funeral. A few minutes later I violently exploded an air-filled paper bag on the landing, and gave a stage moan that could have been heard in the cellars. Then I pursued my original intention and went to bed. The noise those people made in forcing open the good lady's door was positively indecorous; she resisted gallantly, but I believe they searched her for bullets for about a quarter of an hour, as if she had been a historic battlefield."

Less impromptu, and probably less amusing to everyone but Ethel, who called it "a gorgeous hoax," was the crowning stunt of Hector's stay in Davos. It was the custom for each of the town's four hotels to plan the season's dances, concerts and plays. The guests took up a collection to cover expenses and asked everyone from other hotels to join them for the events. When Hector played the part of an old lawyer in a play called *Two Roses,* all the other foreigners in Davos were invited to attend. The only exception to this bonhomie arose at the Hôtel des Iles. Its guests refused to spend money on anyone outside their walls and proposed to give themselves instead a banquet with the funds they had raised.

This display of miserliness roused Hector to action. Purporting to be the hotel's management, he wrote to request the company of guests throughout Davos at the Hôtel des Iles on the evening of March 20, 1893, to see a production of *Box and Cox.* The Push understood that play to be risqué and thus irresistible to any continental visitor.

The parallels between that stunt, as it happened, and the one Hector wrote some years later show the pattern to his imagination. The victim must give himself airs, as did both Miss Langshan-Smith and the guests at the hotel, who kept to themselves, Ethel sneered in the Highland tongue, because they "were so unco' guid." Any discomfiture to the unwitting participants must be kept to a humane minimum. Although Hector sent his bogus invitations around Davos to Russian princes, German barons, and Italian counts, he omitted any of the distant chalets, to save their inhabitants the expense of hiring a sleigh. This fine calibration of indignities persuaded some later critics that Hector's stories were never really cruel. In neither life nor art did the perpetrator feel impelled to watch the confusion he had produced. To remain on the premises would be gauche, akin to laughing at one's own jokes. The young prankster who hangs the sign on the lady's door goes off to bed, and Hector overruled Ethel, who wanted to stay and see the fun, and insisted they remain in their rooms. He explained that he lacked the nerve to look innocent. Instead, they delegated a Scots girl from the Push to go in their place, and she reported afterward about the uproar when the unbidden guests arrived. It had all gone exactly as Hector planned. A full contingent of Germans came from the Kurhaus, and when the hotel looked around for a culprit the blame fell on an American, a man who knew nothing of the Push.

That prank ended Hector's protracted boyhood. With his father and sister he returned to Devon, where the aunts had taken separate lodgings—Tom in Pilton, where they stayed, Augusta in Barnstaple. April passed, and May. Then, in June, Hector went off to his first job.

3

A Touch of
Realism
(1893-1894)

Since Charlie had adapted easily to Burma and the military police, Colonel Munro had arranged a similar post for Hector. Hector's frail health, like Charlie's weak eyes, kept him out of the army. But if he could not wear a scarlet coat, he could at least serve his Queen as a policeman. Did Hector wish to go to Burma? He wished to please his father, but the evidence suggests he would have preferred that the pleasing be nearer home. Later he said that he had been writing of himself when he sent a fictional young man to a distant land because there was no life for him in London. And sometimes he could make a joke of the dilemma:

"At the age of eighteen, Bertie had commenced that round of visits to our Colonial possessions, so seemly and desirable in the case of a Prince of the Blood, so suggestive of insincerity in a young man of the middle-class. He had gone to grow tea in Ceylon and fruit in British Columbia, and to help sheep grow wool in Australia. At the age of twenty he had just returned from some similar errand in Canada, from which it may be gathered that the trial he gave to these various experiments was of the summary drum-head nature."

But when he drew a truer self-portrait, Hector did not disguise the misery he had felt. He sent his young hero to the theatre during one of his last nights in London, and as the sparkling crowd enjoyed one evening among others that would be equally brilliant, the boy reflected on his fate:

"He would be in some unheard-of sun-blistered wilderness, where natives and pariah dogs and raucous-throated crows fringed round mockingly on one's loneliness, where one rode for sweltering miles for the chance of meeting a collector or police officer, with whom most likely on closer acquaintance one had hardly two ideas in common, where female society was represented at long intervals by some climate-withered woman missionary or official's wife, where food and sickness and veterinary lore became at last the three outstanding subjects on which the mind settled, or rather sank. That was the life he foresaw and dreaded, and that was the life he was going to."

One woman offers him the best sort of sympathy, none at all. "I'm not going to talk the usual rot to you about how much you will like it and so on," she says. "I sometimes think that one of the advantages of hell will be that no one will have the impertinence to point out to you that you're really better off than you would be anywhere else."

That was written after Hector had been to Burma and returned, and it is likely that curiosity at least prevented his mood from being quite so bleak on the eve of his departure. Whatever his misgivings, Hector boarded a ship for Rangoon.

William Somerset Maugham, born four years after Hector, was to find a treasury of stories in ocean crossings; Hector found none. Rudyard Kipling, born five years before Hector, had mined west Asia for material. His *Barrack-Room Ballads* had appeared the year before Hector reached Burma, but their success did not tempt Hector to exploit the exotic background that fate and his father had put in his hands. Possibly the difference lay in their expectations. Kipling had been a precocious journalist of seventeen when he set out for Lahore and he intended to make his way as a writer. Hector's social class decreed that he could not be Tommy but he seemed destined to be no more than Tommy's commanding officer.

Hector's tour started with the proper civilities. Charlie met him in Rangoon, where they were both invited to stay with a friend of their father's, the Deputy Inspector General of Police. The 1890s were a quiet period for the English in Burma. Twenty-five years earlier, about the time of Ethel's birth, Major Munro had lived through a tightening of restrictions on British officers, and when word spread that the police could no longer act so high-handedly, there had been a brief upsurge in petty crime. But by the time Hector arrived, cattle theft had been dropping year by year and opium arrests in a typical district were running fewer than twenty. A notorious outlaw, Nga Kyaw, had recently been arrested in the Singu district, where Hector was to be stationed, and headquarters anticipated that his capture would reduce the cases of dacoity—the Hindu word for robbery by armed gangs.

Life for the British officer might be improving but the native troops still found their lot a hard one. In any given year it was cholera, not crime, that was killing half of the policemen who died, and the patrolmen who survived were badly armed and dressed—in Mandalay they wore patched uniforms—and were shivering from the cold. At least, the British inspectors recommended, the natives should be issued greatcoats and serge suits. A want of *esprit de corps* affected the English officers as well, but there was one blessing and not a small one. The inspectors' report concluded, "There is, however, wonderfully little real bad crime in the force."

From his letters as Ethel edited them, Hector does not appear to have taken great interest in Burmese police routine. Since Ethel shared his fascination with animals, he dwelt largely on creatures wild or tamed. But even with Ethel's excisions, or because of them, Hector's are exemplary letters, always clever, often brilliant. And since no young man writing in rustic quarters would rewrite his correspondence for an indulgent older sister, the letters speak as well of a quick, careless flow to his thoughts.

Almost immediately the heat felled Hector, and lying in bed he was beset by the noises of Singu. "There are the children: the little brats have a remarkably good time of it, they are never whacked or scolded, and they take a deliberate pleasure in howling at the slightest opportunity; you never heard such yells, they throw all their little heathen souls—if they have any—into the performance. I should like to spank them for ever, stopping, of course, for meal times."

Even after he had recovered and was exploring his territory, the children could unnerve him. "When I was out of the district if a child howled in any neighboring hut men were sent at once to stop it; if it wouldn't stop it was conducted out of earshot; wouldn't you like to do that with English brats! How rabid the mothers would get!"

Children were not the only offenders. "Then during the night, the frogs and owls and lizards have necessarily lots to say to each other, and whenever my pony hears another neigh she whinnies back, and being a mare always insists on having the last word. As to the dogs they go on at intervals during the twenty-four hours, like the Cherubim which rest not day or night."

Given the slumberous climate, Hector was amused but not surprised to catch a dog barking and yawning at the same time. It reminded him, he wrote to Ethel, of a person saying responses in church. But through all the din, one noise was always welcome to the homesick young officer —the whistle of the steamboat bringing mail from England.

For the first time in his life, Hector had servants of his own choosing, not cooks and cleaning women from the towns around Barnstaple, and throughout the rest of his life he was seldom without a houseboy. His stories make explicit the attraction that Hector felt for naked brown boys, and in one passage he seemed to define his ideal: "about sixteen years old, with dark olive skin, large dusky eyes, and thick, low-growing blue-black hair." In Burma, although he might have been able to find such a youth as an intimate, he was representing his country and his father in a post not far from his elder brother. His letters to Ethel speak of a patronizing affection for his servants but they do not, in what she preserved, suggest more.

"I am agreeably surprised with my servants, they are quick, resourceful, seem honest, and are genuinely attached to their master's interests; of course they are more or less stupid, they are human beings."

"My boy continues to give satisfaction in regard to cooking. The way he serves chicken up as beefsteak borders on the supernatural."

"I hope you will have no more bother with servants; my boy gives me notice about once a month but I never think of accepting it; if he doesn't know a good master I know a good servant, to paraphrase an old remark. He has a great idea of my consequence and of his own reflected importance; I sent him to a village with a message, and Beale A.S.P., who was expecting some fowls from that place, asked if they had been sent by him; he told me he should never forget the tone in which he said 'I am Mr. Munro's boy!' Civis Romanus sum."

Duty took Hector to other remote towns—Mwéhintha, Madaya, Mandalay—usually to provide a ceremonial presence at native rituals. "No martyr," he complained to Ethel, "ever suffered so much on account of religion as I have." Through it all, Hector maintained his instinct for the telling detail and a sense of twin ridiculousnesses, his own and that of his hosts. Of one festival he wrote, "The hours of performance are from 10 a.m. to 3 p.m., and from 8 p.m. to 6 a.m. There are two bands. During performances my dining-room is a sort of dress-circle, so I have to get my meals when I can. As to sleep, it's not kept on the premises, while the heat is so great that you could boil an egg on an iceberg. There are also smells. The acting is not up to much but the audience are evidently charmed with it. I go to bed at ten, finding two hours quite enough, but when I get up at 5:30 the audience are applauding as vigorously as ever."

The presence of a handsome young sahib from England excited local hearts, and Hector was flattered by the interest even as he bemoaned it to Ethel. "The 'Mandalay Herald' had an article on the Toungbein Pwe, in which it was said, 'Many Europeans graced the proceedings with their presence, but the one who was most generally noticed and admired was a policeman in full khaki uniform.' This is rough on me, as I was the only European in uniform there."

"Then I am worried to death by princesses; some of the native magistrates' wives are relatives of the ex-king and fancy themselves accordingly. One old lady, who carries enough jewels for twenty ordinary princesses, takes an annoying interest in me and is always pressing me to partake of various fruits at all hours of the day. She asked me, through Mrs. Carey, how old I was, and then told me I was too tall for my age, obligingly showing me the height I ought to be . . . I told her that in this damp climate one must allow something for shrinkage, and she did not press the matter."

"Tell Mrs. Byrne there is no immediate danger of my marrying a Burmese wife; there was a woman at Singu— ugly as a Fury—who, I think, had great hopes, but my boy, always ready to save me trouble, married her himself; he had one wife already, but that was a trifle. I impress upon him that he may have as many as he likes, within reasonable limits, but no babies."

Speaking the dialects of Burma was not a requirement for a Queen's officer, and Hector was wry about his own limitations. "I was in terror lest they might expect a speech, and how could I get up and tell this people, replete with the learning of Eastern civilization, 'This animal will eat rice'?"

Animals, true ones, were the chief compensation for his desolation and the lack of agreeable companions. Hector found on his doorstep a large silver-gray squirrel, which he described as tame and "snoomified," and soon afterward a duckling. "I thought of putting it with the squirrel, but the latter looks upon everything as meant to be eaten and the duck had broad views on the same subject, so I thought they had better live in single blessedness."

The flowers of the area were a disappointment. Except for one species of magnolia, he found none of the flora to his liking. But he did discover a curious pony to record, one with zebra markings on its legs. "Darwin believed that the horse, ass, zebra, quagga and hemonius were all evolved from an equine animal striped like the zebra but differently constructed, and in his book on the descent of domestic animals he attached great importance to some zebra-like markings which he observed on an Exmoor pony; so my discovery may be of some interest."

Hector's favorite beasts, however, were a more commonplace pony—which he named the Maid of Sker, after a novel by R. D. Blackmore, the writer more famous for *Lorna Doone*—and a baby tiger, which he had to leave behind at Singu when he traveled. "I found the tiger-kitten quite wild; pretended it had never seen me before, so I had to go through the ceremony of introduction again. I soon made it tame again, and we have great games together. It has not learnt how to drink properly yet and immerses its nose in the milk, then it gets mad with the saucer and shakes it, which sends the milk over its paws, upon which it swears horribly."

"The kitten throws off the cat and assumes the tiger when it is fed; I have to throw it its food (generally the head of a chicken) and then bolt; it is making the day hideous with its growling now, as I gave it the head and the wing, and it is trying to eat both at once."

"The tiger-kitten has had a nice cage made for it, with an upstairs apartment to sleep in, but every afternoon it comes out into my room for an hour or two and has fine romps. It would be a nice pet for you but it would be an awful trouble sending it—it might die—and it won't be safe when it grows up. It goes into lovely tiger attitudes, when it thinks I'm looking."

"An old lady came to the hotel last week, one of those people with a tongue and a settled conviction that they can manage everybody's affairs. She had the room next to mine—connected with a door—and I was rather astonished when the proprietor came that evening, and with great nervousness, said that there was an old lady in the next room and er—she was rather er—fidgety old lady and er—er—er—there was a door connecting our rooms. I was quite mystified as to what he was driving at but I answered languidly that the door was locked on my side and there was a box against it, so she could not possibly break in. The proprietor collapsed and retired in confusion; I afterwards remembered that the 'cub' had spent a large portion of the afternoon pretending that this door was a besieged city, and it was a battering ram. And it does throw such vigour into its play. I met the old lady at dinner and was greeted with an icy stare which was refreshing in such a climate."

That night the tiger cub found its voice and began to roar. The more Hector tried to quiet it, the louder the noise became. Hector was sure that on the other side of the door, the old woman was reciting the litany of the Church of England. "Then I heard the rapid turning of leaves, she was evidently searching for Daniel to gain strength from the perusal of the lion's den story; only she couldn't find Daniel so fell back upon the Psalms of David. As for me, I fled, and sent my boy to take the cage to the stable. When I came back I heard words in the next room that never came out of the Psalms; words such as no old lady ought to use."

Confronted with sights that were generally thought repellent, Hector took pride in maintaining his equanimity. That detachment, hard won from contending with Augusta's meaning smile, does not seem to have been the pose of a young man feigning urbanity. Hector's was already a character that observed and noted, took a muted delight in the underside of life and yet could respond to errant flashes of nature's beauty. "I am very interested in watching the vultures which congregate in great numbers just here; there are three kinds, 2 brown and 1 black; the latter is a fine bird and very much cock of the walk; whenever one comes to a carcase the brown birds have to leave off eating and wait till he's finished, trying to look as if they weren't in the least hungry. Usually only one eats at a time at a small carcase, but this morning there was a regular Rugby scrimmage over a particularly 'ripe' pariah puppy, about 14 birds struggling for the choice morsel. Among the vultures I was astonished to see a lovely black eagle (Neopus Malayensis) but just as I got my field-glasses to bear on him, off he flew."

The surface of Hector's days passed agreeably. He regretted not having time for polo, a sport he enjoyed, and

Burma proved to be his last chance for a mount; over the rest of his life, the cost of maintaining the ponies was beyond him. There were brother officers with whom to dine and play whist, and his exile provided him with an unawed perspective on the ogres of his youth. "Aunt Tom's first letter was full of her grievances—so interesting to read; really, if Providence persecuted me in the way it does her, I should be too proud to go to Heaven."

Only occasionally did Hector's sense of frustration erupt in a letter. "Owl and oaf thou art," he berated Ethel, "not to see 'Woman of No Importance' and 'Second Mrs. T.' *the* plays of the season; what would I not give to be able to see them!" It was probably no coincidence that both of the plays Hector regretted missing, the Wilde and Sir Arthur Wing Pinero's *The Second Mrs. Tanqueray,* dealt sympathetically with a woman of dubious propriety. However conservative his politics, Hector had to be intrigued and perhaps unsettled by the theme of society ostracizing one of its members for a sexual indiscretion.

Throughout his service in Asia, Hector had been protesting his lot far more directly than through an occasional lament to Ethel. In fourteen months he contracted a fever seven times. When the last of them proved to be malaria, Hector was bundled up to be shipped home to an ecstatically happy sister. Just before boarding the ship, he was lying feverish in a dismal hotel when he developed a great thirst. He had no luck in rousing a servant; at last he heard footsteps in the corridor and called out. It was a fellow guest. Please find a servant who can bring me something to drink, Hector said. It is none of my business, the man replied; I cannot be expected to attend to sick people or to deliver messages for them. With that, the man left. Repeating the story, Ethel was charitable enough to speculate that the man might have been mad. What was indisputable was that he had been German.

Ethel and her father were living eleven miles west of Barnstaple in a community named Westward Ho! In the town was a public school, quite new and minor, called United Service College. Kipling had been a USC boy but otherwise it was filled largely with dim or troublesome young men whose parents hoped all the same to get them into Sandhurst. Colonel Munro may have been attracted to the town by its colony of retired military men. The colonel went to London to meet Hector's boat, but Hector was still too weak to make the trip to Devon. His father hired a nurse and waited with Hector until he could travel. When at last they reached home, Ethel's joy was tempered by his appearance. Around the neighborhood the story spread that Colonel Munro's son had come home to die. Hector did regain his strength but only very slowly. Although he bought a horse for the hunting, the season had ended before he could spend a day out with the hounds.

Throughout his life, Hector continued to accept invitations to shoot but never with marked enthusiasm, and he wrote, "There's such a deadly sameness about partridges; when you've missed one, you've missed the lot . . ." As a satirist, Hector found better sport in the boasting that accompanied a kill. "There was a Major Somebody who had shot things in Lapland, or somewhere of that sort; I forget what they were, but it wasn't for want of reminding. We had them cold with every meal almost, and he was continually giving us details of what they measured from tip to tip, as though he thought we were going to make them warm underthings for the winter."

Again his months passed smoothly, a year, then more. In the summer the family went to the seashore; Hector played tennis, a game he had come to love; his father set up a putting green on the lawn, though Hector, unlike Charlie, never became devoted to golf. Then the day came when Hector was unmistakably recovered, and once again the question of an occupation presented itself. As a woman, Ethel could stay with her father and make a home for him. Of men more was required. This time Hector set out for the more congenial destination of London. What he would do there, a career appropriate to his interests and his position, required some original thought. Certainly it would not be business; Hector had the patronizing contempt of his class for men who bought and sold. In a later essay he gave his spokesman a long screed against the businessman, married early and working late, who lived with drab multitudes of his kind in little villas outside big towns. "He is buried by the thousand in Kensal Green and other large cemeteries; any romance that was ever in him was buried prematurely in shop and warehouse and office. Whenever I feel in the least tempted to be businesslike or methodical or even decently industrious I go to Kensal Green and look at the graves of those who died in business."

4

The Blind Spot (1894-1900)

H ector went to London to write. Because of the number of letters that Ethel destroyed, we have a better idea of how he dressed than what was on his mind. Fawn-colored overcoats had come into fashion, and Hector was never inclined to flout the current mode. A gray bowler with a black ribbon, trousers with a check in gray or green, completed an approved outfit. Monocles had become stylish, and as far away as Burma Charlie had screwed one into his weaker eye. Some men carried a short cane, hardly more than a swagger stick, but Hector detested affectation and probably forwent one. Venturing out, he confronted women in bonnets piled high with black and cream lace and gowns with a décolletage made the more alluring with frills and velvet ruffles. A wasp waist gave a woman the desired hour-glass figure; at the back, her train was gathered and went on to sweep the floor.

Older women in society observed that by the mid-1890s

an unseemly to-do had begun to roil the London gentry. People now craved entertainment. They were drinking champagne all through dinner, and afterward the women had hardly settled themselves in a drawing room before the men were bursting in upon them. Surgeons, actors and Jews were being received by otherwise irreproachable hostesses, and fads, such as painting one's walls a certain hue, spread in an instant across London. It was just such a sweeping enthusiasm for the shade of mauve, and nothing to do with an off-color morality, that had given the decade its name.

Hector was not immune to the contagion. He might intend to pass his days in research for a book, but he would definitely spend his evenings at the theatre or ballet. A cousin of his, Willie Mercer, came to London with his mother later during this London interlude, and relatives arranged that Hector should meet them. After an introduction at dinner, Hector was their host at the ballet *Old China* at the Empire Theatre. Young Mercer was fifteen or sixteen at the time; when he was grown, he took as his pen name, Dornford Yates. In his teens he was charmed with his cousin, with his easy talk and with that talent for adapting to his surroundings that allowed Hector to return regularly to Devon and treat his aunts with the utmost propriety.

Willie noticed, as everyone seemed to do, Hector's extreme neatness and good grooming, and he thought him attractive—lean, not tall, clean-shaven, ready to smile. The sallowness of his complexion could have been a residue from the malaria. With the eye of an adolescent, Willie decided that Hector's face looked better in repose. When he spoke, he tended to articulate too much, to use his mouth and lips in ways that lessened his appeal. Another man who noticed this same tendency wrote it off as some slight muzziness to Hector's features, as though the sides of his face were slightly out of alignment. Most people did not see it at all. Nor, then or later, did those who praised Hector's kind nature speculate on how easily indifference, combined with good manners, can establish a reputation for kindliness.

Hector had received a card that allowed him entry to the Reading Room of the British Museum. There, only a few years before, Karl Marx had labored over *Das Kapital*, and if Hector's intention was not so ambitious as the reforming of political thought, his undertaking was daunting enough. He would write a history of the rise of the Russian Empire. Obviously it would be a lengthy project and apparently Colonel Munro was willing to underwrite it. There is no indication that Hector earned a penny during the three years he spent in the research and writing. With one exception. In February 1899 he published what seems to have been his first story.

The forum was a magazine of no great distinction called *St. Paul's,* and his trifle appeared among pen-and-ink sketches of music-hall life and photographs of such entertainers as Lionelle Warton, "a very quaint and clever little dwarf." Hector's story was signed only with his initials to protect his impending scholarly renown. "Dogged" glistens only in patches but it is not merely rough paste. Its hero's name indicates that history was not far from Hector's thoughts during its composition. "Artemus Gibbon was, by nature and inclination, blameless and respectable, and under happier circumstances the record of his life might have preserved the albino tint of its early promise; but he was of timid and yielding disposition and had been carefully brought up, so that his case was clearly hopeless from the first."

Gibbon, a bachelor, goes to a church bazaar, where he is bullied by an implacable matron into taking away a yelping terrier named Beelzebub. The dog sounds like Hector's baying Gillie crossed with the lethargic dogs of Burma: "A rakish-looking fox terrier, stamped with the hall-mark of naked and unashamed depravity and wearing the yawningly alert air of one who has found the world is vain and likes it all the better for it . . . ."

The misdeeds of his new pet get Gibbon expelled from his rooms and dropped by his friends. Beelzebub brings Gibbon instead into the company of "smart, sporting youths lurid in waistcoats and conversation" and of a woman "young and pretty and birdlike—especially with regard to her hair, which was of the tint a Norwich canary aspires to but seldom attains." Gibbon invites her to tea. On her departure, they kiss, which does not prove addictive; at least none of Hector's young men ever cared to try it again.

At about the time she was having her row with Graham Greene, Ethel Munro assured a correspondent that the lack of romance was not due to absent-mindedness on her brother's part. "One subject he never wrote on, was sex, and I am certain if he had, he would have made fun of it. The only way to treat it!"

In the spring of 1900, with Hector approaching thirty, the publishing house of Grant Richards brought out *The Rise of the Russian Empire*. One incident marred the family's enjoyment of his success: coincidentally with publication, Augusta Munro died in Barnstaple. Less than three weeks before her death she made her will, leaving an estate of six hundred eighty-one pounds to Aunt Tom throughout her lifetime and thereafter to their three nieces, one of them Ethel. Bequests of the period constituted something of an old girls' network, an acknowledgment that male children could shift for themselves but females, particularly if they did not marry, needed some support. On her deathbed Augusta had shown herself less absolute than in her prime: "I wish to be buried at Tawton with my father and mother, if there is room."

As Hector's title indicated, his Russian survey owed much to the great eighteenth-century ironist who had written *The History of the Decline and Fall of the Roman Empire*. He aspired to Gibbon's sweep, his graceful phrasing, his mocking eye cocked at Christianity. But from the outset Hector also struck a combative note; he indicated, for example, that he knew better than the geographers the tactile surface of this land he had not yet seen. And throughout his book ran a bright romantic thread, less descriptive of Russia than of Russia as Hector wanted it to be. The imagination of Russia's slaves, he wrote "gave deific being to the sun, moon, stars, wind, water, fire and air, but most of all they reverenced the lightning. In their dark, overshadowed forest homes it was natural that the sun, which exercised such mystic sway in the blazing lands of the Orient, should yield place to the swift, dread light which could split great trees with its spasm of destruction and shake the heavens with its attendant thunder."

Did the irony occur to him of an impeccably dressed young man with self-effacing manners unleashing elemental passions in the Reading Room of the British Museum? The entire book echoes with the frustration of an adventurer's soul locked in the body of a clerk, and when a roll call of battles impresses him as sounding too much like an inventory, Hector's bolder self overrides the facts to discard the two centuries from A.D. 1050. "The history of Russia during the next two hundred years is little more than a long chronicle of aimless and inconsequent feuds between the multiple Princes of the Blood."

At times, Hector's appetite for the horrors of the past seems to strike him as imprudent and he pauses for an unfelt lamentation over the rampaging cruelty. Telling of the massacre of 1183, "when the head of the Pope's Legate, severed from its legitimate body and tied to the tail of a dog, went bumping and thudding along the public streets to the accompaniment of hymns of praise and thanksgiving," he expects readers to respond not to his excitement but to the enormity of the crimes. He is rarely subtle. When he describes the population kneeling in supplication against the Mongols, he adds, "From cathedral, church and roadside shrine wails the pitiful litany, 'Save us from the infidels!' Candles burn and incense swings, and anguish-stricken hearts yearn out their prayer, 'Save us from the infidels!' Call Him louder. Perchance He sleepeth."

Or, deploring the misery of the early 1600s, "The ideal of God is usually that of a being who derives some not very comprehensible satisfaction from the contemplation of self-inflicted sacrifice or suffering of some sort, and it was quite in keeping with accepted ideas that the only remedy for the misery of a nation was—more suffering."

Jesus of Nazareth was no more immune from Hector's scorn, and the impalement of Dmitri Shaferov in 1560 gave him a chance for righteous blaspheming. "All day long, it was said, he lingered, bearing his pain heroically; and Church and Tzar looked on impassively at a deed more meanly cruel than that monk-taught tragedy, the memory of which they bewailed every Good Friday."

By the time Hector left off his account at 1619, with the dynasty of Theodor and Mikhail Romanov, he had sounded other themes and vented many of the obsessions that underlay his literary imagination. Writing of a victory of the Mongols, he noted, "The Russians dreamed that they were free. Not so lightly were they to be rid of these dusky wolf-eyed warriors, who teemed in the wide, arid plain land of Asia like rats on an old threshing-floor." Through it all coursed blood, though not always enough to speed the clotted narrative. Here Hector is describing the rule of Ivan the Terrible:

"Grim and dreary, mean and monstrous, as the Moskovy of this period seems, with its Aleksandrovskie slobada, its gibbets, axes, impalements, and boiling cauldrons, its man-devouring hounds and blood-splashed bear-dens, its kromiesniki and dumb driven population, its gutters running red and carp growing bloated on human flesh, and, above all, everywhere those glittering crosses. . . ." If that catalogue does not sate his readers, Hector then detours to Italy to compile the atrocities underway there.

Hector committed his saga to the reviewers at a time when book publishing in England was more given to humor and suspense than to historical surveys. According to the *Bookman*—where Hector's volume was advertised at ten shillings sixpence—the book of the hour was Booth Tarkington's *The Gentleman from Indiana,* and other popular offerings were Mark Twain's *The Man That Corrupted Hadleyburg* and the short stories of W. W. Jacobs. The price of Hector's book was not cheap for nonfiction; a more appealing theme than his, *How England Saved Europe,* was selling at six shillings, and a life of Edward Fitz-Gerald, acclaimed for his translations of Omar Khayyam, was seven and six. Yet Hector's gender guaranteed that even if his book did not sweep the country it would receive sober notice. Had Ethel written the book, she could have expected this treatment from a *Bookman* columnist: "An author stands or falls by his book. Not so a lady. She has, or should have, a crushing retort always ready . . .

'You say my books are bad. Well, sir, what of that? *Have you tasted my pies?*' "

As it turned out, in several instances Hector could have used a ready retort. The *Bookman* called on Edward Garnett for a notice in its August 1900 edition. Garnett was the editor who had discovered Joseph Conrad and rejected Somerset Maugham's first stories, and he began his review with an analogy: History is to life what a skeleton is to the living body. He animadverted on that theme for one-third of his allotted space before turning to the volume that had provoked his meditation. Then, although he praised Hector's work as "courageous and intelligent," Garnett complained that the skeleton he had provided merely whetted the appetite for studies by scientists, ethnologists, economists, philologists and a host of other experts. "Mr. Munro's stimulating and conscientious sketch"—the book ran 334 pages—only led to frustration, since "we find ourselves therefore perpetually wishing for a new race of historian to arise."

In its review, the *Athenaeum* was the first journal, but not the last, to complain about Hector's pedantic spelling of Russian names—the rendering of Moscow as "Moskva" and the Kremlin as "Kreml." On the whole, its critic believed he could "greatly commend Mr. Munro's volume," even though he treated the Borussians, or Prussians, as a subtribe of Liths when there was more reason to consider them Slavs.

It was one of the first reviews of Hector's first book, and he violated twofold a sensible rule regarding criticism: he not only quarreled with a review, he quarreled with a favorable one. His contentiousness was phrased at least in the most cautious and circuitous language: "—and in this connexion I should like, in a spirit of inquiry, rather than controversy—" And when the padding was stripped away, Hector's point turned out to be a minor one. He was merely defending his thesis that Christianity had merged with Russian pantheism and not extinguished it. To bolster his argument, Hector claimed the authority of an eyewitness, although what he had observed had taken place in Devon, not Russia: "Among the yeomen and peasantry of the west of England, where Christianity in its most rigid dogmatic form flourishes, I imagine, as heartily as anywhere in the kingdom, there still lingers a genuine and practical belief in witches and black and white magic, presumably a relic of a much earlier cult."

In defense of his eccentric spelling, Hector invoked arcane authorities. As for his classing the Borussians as Lithuanian, Hector offered a sly defense. Among his sources he named the Encyclopaedia Britannica, adding, "which makes me the more remorseful if I have furthered so substantial an error."

Had Hector been patient, he would have found ample chance to respond to reviews that were genuinely unfavorable. But he seems to have spent his indignation on the *Athenaeum* and his later critics went unchallenged. The following spring, when the book was issued by L. C. Page of Boston, the American reviews could only confirm Hector's early antipathy toward the United States. In England, editors were still guided by Martial's sentiment that a good man is always a novice, and no one had objected that a man with no diplomas or degrees had written a scholarly history. In the United States, where scholarship was further along to becoming a closed shop, Hector's book was received with impatient and detailed cavils. To Puritan America, his humor at the expense of religious feeling proved distressing. The *Nation*'s critic did grant Hector "a genuine talent for picturesque and telling double-barreled adjectives," but he deplored the flippancy that had crept into even the gravest episodes and wondered as well at the pomposity of revising the English spellings of Russian places and persons. The critic caught Hector out on a host of points: Why, for example, change the perfectly intelligible "Cossack" to *Kozak,* when Hector's own rules called for "Kazák"?

Archibald Cary Coolidge, writing in the *American Historical Review,* struck even harsher blows. He was not content to denigrate Hector's bibliography but went on the attack as well against his prose style, especially those dual adjectives that the *Nation* had admired. "It may be a writer's misfortune, not a fault, that he has not a positively good style, but there is no excuse for the badness of pages of turgid rhetoric mixed with ineffective sarcasms, not infrequently in bad taste. The countless similes too, in which the author indulges are hardly ever happy; the masses of double-barreled adjectives are very exasperating, the whole is confused and wearisome."

Loyally, Ethel mined the few reviews and the reaction of friends for whatever mild praise she could extract and included it in her memoir. Hector, whether or not he saw the Coolidge review, seldom again lapsed into the style that had provoked it. When the book was safely remaindered, he enjoyed repeating a remark by his father's coachman, who had borrowed it and later handed it back, saying, "I've read your book, sir, and I must say I shouldn't care to have written it myself."

Telling the story, Hector added bravely that it was the biggest compliment he had ever had.

5

A Bread and
Butter Miss
(1900-1901)

As Hector had been finishing his history and seeing it through publication, another avenue for his writing —somewhat less respectable but undeniably alluring— was opening to him. Friends from Devonshire had introduced him to the most popular and influential political cartoonist in London, Francis Carruthers Gould. Gould, who had been born in Barnstaple, was fifty-six years old as the new century began, and he was not the obvious patron for a dapper Tory bachelor. Gould's political viewpoint was a thoughtful Liberalism, and his happiest moments came when, surrounded by his large and loving family, he could crouch in a worn dressing gown over his drawing board, a cigarette stuck like a spare pencil in the corner of his mouth. He would have admitted that other cartoonists were better draftsmen. Tenniel and Partridge at *Punch* were considered true artists. But they could be bland where Gould was always sharp; a man had no right to do a caricature, Gould said, except in the same way that he makes a statement he believes to be true.

Yet, while he used his pen to advance the Liberal Party, Gould's kind heart was so obvious that even his opponents praised his talent. Gladstone and Lloyd George had bought the originals of the cartoons in which they were the victims, and Joseph Chamberlain, often a target, wrote urbanely to Gould, "The subject of so many of your cartoons is not a pleasant character, but I am able to regard him impartially as a work of imaginative art and I congratulate you on adding another interesting personality to the gallery of English fiction." It was Chamberlain's style to say he admired even those cartoons that drew blood, and so months passed before word reached Gould that the Liberal Unionist did have one demurrer. In a celebrated cartoon after the election of 1900, Gould had portrayed Chamberlain as a muddy retriever laying a khaki bird at the foot of fastidious masters who were disdaining his methods. If it was all the same, Chamberlain confided, I would prefer not to be represented as a dog. Hearing that the device was offensive, Gould never resorted to it again.

Carruthers Gould had started his career at the *Pall Mall Gazette,* but by the time Hector came to call on him, he had transferred to the *Westminster Gazette,* a paper aimed at educated and politically influential circles. Bernard Shaw called it "the only daily paper one can read with the sensation of being in decent company." Such journals rarely attract enough revenues to balance their accounts, and the *Westminster's* deficit was regularly underwritten by a few wealthy and sympathetic businessmen. Thirty to forty thousand copies were printed each evening, but because they were read and passed along, a hundred thousand people saw the *Westminster* each day. They were men and women who could make a reputation overnight, and that is what they did for Hector Hugh Munro. Except that the name they made for him was Saki.

Self-baptism, the taking of a pen name, is one of those decisions, like swearing off drink, that makes a man for the moment his own father. Parents usually choose names for their children as a revelation, a trumpeting to the world of the sort of offspring they intend to raise. Often they are proved wrong. The pen name is the opposite. The writer takes it for concealment, and yet his choice invariably reveals his character. At least that was true of Hector when he turned for secrecy to the *Rubaiyat*.

If there is a modern parallel to the enthusiasm that came over London in the 1900s for the eleventh-century quatrains of a Persian tentmaker's son, it may be in the persisting vogue of Kahlil Gibran. Edward FitzGerald had first translated the *Rubaiyat* of Omar Khayyam in 1859, and as the Victorian spirit weakened and sank, his sentimental tribute to transient pleasures, that ode on a Persian jug, won the hearts of a generation who could not wait for the Prince of Wales to assume the throne before they launched the Edwardian Age.

Ethel Munro had succumbed rapturously to Omar Khayyam, and she bought not only the FitzGerald translation but a rendering by "E. H. Whinfield, M.A., Late of the Bengal Civil Service." Ethel's pleasure in what she read was never covert. She marked approvingly and copiously throughout any book with a line along the margin, two for emphasis. What did not win her favor— fatuous lines by Matthew Arnold—she crossed out with a furious scribble. Those passages she endorsed treated life as an unjust burden or celebrated heedless love. She accorded this quatrain a double line: "Hearts with the light of love illumined well, / Whether in mosque or synagogue they dwell, / Have *their* names written in the book of love, / Unvexed by hopes of heaven or fears of hell."

Hector did not deface his books. Rather, he copied out choice bits of poetry into a commonplace book. It was there that he set down selections from Hafiz of Shiraz and "My Home," by James Clarence Mangan. "Take up the goblet," he copied from Hafiz, "for sweet life, when gone will not come back." And with that, five stanzas from Omar, meticulously copied in Hector's spiky bold hand:

"Yet ah, that Spring should vanish with the Rose!
That Youth's sweet-scented manuscript should close!

The Nightingale that in the branches sang,
Ah whence, and whither flower again, who knows!"
★   ★   ★
"Yon rising Moon that looks for us again—
How oft hereafter will she wax and wane;
How oft hereafter rising look for us
Through this same Garden—and for one in vain!

And when like her, oh Sákí, you shall pass
Among the guests Star-scattered on the Grass
and in your joyous errand reach the spot
Where I made One—turn down an empty Glass!"
★   ★   ★
"Perplext me no more with Human or Divine,
Tomorrow's tangle to the winds resign
and lose your fingers in the tresses of
The Cypress-slender Minister of Wine.

So when that Angel of the Darker Drink
At last shall find you by the river-brink,
And, offering his Cup, invite your Soul
Forth to your Lips to quaff—you shall not shrink."

Afterward, when critics searched for the meaning in
Hector's choice of pen name, they quoted only the second
and third stanzas, catching the wistfulness but missing the
martial injunction, the call to courage in the face of death.
But Hector had copied out all five verses and he embodied
both spirits or sought to do so. In 1886, *Dr. Jekyll and Mr.
Hyde* had chilled hearts because readers knew that it was
less horror story than confession. In the years since Stevenson wrote, the man has come to look fortunate who
has only two natures, and Hector Munro had at least two.
He was young and merry and bright. And from the age of
five, fifteen and thirty, he was old and sad and cruel. It
was Hector who would write the best of the stories; it was
Munro who would go off to war. But the name of Saki
could stand for both of them—for Hector when he passed
on his joyous errand among the guests, for Munro when
he sought the cup at the river-brink. In Omar Khayyam,
Hector Munro found an ambiguous pseudonym more appropriate than he could know.

But why had he looked there at all when his first published sketches were parodies of Lewis Carroll and when he had no intimation that this careless choice would follow him through his life? There is a clue in the files of the *Westminster Gazette*.

In March 1901, with his Alice series launched, Hector published two parodies of the *Rubaiyat*, both signed, as the early Alices had been, SAKI. Exigencies of printing did not permit the diacritical marks that he had carefully used in his notebooks; the name appeared unadorned but in uppercase letters. These columns were headed, "The Quatrains of Uttar Al Ghibe, With Explanations and Conjectural Notes," and, like the Alice sketches, they lampooned political figures of the day. Hector gave them this introduction: "The following recently-discovered Quatrains have been ascribed with some certainty to a Persian poet of the above name who flourished at Baghdad, or, as some authorities are inclined to believe, El S'where, under the Sessyl Dynasty." The last phrase was a gibe at the family whose members had so penetrated the government that it was sometimes called the Hotel Cecil. One verse concerned Winston Churchill, who had come to Parliament after making his name as a correspondent for the *Morning Post* in South Africa. There he had been captured by the Boers and managed a thrilling escape, and Hector's rhyme celebrated the uses of publicity to an ambitious young adventurer:

"An ample note-book underneath the Bough,
A jug of ink, a ready pen—and Thou
Beside me sitting in the Wilderness—
Oh, Wilderness were Paradise enow.

"For 'Paradise' some translators read 'paragraphed.' "

That first column inspired a sequel two weeks later before Hector returned to Alice. But it may well be that the first parodies he had taken to Carruthers Gould had been based on the *Rubaiyat* and signed with a pen name drawn from their source. The two pieces that appeared may have been those samples, emended to bring them up to date. Gould had an affinity for drawing Alice, and if he had pressed his new protégé to begin with the Wonderland satires, Hector may have retrieved the pen name as the only thing he could salvage from that apprentice work.

Whatever the circumstances, Hector's career was determined on the day in 1900 when Gould took him into the office of John Alfred Spender, editor of the *Westminster Gazette*. At forty-three, Spender was fourteen years older than Hector, and he noticed that after the introductions Munro left the talking to Gould. They proposed to collaborate on a series that would take Alice through the political mire of the Boer War. Spender was not immediately taken with the idea. Writers had often sent him parodies of Lewis Carroll, and he had found most of them dismal. To succeed perfectly—and anything less was abject failure—they had to catch the skewed logic of the original. Could Hector succeed perfectly? Spender worked hard to extract some word from the silent young writer, and at last it came. In his memoirs, Spender did not reproduce the conversation, only his reaction that Hector's mind was pungent and original, and that Gould could take pride in his discovery.

Spender displayed the first article, with Gould's inspired caricature of Arthur James Balfour, on his front page of Wednesday, July 25, 1900. " 'Have you ever seen an Ineptitude?' asked the Cheshire Cat suddenly; the Cat was nothing if not abrupt.

" 'Not in real life,' said Alice. 'Have you any about here?' "

The Cat in reply points to a large hapless bird with a drooping neck, "something like a badly-written note of interrogation." It is Balfour, nephew of Robert Cecil, the leader of the Conservatives in the House of Commons, drawn with eyeglasses, mustache and spats and, for hands, ineffectual little wings.

" 'What is it?' Alice asked, after surveying Balfour for a few moments in silence. 'And why is it here?'

" 'It hasn't any meaning,' said the Cat. "It simply *is*.'

" 'Can it talk?' asked Alice eagerly.

" 'It has never done anything else.' "

Balfour was a likelier subject for satire than he was a

political leader. At Cambridge thirty years before, his taste for velvet and blue china had led him to be called "Pretty Fanny" and "Miss Balfour" and, arriving in Parliament, he played to his languor and his taste for elegance. When Robert Cecil unexpectedly settled on Balfour a critical appointment as Chief Secretary for Ireland, the choice had provided English street boys with the jeer "Bob's your uncle!" Many of those who admired Gould's deft pen also believed, however, that no caricature could be more clever, or deceiving, than the poses Balfour struck to conceal a ferociously ambitious politician with a great capacity for ruthlessness and hard work. Now, with the Boer War, Balfour was facing a test of both qualities.

The war in South Africa had begun as a popular crusade. Britain's troops set out to protect English settlers and make secure from the Dutch farmers, the Boers, all claim to the Transvaal, where gold had been discovered. Four and a half years earlier, the British had failed in that objective with the Jameson raid, a botched coup intended to snare the Transvaal. Now with another quick incursion, the matter was to be resolved to England's satisfaction.

But, as happens, the Dutch guerrillas protracted a battle they were supposed to understand was impossible for them to win. During England's reverses, Balfour's imperturbability met a public test; with British troops pinned down at Ladysmith, Balfour called the situation "an unhappy entanglement" and lamented in public having to give up his Christmas holiday. Historians later suggested that this foppish indifference, derided in his day, may have imparted confidence to the nation and led, after more disastrous losses, to the ultimate British victory. Hector saw matters differently:

" 'Can you tell me what you are doing here?' Alice inquired politely. The Ineptitude shook its head with a deprecatory motion and commenced to drawl, 'I haven't an idea.' "

The Cat tries to explain: " 'Its theory is,' he continued, seeing that Alice was waiting for more, 'that you mustn't interfere with the Inevitable. Slide and let slide, you know.'

" 'But what do you keep it here for?' asked Alice.

" 'Oh, somehow you can't help it; it's so perfectly harmless and amiable and says the nastiest things in the nicest manner . . . but you can't push an Ineptitude. Might as well try to hustle a glacier.' "

Hector's first Alice was not immediately followed by another. More than three months passed before she traveled again, this time to Pall Mall. It was her second appearance that made Saki famous. Alice's quarry was the White Knight, Henry Charles Petty-Fitzmaurice, the fifth Marquess of Lansdowne, who, having been an indifferent Secretary of War for five years, was rewarded for Britain's reverses with the title of Foreign Secretary. Hector entrusted to this steward of the South African war a prime example of Carroll's unassailable backward logic. " 'In my Department one has to be provided for emergencies. Now, for instance, have you ever conducted a war in South Africa?'

"Alice shook her head.

" 'I have,' said the Knight, with a gentle complacency in his voice.

" 'And did you bring it to a successful conclusion?' asked Alice.

" 'Not exactly to a *conclusion*—not a *definite* conclusion, you know—nor entirely successful either. In fact, I believe it's going on still . . . but you can't think how much forethought it took to get it properly started.' "

Alice observes a number of obsolete and impractical weapons hanging from the Knight's saddle.

" 'You see, I had read a book,' the Knight went on in a dreamy far-away tone, 'written by some one to prove that warfare under modern conditions was impossible. You may imagine how disturbing that was to a man of my profession. Many men would have thrown up the whole thing and gone home. But I grappled with the situation. You will never guess what I did.'

"Alice pondered. 'You went to war, of course—'

" 'Yes; *but not under modern conditions.*'

"The Knight stopped his horse so that he might enjoy the full effect of this announcement.

" 'Now, for instance,' he continued kindly, seeing that Alice had not recovered her breath, 'you observe this little short-range gun that I have hanging to my saddle? Why do you suppose I sent out guns of that particular kind? Because if they happened to fall into the hands of the enemy they'd be very little use to him. That was my own invention.' "

Spender wrote that in his years as an editor he had never known a political satire to be so combustible. They were laughing in Westminster and Mayfair, Bond Street and Belgravia. Lord Lansdowne's ingenious solution was quoted everywhere. Earlier in the year, H. H. Munro had been received with severe reservations as an historian. Now Saki was welcomed uproariously as a social critic. His tone had proved exactly right. The war might be tragic but the buffoonery of its management was fair sport for satire.

After that success the Alices followed more rapidly through the next thirteen months. During that time Victoria died and Edward took the throne in January 1901, but Hector's humor never impinged on the monarchy. He attacked instead the Liberal Party for its feuding and factions, and he made fun of the intractable Dr. Frederick Temple, Archbishop of Canterbury, who was also beset by doctrinal disputes. "Of course something must be done," the Archbishop tells Alice, "but quietly and gradually—the leaden foot within the velvet shoe, you know."

In another encounter, Alice tries to get the attention of a large and solemn caterpillar, whom readers recognized as the Speaker of the House. Spender considered their dialogue ageless, true of any speaker dealing with an obstreperous member.

" 'If you please—' she began.

" 'I don't,' said the Caterpillar shortly, without seeming to take any further notice of her.

"After an uncomfortable pause she commenced again.

" 'I should like—'

" 'You shouldn't,' said the Caterpillar with decision.

"Alice felt discouraged, but it was no use to be shut up in this way, so she started again as amiably as she could.

" 'You can't think, Mr. Caterpillar—'

" 'I can, and I often do,' he remarked stiffly; adding, 'You mustn't make such wild statements. They're not relevant to the discussion.' "

Hector and Gould would consult for hours before they went their own ways, one to write, one to draw, and one day the cartoonist enlisted Hector in a favorite pastime, tweaking the nose of the Poet Laureate, Alfred Austin. Austin's latest offense had been to celebrate with his usual orotundity the return from Australia of the Duke of York, later to become King George V. In his piece, Hector responded by presenting Austin as the White Rabbit. (The poet demonstrated his imperviousness to ridicule by going on to write verse with such lines as "Show me your garden and I shall tell you what you are.")

" 'The Duke and Duchess!' said the White Rabbit nervously as it went scurrying past; 'they may be here at any moment, and I haven't got it yet.'

" 'Hasn't got what?' wondered Alice.

" 'A rhyme for Cornwall,' said the Rabbit, as if in answer to her thought; 'borne well, yawn well'—and he pattered away into the distance, dropping in his hurry a folded paper that he had been carrying.

" 'What have you got there?' asked the Cheshire Cat as Alice picked up the paper and opened it.

" 'It seems to be a kind of poetry,' said Alice doubtfully; 'at least,' she added, 'some of the words rhyme and none of them appear to have any particular meaning.' "

After excursions into poetry and church doctrine, the series ended as it had begun, with scorn for the Boer War, which the government had promised to end by September 1900, and which was still taking lives fourteen months later. Hector gave Balfour, as the March Hare, a refrain to sing:

"Dwindle, dwindle, little war,
How I wonder more and more
As about the veldt you hop
When you really mean to stop."

It was 1926 before the Viking Press in New York brought out a collected edition of Hector's work for

American readers; a quarter of a century had passed since the Alice series first appeared in London. The press run for *Alice in Westminster* was substantially smaller than that for the Viking volumes of Saki stories. The publishers were sure that an American public would find its political satire dated and obscure. But the demand was so great that a second printing had to be made; and after another forty-odd years had passed, Hector's disdain for a great power enmeshed in a squalid and distant war could have touched an even more responsive chord in America.

As the new Alice adventures were unfolding in the *Westminster Gazette,* Hector was experimenting with other styles. At home, he continued to copy his favorite quotations into his notebook, mingling sighs from the Romantic poets with sterner stuff. "Deep as first love," he copied out from D'Annunzio's "Triumph of Death," "and wild with all regret, O Death in Life, the days that are no more." On the same page he quoted from Stendhal: "—examine yourself; get at your most spontaneous, indubitable tastes, desires, ambitions; follow them; act from them unceasingly; be turned aside by nothing."

Mixed with such bracing maxims were paragraphs of Hector's own, either sententious or in pursuit of a style. "Man was a being with myriad lives and myriad sensations, a complete multiform creature that bore within itself strange legacies of thought and passion, and whose very soul was tainted with the monstrous maladies of the dead." And: "The evening darkened in the room. Noiselessly, and with silver feet, the shadows crept in from the garden. The colours faded wearily out of things."

Hector had not found his voice, nor did his use of Saki on the Alice parodies indicate a firm decision about which name to use when he met his true public. Early in 1901 he published a short story in the *Westminster* and signed it, as he had the piece two years earlier in *St. Paul's,* with his initials. The story was "The Blood Feud of Toad-Water," based on a story told the Munros by their rector in Devon about the hen who strayed into a neighbor's garden. Hector allowed the piece to be reprinted nine years later to eke out a collection of short stories, but it had little in common with the work that would define his reputation: no society figures, only isolated farm folk; no repartee, indeed, no dialogue at all; no invention, the plot coming unaltered from the clergyman. But his writing was already invested with humor, even though his distinctive precision, the sense he conveyed that each of his words was inevitable, was still beyond his grasp.

"Mrs. Saunders, sauntering at this luckless moment down the garden path, in order to fill her soul with reproaches at weeds, which grew faster than she or her good man cared to remove them, stopped in mute discomfiture before the presence of a more magnificent grievance. And then, in the hour of her calamity, she turned instinctively to the Great Mother, and gathered in her capacious hands large clods of the hard brown soil that lay at her feet. With a terrible sincerity of purpose, though with a contemptible inadequacy of aim, she rained her earth bolts at the marauder, and the bursting pellets called forth a flood of cackling protest and panic from the hastily departing fowl."

By the time the story was reprinted, Hector had returned from years of writing daily dispatches under the pressures of a deadline and paying by the word to wire them across Europe. He had pared away any excesses from a way of thinking that was naturally graceful. If he had taken the time to rewrite the tale of Toad-Water, he might have cut out references to "her good man" and "the Great Mother" and found ways less arch of describing "earth bolts" and "bursting pellets." Retained, and standing in sharper relief, would have been the even-handed judgments—"terrible sincerity," "contemptible inadequacy"—that gave to his later work the air of having been composed by a magistrate, albeit one with his feet propped up jauntily on the bench.

By 1901 Hector had much to tell Ethel of life in London, and he wrote often to Westward Ho! Just as faithfully she destroyed his letters to keep them from their father, who insisted on seeing any message from his younger son. ". . . Hector and I sometimes had plans which we did not divulge to him at once," Ethel explained in her memoirs, leaving a suggestion that Hector's notes were filled with impromptu travel arrangements or thoughtful surprises for the Colonel. More likely, Hector had preserved the intimacy with Ethel that they had enjoyed from the nursery, and although in Burma propriety and his position had conspired to guarantee that Hector's life would be chaste, London provided no such restraints. Hector and Ethel both subscribed to the theory that nothing should be denied the superior man, and they were agreed, too, on Hector's superiority. He seems to have pursued less a secret life than a discreet one, to which Ethel was an appreciative audience. And with all her tolerance going to her younger brother, there was very little left for the rest of the world. It would not be enough to say that in her eyes Hector could do no wrong. Rather, when he did wrong it was delightful. In his later years, Charlie described to his daughters a game that he had played as a young man with Ethel and Hector. They all closed their eyes and tried to identify certain sounds. To universal merriment, Hector found a way to pour crumpled paper from one bowl to another so that it sounded like urination. Charlie's daughters could scarcely believe it. Aunt Ethel was there? Wasn't she furious? If I had done it, she would have been, said Charlie, not bitter, simply recognizing a bond that had never fettered him.

When Ethel had to acknowledge that Hector was spending a good deal of time with a young man, even sharing quarters with him, she called it "chumming." Such was the case with a friend named Tocke but affectionately called "Tockling" by Hector in a letter Ethel preserved.

"The duck was a bird of great parts and as tender as a good man's conscience when confronted with the sins of others. Truly a comfortable bird. Tockling is looking well and is in better health and spirits generally, and everything in the garden's lovely. Except the 'Cambridgeshire' which we all came a cropper over. We put our underclothing on the wrong horse and are now praying for a mild Winter."

Occasionally Ethel went to visit friends or family, and Hector traveled to Devon to amuse his father, whom he called "Gov," and keep him safe from Aunt Tom. As

Ethel stepped out the door, Tom was at the gate ready to take charge, and it was Hector's duty to see that the only spinster to bully the Colonel these days was his daughter.

"Aunt Tom came to visit the day Ker left," Hector wrote to Ethel, "but I am still understudying your place. She is horrified at the rapidity of my marketing (which has been so far successful), but I pointed out to her that it was doubtful economy to spend an hour trying to save a few halfpennies on the price of vegetables when other people spent pounds to snatch a short time by the seaside—and the quicker I marketed the sooner I got back. Of course she was not converted to my view . . . On Wednesday we drove to Bucks and met a menagerie, so with two other traps we turned into a field to let it pass. Bertie and I went in on both nights to see the beasts, and made friends with the young trainer, who was quite charming, and had sweet little lion cubs (born in the first coronation week) taken out of their cage and put into our arms, also seductive little wolf-puppies which you would have loved."

All the Munros were proud of their Highland blood. When a *History of the Munros of Fowlis* appeared in 1898, Aunt Tom at once bought a copy even though its research did not link her branch directly with the head of the clan. And Charlie in later life often signed his irate letters to the editor of the local papers "Highlander." But the family seldom felt obliged to travel to its font. Charlie went to Scotland but once, on his honeymoon. Three years before, Hector had made his one trip to Edinburgh, but his companion was Aunt Tom and it was no honeymoon. He wrote to Ethel:

"Travelling with Aunt Tom is more exciting than motorcarring. We had four changes and on each occasion she expected the railway company to bring our trunks around on a tray to show that they really had them on the train. Every 10 minutes or so she was prophetically certain that her trunk, containing among other things 'poor mother's lace,' would never arrive at Edinburgh. There are times when I almost wish Aunt Tom had never had a mother. Nothing but a merciful sense of humour brought me through that intermittent unstayable outpour of bemoaning. And at Edinburgh, sure enough her trunk was missing!

"It was in vain that the guard assured her that it would come on in the next train, half-an-hour later; she denounced the vile populace of Bristol and Crewe, who had broken open her box and were even then wearing the maternal lace. I said no one wore lace at 8 o'clock in the morning and persuaded her to get some breakfast in the refreshment-room while we waited for the alleged train."

Aunt Tom had once read in a Devon paper that a man who sometimes left his home in Edinburgh would rent it in his absence. That had been thirty years ago, but Tom believed he ought to be doing it still. When it turned out he did not, Hector, Tom and the recovered baggage went by horse-drawn cab from one small hotel to another, seeking accommodations. Tom had always been a prodigy of vigor. Trailing in her wake, Hector was given to strain, much of it nervous. "Anyhow," Tom had declared after another fruitless stop, "we are seeing Edinburgh," a consolation Hector thought was much the same as Moses informing the companions of his forty years' wandering that they were seeing Egypt.

"Then we came here," Hector concluded his letter—signed "y.a.b.," your affectionate brother—"and she took rooms after scolding the manageress, servants and entire establishment nearly out of their senses because everything was not to her liking. I hurriedly explained to everybody that my aunt was tired and upset after a long journey, and disappointed at not getting the rooms she had expected; after I had comforted two chambermaids and the boots, who were crying quietly in corners, and coaxed the hotel kitten out of the waste-paper basket, I went to get a shave and wash—when I came back Aunt Tom was beaming on the whole establishment and saying she should recommend the hotel to all her friends. 'You can easily manage these people,' she remarked at lunch, 'if you only know the way to their hearts.' She told the manageress that I was frightfully particular. I believe we are to be here till Tuesday morning, and then go into rooms; the hotel people have earnestly recommended a lot to us.

"Aunt Tom really is marvelous; after 16 hours in the train without a wink of sleep, and an hour spent in hunting for rooms, her only desire is to go out and see the shops. She says it was a remarkably comfortable journey; personally I have never known such an exhausting experience."

6

The Stampeding
of Lady Bastable
(1901-1902)

In London, recovering from his holiday, Hector interrupted his Alice parodies to introduce a character of his own devising, a young dandy and debtor around town named Reginald. With limited success, Hector had tried to write like Gibbon; to great acclaim, but with no particular artistic satisfaction, he had written like Lewis Carroll. Now, writing in that tone in which he wrote to Ethel, Hector was sounding his authentic note at last. "I did it," the narrator begins the first story. "I should have known better. I persuaded Reginald to go to the McKillops' garden-party against his will."

The teller of the tale is older than Reginald and stuffier. Not well enough connected to be indifferent to his social position, he sometimes introduces Reginald as his cousin and perhaps he is. Whatever their relationship, the narrator is fond, even doting. Reginald can always call on him for a loan, which, with Reginald, means a gift. And the narrator is self-effacing. When he must speak of himself at all, he calls himself "the Other."

This Other assures Reginald that Mrs. McKillop will be pleased to welcome him to her house. " 'Young men of your brilliant attractions are rather at a premium at her garden parties.'

" 'Should be at a premium in heaven,' remarked Reginald complacently.

" 'There will be very few of you there, if that is what you mean.' "

Agreeing to go, Reginald takes two and a half hours to dress, debating fretfully over which necktie to wear and inveigling his feet into shoes a size too small. At the party, the narrator seats him close to a dish of *marrons glacés* and as far as possible from the Archdeacon's wife. But Reginald is too fleet to be anchored. First he twits old Colonel Mendoza about his advanced age. ("Reginald in his wildest lapses into veracity never admits to being more than twenty-two.") He teaches the youngest son of the local temperance beldame how to mix absinthe. And he beards the Archdeacon's wife to talk about a recent scandal in the theatre. As Mrs. McKillop explains to the narrator, " 'Your cousin is discussing *ZaZa* with the deacon's wife; at least, he is discussing, she is ordering her carriage.' "

As the brief anecdote ends, Reginald is reclining in a comfortable chair "with the dreamy, far-away look that a volcano might wear just after it had desolated entire villages." As the Other upbraids him, "a shade of genuine regret for misused opportunities passed over Reginald's face.

" 'After all,' he said, 'I believe an apricot tie would have gone better with the lilac waistcoat.' "

That was all, a slender curiosity, barely a column long in the most disposable form of publication, the daily newspaper. It was signed Saki, an indication that Hector felt there was something *outré* in its manner and that he expected Reginald to be as perishable as the topical Alice. Certainly the influence behind his inspiration was as obvious as Lewis Carroll had been. Being in Burma, Hector had not seen a one Oscar Wilde play, but there was not much else to Wilde that he had missed.

"History is merely gossip," Wilde had said in *Lady Windermere's Fan*. Eight years later, Reginald remarked, "I hate posterity—it's so fond of having the last word." And yet it was not mere imitation on Hector's part. It is hardly surprising that men with inconvenient lusts that could send them to jail should hold some opinions in common. And since each man was a wit, he would express himself in the epigrams that only wit can fashion. Hector was influenced by Wilde but wit cannot be learned. The two did, however, ring harmonious changes on the same themes:

Wilde: "No woman should ever be quite accurate about her age. It looks so calculating." Saki: "To have reached thirty is to have failed in life."

Wilde: "When a woman marries again it is because she detested her first husband. When a man marries again, it is because he adored his first wife. Women try their luck; men risk theirs." Saki: "No really provident woman lunches regularly with her husband if she wishes to burst upon him as a revelation at dinner. He must have time to forget; an afternoon is not enough."

Wilde: "There is no sin except stupidity." Saki: "Scandal is merely the compassionate allowance which the gay make to the humdrum."

Wilde: "They say when good Americans die they go to Paris." Saki: "She believed in the healthy influence of natural surroundings, never having been to Sicily, where things are different."

Sheridan, Thackeray and Shaw stand by to testify, were testimony needed, that wit is not a monopoly of homosexuals. But wit is often rueful, and homosexuals have reason to rue; wit is often intolerant, and intolerance is a quality that they know; wit can be self-mocking, and it is when homosexuals mock themselves that society allows itself to relax in their presence. Oscar Wilde once illustrated perfectly the special quality of homosexual wit when he expanded upon the common lament that life is unfair. "Life is unfair," said Wilde, "for which most of us should be very grateful."

If Wilde's wit and Hector's sprang from shared assumptions, there were differences worth noting between the two of them. When Wilde has a character say, "I can resist everything but temptation," one hears the sigh behind an admission that from Hector would have been a boast. And Wilde appreciated women enough to treat them with a kindliness that was foreign to Hector. "Why are women so fond of raking up the past?" Reginald asks. "They're as bad as tailors, who invariably remember what you owe them for a suit long after you've ceased to wear it." Wilde understood why men were attracted to women; very likely he even remembered. His women are vain, giddy and infinitely more scheming than men. Yet when the final artful touch of rouge has been applied and the last curl pressed carefully out of place, they float upon the scene so gracefully that only a churl would fail to appreciate them, and only a greedy naturalist would care to pin one. But in Hector's world, Reginald is the butterfly, and there are currents of more genuine, if faintly nasty, desire in any of the Reginald stories than in Wilde's airy plays with their admirable beauties and cold-handed gallants.

Late in November 1901, Hector sent Alice on her last adventure, to take tea at the Hotel Cecil. Within three weeks, Reginald was back, discoursing now on Christmas presents. The piece is distilled Reginald: teasing, vain, and —his charm—unrepentantly self-centered. "I wish it to be distinctly understood," he begins, "that I don't want a 'George, Prince of Wales' Prayerbook as a Christmas present. The fact cannot be too widely known." Reginald wonders why no one offers technical education classes on the science of present giving; his problems stem from the intractability of his aunts.

"There is my Aunt Agatha, par exemple," Reginald says, cutting as close to reality as Hector's prudence would permit him, "who sent me a pair of gloves last Christmas, and got so far as to choose a kind that was being worn and had the correct number of buttons. But—they were nines! I sent them to a boy whom I hated intimately; he didn't wear them, of course, but he could have—that was where the bitterness of death came in. It was nearly as consoling as sending white flowers to his funeral."

As the creation of a man indebted to the *Rubaiyat,* Reginald shows little appreciation of his heritage. "I am *not* collecting copies of the cheaper editions of Omar Khayyam. I gave the last four that I received to the lift-boy, and I like to think of him reading them, with Fitz-Gerald's notes, to his aged mother. Lift-boys always have aged mothers; shows such nice feeling on their part, I think." And such nice feeling on Reginald's part that he should inquire about the lift-boy's living arrangements.

Despite his list of prohibitions, Reginald turns out to be easy enough to shop for. "No boy who had brought himself up properly could fail to appreciate one of those decorative bottles of liqueurs that are so reverently staged in Morel's window—and it wouldn't in the least matter if one did get duplicates. And there would always be the supreme moment of dreadful uncertainty whether it was *crème de menthe* or Chartreuse . . . People may say what they like about the decay of Christianity; the religious system that produced green Chartreuse can never really die."

Months passed before Reginald popped in again on *Westminster* readers, and during that time Hector experienced two setbacks and a compensating success. In London, he contracted double pneumonia. It was a severe attack, but when Hector recovered Ethel found him stronger than he had ever been before, strong enough even to consider traveling again. Hector's second discouragement was professional. Buoyed by the success of Alice, he and Carruthers Gould collaborated on another set of parodies, this time of Kipling, called "The Political Jungle Book" and later "The Not-So Stories." Gould was in fine form, drawing his caricatures in double profile so that they were equally recognizable as animal and politician. Hector's text caught the sound of Kipling but seldom managed so clean a kill. His one inspiration was to portray Balfour, always an accommodating target, as a tiger named Sheer Khan't. ("When he went foraging his quarry was usually a scape-goat.")

The series appeared throughout 1902, five attempts in all to win a public, but this time there was no clamor for more. The problem may have been due to the material being parodied. Lewis Carroll's original had appeared thirty years before Hector's Alice, long enough for the generation that first loved her to grow up and embrace her reappearance in the *Westminster*. The *Just So Stories* had appeared earlier in the same year that Hector had sport with them.

A more successful jape that year was an editorial that Hector offered in the guise of a story and called "The Woman Who Never Should." In it the languorous Balfour, newly installed as Prime Minister, is visited in his chambers by a woman from his past. While it is only a political satire, its breathy, insinuating style suggests that, had Hector taken the genre seriously, he might have duplicated the melodramatic success of the early Maugham. Balfour "turned to find a woman standing beside him—a woman with pale, almost frightened face, but with an underlying air of resolution that bordered on defiance.

" 'Efficiency!' he said; '*you* here. Here, of all places!'

" 'You are displeased to see me here?'

" 'Not displeased, exactly, but I can scarcely believe it. You must see that you cannot possibly stay here.'

" 'Yet at one time you used to be proud to be seen with me. I suppose I was useful to you at election times, when things did not go so easily for you as they do now. You used to take me to your arms then, and I think you really cared for me—just a little.'

" 'Of course I admire you very much still, and I often talk about you—really I do, though we've seen so little of each other lately. But you can't reasonably expect me to dislocate my whole career and habits.' "

The best news for Hector that year was Spender's decision to publish the Alice series as a paperbound volume. The success of that pamphlet then prompted a "library edition" at two shillings sixpence. Despite Gould's enormous popularity, Hector had top billing on the cover: Written by H. H. Munro ("Saki"). Satire had proved respectable enough, or at least lucrative enough, to merit his name. He provided Charlotte Munro with a copy inscribed, "Aunt Tom, With the author's love, H. H. Munro." Even warmer was the inscription on the copy he kept for himself: "Presented to the author by himself, as a mark of affection and esteem. H. H. Munro." His signature ran together, as he would always write it, making the tops of the capital letters a sharpened barricade.

When he had recovered from pneumonia, Hector turned out a spate of Reginald stories. Some were Reginald's monologues, some conversations between Reginald and the Other. In two stories Hector introduced a third character as foil for his young man, a duchess who sounds much like Aunt Tom. Once in a while the Other is permitted a joke; it is he who remarks, "To be clever in the afternoon argues that one is dining nowhere in the evening." More often Reginald insists upon the last word:

" 'After all,' said the Duchess vaguely, 'there are certain things you can't get away from. Right and wrong, good conduct and moral rectitude, have certain well-defined limits.'

" 'So, for the matter of that,' replied Reginald, 'has the Russian Empire. The trouble is that the limits are not always in the same place.'

" 'Of course,' she resumed combatively, 'it's the prevailing fashion to believe in perpetual change and mutability, and all that sort of thing, and to say we are all merely an improved form of primeval ape—of course you subscribe to that doctrine?'

" 'I think it decidely premature; in most people I know the process is far from complete.' "

Reginald and the Duchess are conducting this symposium at the theatre, and Reginald deplores the thoughtless intrusions from the actors on stage. "That is the worst of a tragedy," he observes, "one can't always hear oneself talk." When they can resume their debate, Reginald tells the Duchess about "the man I read of in some sacred book who was given a choice of what he most desired. And because he didn't ask for titles and honours and dignities, but only for immense wealth, these other things came to him also."

"I am sure you didn't read about him in any sacred book."

"Yes; I fancy you will find him in Debrett."

Naturally, Reginald is an expert on house parties, that uniquely British ruse for making London habitable on the weekend by luring bores and fools to the country. He can categorize for the Other the girl who wears "a frock that's made at home and repented at leisure." Or the seeker after rural truth who asked Reginald how many fowls she could keep in a run ten feet by six. "I told her whole crowds, as long as she kept the door shut, and the idea didn't seem to have struck her before; at least, she brooded over it for the rest of dinner."

Against his better judgment, though in accordance with his worst instincts, Reginald allows himself to be taken hunting, the least of its drawbacks being that it requires him to get up at dawn. Reginald realized that it was dawn because "the grass looked as if it had been left out all night." He does bag a bird; he shoots his host's pet peacock. "They said afterwards that it was a tame bird; that's simply silly, because it was awfully wild at the first few shots."

Occasionally throughout the series of stories Reginald troubled to take aim but fired only blanks. "I always say, beauty is only sin deep," for example, and, "Never be a pioneer. It's the Early Christian that gets the fattest lion."

That particular attempt to amuse had been directed by Reginald to the person Hector identified as "his most darling friend," a phrase that marked Hector himself as a pioneer. For the initiated, an added charm to the stories was an occasional word to suggest that Reginald refused to play by the rules of the Marquess of Queensberry, that Reginald was not merely posing. That pleasure was increased by the slyness with which his creator allowed the young fop to declare himself. Here were his adventures, gracing the front page of a respectable journal, whose unsuspecting readers clasped him to their bosom and repeated his jokes. For the love that could not speak its name, Saki had spoken, and the name was Reginald.

Although words never failed him, Reginald's ingenuity

could extend to action as well. He takes a group of choir boys—"shy" and "bullet-headed"—to a woodland stream, confiscates their clothes while they bathe, and leads them naked through the streets of their village singing temperance hymns. Reginald wanted to outfit them with panther skins, but since none is available, the boys who had handkerchiefs with a spotted motif are allowed to wear them, "which they did with thankfulness."

Hector flirted with endangering his reputation by these gestures to a coterie, but in his treatment of another minority he was unimpeachably on the side of the prevailing prejudice. Twice Reginald mentions Jews in his conversation, and although each time he is careful to say something placating about their virtues, Hector's own disdain shows through. In one instance, Reginald describes the Anglo-Saxon Empire as becoming a suburb of Jerusalem. "A very pleasant suburb, I admit, and quite a charming Jerusalem. But still a suburb." At another point, he remarks, "Personally, I think the Jews have estimable qualities; they're so kind to their poor—and our rich."

One man who knew Hector suggested that his remarks betrayed no anti-Jewish feelings—even though Ethel, who lived to see the results of Hitler's final solution, harbored them through an unshakable lifetime. Rather, he said, they represented the response of a social satirist to the pavan of changing mores. The same man pointed out that Hector never scorned Jews as Jews, only as people with pretensions, figures fit for ridicule whether Jewish or Gentile. But Hector's response to Jews, as he would show in his newspaper dispatches, was more complex than that. He was a product of his age, and his rebelliousness was spent on Christianity and conventional sexuality. Otherwise, he accepted with the air he breathed the monarchy, the Empire and a wariness toward Jews.

When Reginald got off his line about reaching thirty, Hector, who had been thirty for eighteen months, was indulging in self-reproach. Who could have believed, romping through Davos, that men became thirty or, if they must, that they had not made their mark by then. For a day or two Hector had amused the politically literate members of his society, but that, he was finding, was no career. With Gould to illustrate his whimsy and Spender to publish it, Hector might have stayed on in London to build upon his slender reputation. Instead, he went to Macedonia, not exactly as a writer or a historian but as that mixture of breeds, a journalist. Hector would never have acknowledged a thirst for respectability, but his was strong, if unspoken, and to it the job offered these sops: when he left London this time, at least it was not as a policeman; and if he must leave as a reporter, at least it was for the *Morning Post*.

From its early days in the 1770s, the *Morning Post* was regarded as the most English of newspapers. It was politically conservative, yet it had opposed Pitt during the American Revolution. It supported national education at a time when even schoolmasters advocated sending children to the loom. Thackeray, like its other readers, regarded the *Morning Post* as speaking for the gentry, yet it was widely read in the poor industrial regions of North England. Whatever else, the *Morning Post* was well written. Dr. Johnson first published his travel journals there, Samuel Coleridge wrote leading articles for it, and William Wordsworth published sonnets in its pages. When, to lighten the mood, the paper paid Charles Lamb sixpence each for jokes, a literary consensus held that he was being overpaid.

The *Morning Post*'s more recent correspondents were equally distinguished. George Meredith went to Italy to cover the wars of liberation, and Kipling and Thomas Hardy regularly submitted their verse. During the war in South Africa the newspaper had stanchly defended the conflict as a fulfillment of its own prophecy. For twenty years its leader writers had been warning the Boers that England would use full force to crush any insurrection. But in its news columns the paper trumpeted every military ineptitude so loudly that Winston Churchill wrote from South Africa to suggest that this constant criticism of a conservative government came ill from a conservative newspaper. Hector's Alice satires in the liberal *Westminster* had, by contrast, represented gentle chiding.

What role his father played in Hector's decision to go

abroad for the *Morning Post* is open to speculation. Hector greatly admired the Gov, and the admiration was returned uncritically. But perhaps with his health seemingly restored, Hector was tempted to do something that was dashing, or enterprising, or, at the least, self-supporting. It does not seem likely that any of the young men he had chummed with had influenced his decision. From the sound of his letters and his first dispatches, Hector went out to the Balkans exhilarated and alone.

7

The Yarkand Manner (1902-1904)

The Balkan states were relics of the Ottoman Empire —"Balkan" being the Turkish word for "mountain" —and in recent years they had begun to quarrel over Macedonia, which represented the last large parcel of land in Europe still held by the Turks. In itself the territory, north of Greece and southwest of Bulgaria, was not worth a great deal. Only three million people lived on it, and most of them were Slavs who spoke a dialect much like Bulgarian. The question troubling Europe had become, Should the Macedonians be permitted to form a separate state, or should the territory be carved up among their neighbors? And if that latter alluring solution were accepted, how would the slicing be done? The issue was a matter of race and language on its surface, of conventional power politics at its core, and it so agitated the region that the *Morning Post* simply ran a standing headline, "The Balkan Troubles," under which it reported each day's tangled developments.

Late in 1902, as Hector departed for the region, rumors were circulating in world capitals that the Great Powers were tempted to intercede since the feeble Turkish government could not stop either the sharp local clashes or the growing reliance on terror. A year earlier, a Bulgarian cell had kidnaped Miss E. M. Stone, an American missionary in Macedonia, and released her only after the Turkish government paid $70,000. Hector would be facing at least as much danger from the Bulgarian guerrillas as he had from marauding bands in Burma. During the week of his arrival, Bulgarian rebels launched another skirmish, apparently aimed at drawing the major powers deeper into the quagmire.

Despite this portentousness, Hector's first dispatch from Vuchitrn was marked by the same flippancy that had put off critics of his Russian history. Although his byline read only "From Our Correspondent," Hector engaged freely in first-person narration, a style denied to competing correspondents for Reuter's Telegrams: "I am within sight of Mitrovitza, which is now the centre of Albanian effervescence." His dispatch ran to seven brief paragraphs and contained several of the themes to which Hector would return often as a war correspondent. He placed a premium on physical courage, and with a sneer he reported that the Albanians would never stand up to cannon fire but preferred to tear up the railway tracks between his lookout post and the town of Mitrovitza. In this admiration for war in its traditional form, Hector was again reflecting his time. Dedicating a rifle range outside London, Rudyard Kipling had lately deplored the fact that the overwhelming bulk of a white male population could grow up and die absolutely ignorant of the use of firearms, and Kipling's remarks had been cheered by a chorus of "For He's a Jolly Good Fellow."

Hector was always inclined toward optimism in his dispatches, less because of any special hopefulness to his character than because it pleased him to deflate the prevailing alarms. Hector would be ever assuring his readers that things were not so dire as rival correspondents were painting them, a stance that lent to his reportage a detached calm suited to the journal in which it appeared.

Most characteristic of all was Hector's penchant for incorporating into his stories flavorful dialogue and keen descriptions, a technique rediscovered every generation and called New Journalism. "The Kaimakam of this town said to me: 'I have a vineyard in the outskirts, but I never eat grapes'—meaning that the Albanians rendered all work in the fields impossible. When a pope remarked to him in my presence, 'You are such an energetic official that I pray you may long be spared to us,' he replied, 'Choose some other prayer, I beg of you.' "

Hector had been a journalist only briefly when he mastered that indispensable tool of the trade, the sweeping, shameless generalization: "The majority of Albanians," Hector concluded, having been in the Balkans less than a month, "would also welcome the reestablishment of law and order, but they are powerless in the face of the heads of their clan."

Hector traveled to the Aegean and four days later it was from Salonica that he filed his next report, which then took another four days to reach London for the *Morning Post* edition of October 8, 1902. "I hear that Europe has been inundated with rumour of insurrection here, but so far I am assured that nothing serious has happened in this vilayet." In this even briefer report, he added another device to his journalist's kit, the unidentified informant; his facts had come "from a private source." Hector was an untried analyst, and to his reassurances of peace the *Morning Post* appended a Reuter's dispatch from Belgrade that also dismissed the possibility of an uprising in Macedonia.

The following day, Hector identified his source. It was a time when newspaper readers assumed, with their correspondents, that a British diplomat would be the one source of accurate information. "I asked the news of our Consul-General this morning. He said that three reports of affrays had reached him . . . A tax-gatherer came to a Christian village. Taxes had not been paid for a long period and he was forced to distrain. A wedding was taking place at the time, and he, perhaps indiscreetly, seized the bride's dress and wedding presents. This aroused indignation, and some men, who had been indulging in the wedding breakfast rather too freely, rose and killed the tax-gatherer. Then, fearing the consequences, the whole village fled to the mountains."

The other incidents were equally minor. Clearly, Hector sided with those officials who claimed that if the Turks would only fight the Bulgarians with government troops instead of the irregulars—called zapties—the struggle would be brief. "Complete pacification would be easy," Hector wrote. "The zapties are irregularly paid and irregularly fed. They must take bread or other bare nourishment from the villages they visit, and this causes discontent."

Hector's story held no trace of sympathy for the Bulgarian bands that were fighting for independence from Turkey. An artificial movement, he called it, inspired by Sofia and only working to provoke a massacre that would draw in the Great Powers. "The turbulent persons are very few," Hector wrote, summing up, "and the Government is alert." This was hardly yellow journalism; indeed, Hector's talent showed itself in making so essentially colorless an approach sufficiently crisp and detailed that it was journalism at all.

A long hiatus before his next report supports the speculation that at this stage of his career Hector was a stringer for the newspaper, paid only for the dispatches he sent and not yet on the regular stipend that caused him later to feel compelled to file nearly every day. For now, he was a journalistic zaptie, taking his nourishment where he found it, and by the end of November that meant going on to Belgrade, the capital of turbulent Serbia. Once there, Hector took a break from politics and sent the *Morning Post* an explication of the slava, a local holiday. It was the sort of feature story he handled deftly, intrigued as he was by lore that had survived among the people with no endorsement from their religious leaders.

"The 'slava' or family saint's day is a peculiarly Servian institution. If one is ever in doubt about the nationality of Slavs in Macedonia or elsewhere one has only to inquire if they observe the 'slava.' . . . On their 'slava' day Servian families expect to be visited by all their friends and acquaintances. A book is published in Belgrade tabulating all the saints of the various families, and every diplomatic agent who desires to keep on good terms with the people must study it carefully, as the neglect of a friend's 'slava' is a grave social offence." Hector told about legends that predated Christianity and persisted during the slava, and he explained how a local priest, or pope, celebrated the occasion. "The various members of the family advance in turn, kiss the crucifix, and receive a sousing on the head."

Between dispatches, Hector took time to send to Ethel letters as conscientiously phrased as his articles for the *Morning Post*. He had joined as a visiting member the Union Club in Sofia, he wrote, "the social hub of the local universe." His immediate concerns after filing a story were to find a horse to ride, a river for bathing and a game of tennis or bridge. "The English vice-consul and I fell into each other's arms when we each discovered that the other played Bridge." Like Maugham, Hector remained devoted to bridge, a game that allows one to sit for hours in the company of others and say next to nothing. For a man with Maugham's stammer, bridge represented comfortable social intercourse. For a man as diffident as Hector, and as sensitive to banality and pretension, it seems to have provided the same refuge.

Certainly Reginald took bridge with rare seriousness. He told of a Russian boy whose only distinctions were his skill at bridge and his devotion to his family. "When his maternal grandmother died he didn't go so far as to give up bridge altogether but he declared in nothing but black suits for the next three months." When characters in Hector's later stories were made to say, "Cards are such a waste of time, I think," or, "None of my children have been brought up to play card games," the reader could be sure that they were females and would soon receive their comeuppance.

Hector's letters gave Ethel occasional glimpses of his work as a foreign correspondent. "I have voluminous discussions in French with some of the leaders in the Bulgarian parliament; I don't mean to say the discussions take place there; mercifully neither can criticize the other's accent." In his absence, Ethel had inherited some of Hector's London friends, not always finding in them the same attractions. "Don't get humpy with L. B.," he asked of her.

"It's part of his nature to do odd things and he will never be otherwise. I can imagine him walking out of Heaven and saying, 'This place is run by the Jews.' And at heart he is friendly." Another man had sent him a tiny silver crucifix to ward off the vampires endemic to the Balkans, "which," said Hector, "up to the present it has done."

With the new year, Hector's byline now read, "From Our Special Correspondent," and he justified the adjective with a column of speculation about a political scandal that threatened to erupt that very day in the Bulgarian parliament. The possibility caused Hector to hurry to the chamber of the National Sobranje and cast a cool eye upon the native political talent. "On two descending tiers, upholstered in scarlet, are the seats of the President and the Ministers facing the semicircular dark-wood benches, on which are ranged the elect, or at any rate the elected, of Bulgaria. The red-draped rostrum of the clerk and two severely simple tables for the scribes occupy the floor of the House. With a view, possibly, to the requirements of the Greater Bulgaria of a future day, the seating accommodation has been allotted on a scale which gives plenty of elbow room. In leisurely fashion the members drift into their places, some clad in an irreproachable Westminster model, many in primitive and uncompromising peasant garb, and one political group affecting a red fez headgear. The Ministerial Bench is enlivened by the uniform of the Minister of War, and further diversified by the brown tweed coat of M. Ludskanoff, the maligned man of the moment.

"M. Daneff and his civil colleagues sit with an air of smiling depression, as though a double-beaked eagle were plucking continually at their consciences. No Ministerial statement of resignation is forthcoming, however, and as Government catastrophes arrive from above and not from below in this country the interest of the sitting practically evaporates in the first few minutes. With laborious slowness the House votes the order of the day, the voting being by roll-call, apparently read out in the alphabetical order of the Christian names. The preponderating response of 'Da' (Aye) removes any doubt as to the intentions of the Chamber, but there is a considerate silence at the finish while the clerk hurriedly adds up the totals. One member employs himself in the interval—and indeed during the greater part of the sitting—by telling the beads of a huge yellow rosary. The figures are at last ascertained and carried up to the President, who announces that the 'Das' have it. The House resolves itself into committee, and for the present at least there is no crisis."

Early in February, Hector journeyed to the town of Rustchuk, where he pondered whether the Bulgarian government truly wanted peace in Macedonia. He reminded his readers that a fortnight earlier they had read in the *Morning Post* a border proposal only now being publicly put forward. It was Hector's first scoop and he intended to have the credit. His sympathies lay with the Turkish government, less because of the issues at dispute than because he deplored all rebellion except those in which he was the rebel chieftain. Just as the modernist of the period needed an academy to flout, Hector had to be assured of a tranquillity to disturb. For that reason he was skeptical about any reports that would give legitimacy to the uprising against the Turks.

"The frontier monastery of Rilo has been a showcase of samples of alleged Turkish barbarities, a place of pilgrimage for those who wished to hear with their own ears what their interpreters had to tell them."

But he concluded that, justified or not, there would be a revolt of some size in Macedonia in the spring, and by month's end, Hector felt he must firmly affix blame for the growing Macedonian problem: "Without political bias in any direction, the disturbing factor in the region known as Macedonia may be sought and found in the Bulgar-Macedonian, or, as he must be called when met with on this side of the border, the Macedonian-Bulgar. With his strong racial personality, he forces himself into the notice, though not necessarily into the knowledge, of the European public, in whose eyes he ranks somewhere between a brigand and a religious martyr; a city that is set on a hill cannot be hid, but it is always susceptible of Impressionist treatment. In Bulgarian politics he occupies much the same position, apart from the fact that he is merely a local variant of the general population, as the Irishman in the United States. At organization he is an adept, though of necessity his methods are shaped less on the lines of an electoral caucus than on those of an Italian secret society. From the starting-base of 'corner-boy' and, literally, man in the street, he monopolises gradually the outdoor trades, such as light porter, water-carrier, and hawker of small goods—of considerable importance in a Balkan city . . . Without being exactly a thorn in the side of the community, the Macedonian is at least a very crumpled rose-leaf."

Perhaps Hector's readers, accepting his assurance that his was a neutral analysis, could appreciate the justice to his accusation that the brash Bulgar had snatched up the important occupations in Macedonia—porter, water bearer, sidewalk vendor. They would then be susceptible as well to Hector's claim that the Turkish ruler, the Porte, was doing his best to institute political reform. "The fantastic idea that evil comes from above, having its origin in official oppression," Hector wrote, "does not require very elaborate refutation."

Russia and Austria had joined to propose their own reforms for Macedonia. From Rustchuk, Hector reported on the disillusion those proposals had caused among the Bulgars, who objected to the central thesis that Turkey should go on wielding the executive power in the region. Hector permitted himself a weary hint that he was equally disillusioned. "As I have previously contended, no scheme of administrative reform really touches the sources of unrest." For him, the solution was clear: Bulgaria must give up its expansionist aims; all else was temporizing.

Two weeks later, on March 19, 1903, Hector noted that Russia, which had seemed to support Bulgaria in its Macedonian adventure, was now decreeing that "not one drop of blood" was to be expended in the Balkans. Hector gleefully labeled this departure "the anemic policy," but while he took delight in Bulgaria's immediate distress at the retreat of its powerful ally, he feared that the long-range result could be dangerous to Britain. Russia would now be free to intrigue elsewhere. "No one who is opposed to the strengthening of Russian influence in South-Eastern

Europe, at the very threshold of Nearer Asia, can view this outcome of the situation with satisfaction."

On April 1, the *Morning Post,* in a discursive editorial on Macedonia, took a less benign view of Turkish rule than did its own correspondent. "We know also that the Turk has always had the position of the ruling race; that his religion teaches him that he is in every way the superior of unbelievers, who are in comparison with the Faithful but as dogs." The paper also deplored the fact that news about Macedonia was coming from its periphery—from Serbia, Bulgaria and Salonica—rather than from the disputed territory itself. Before the month was out, Hector was on his way to Macedonia.

He traveled in the company of two fellow journalists, one an elderly and bearded Viennese, the other H. N. Brailsford, a correspondent for the *Manchester Guardian.* Henry Brailsford was a rather short, muscular man with bright blue eyes and a passion for Bach and Schubert. He had studied philosophy in Glasgow but his developing political views, which led him eventually to socialism, prevented him from settling in at a university. Both Hector and Brailsford were youthful-looking and clean-shaven, and at the Turkish border an official surveyed the railroad car and concluded that they were the sons of their Viennese colleague. On their passports, he wrote that they were being taken to school in Salonica, an error that may have amused Brailsford and gratified Hector. Brailsford was less amused, however, when some weeks later he was arrested by the Turkish authorities as a runaway from school.

With his instinct for human foibles and his neat prose style, Brailsford made an apt companion for Hector. He scorned Albanians and Bulgarians alike but he found something admirable in the graceful corruption of the Greeks. Since he was contentedly married, he could praise, in language that Hector did not yet feel free to use, the attractions of Serbian manhood. In Belgrade, he wrote, "the women are not striking, but the men—for example, the too numerous officers—are notably tall, well-built in a lithe way, and frequently handsome in feature."

Hector's letters to Ethel from Uskub showed him reveling in the strangeness of his assignment and the rustic nature of his surroundings. "This is the most delightfully outlandish and primitive place I have ever dared to hope for. Rustchuk was elegant and up-to-date in comparison. The only hotel in the place is full; I am in the other. A small ragged boy swooped on my things and marched before me like a pillar of dust, while two blind beggars came behind with suggestions of charitable performances on my part. Then I was walked upstairs and offered the alternative of sharing a bedroom with a Turk or a nicer bedroom with two Turks.

"I pleaded a lonely and morose disposition and was at last given a room without carpet, stove, or wardrobe, but also without Turks. The only person on the 'hotel' staff that I can converse with is a boy who speaks Bulgarian with a stutter. The country round is 'apart'; lovely rolling hills and huge snow-capped mountains, and storks nesting in large communities; everything wild and open and full of life. There are two magpies who seem to have some idea of living in this room with me."

During his assignment in Uskub, the *Morning Post* gave Hector reason to celebrate. After six months as a journalist, he received his first byline, "From H. H. Munro, Our Special Correspondent." Hector justified this show of faith by beginning his next dispatch on an Albanian uprising with the stark declaration, "The situation here is grave."

At the end of April 1903, the *Morning Post* ran three squibs from Hector, all filed from Uskub but on successive days. The third, headed "Rumours of Heavy Fighting," was so muddled that the editors appended a note to clarify for their readers just where the fighting was going on. All that was sure was that Macedonia was rife with fearful stories and that Hector was depending on British contacts whom he frankly labeled "Turcophil."

Along with the truncated reports of fighting, Hector filed another, longer story, of the sort that latter-day reporters deride indulgently as "think pieces." Endeavoring to explain to readers how it could happen that Turkey, a

nation known as the sick man of Europe, could throw off
its infirmities and join with the Russians in agreements
against the Bulgarians, Hector warned that Russia's efforts
in the Balkans must be measured by centuries rather than
decades. With a whirl worthy of a local dervish, Hector
offered a conclusion: "Under the nose of Austrian state-
craft, behind the back of France, and full in the face of the
Bulgarian government, the Porte (of Turkey) and St.
Petersburg have entered into a temporary alliance, which
possibly exists in fact rather than in ink.

"The drift and purport of this compact may briefly be
summed up in the expression that Turkey is letting a room
to Russia in order to be master in the rest of the house."

To his governmental mind reading Hector tacked on
that useful and all-purpose sentence, the advance counter-
rebuttal: "For obvious reasons a very emphatic official
denial will be forthcoming from the quarters concerned."

As Hector's thoughtful piece was on its way to London,
Bulgarian rebels drove carriages past the leading banks in
Salonica and threw out bombs. The Ottoman Bank was
totally destroyed, another was badly damaged, as was the
German Club. Hector left at once for the scene but his trip
was interrupted dramatically. "While traveling from
Uskub to Salonica," he confided to his readers, "I was
seized by a railway picket and had a narrow escape of
being shot, as I was suspected of being a dynamiter."

By midnight Hector had been permitted into Salonica,
and, from the railway station, he filed a fuller account of
the travail. "The reports which reached Uskub on
Wednesday night and this morning of sinister doings at
Salonica, of attempts to dynamite the line to Constantinople, and of the Ottoman Bank having been blown up,
tempered by a cheerful official optimism that parts of the
bank were still standing, prompted an immediate move
towards the scene of disturbance."

With an American reporter he had gone south at about
two in the afternoon, passing by many guards and en-
campments to reach Salonica by nightfall. There he was
told that the city was under a state of siege and no one
could leave the station. "The first duty of a correspondent
is to correspond," Hector noted, "and a tour in the throes

of a revolutionary outbreak seemed to offer more attractions than a railway station tenanted with herded humans.

"In the hope of slipping out by a side exit we therefore picked up our valises and made for an apparent outlet some five hundred yards distant across a waste of inconveniently overgrown grass. As a slight precaution against being mistaken for prowling Komitniki we turned down the collars of our overcoats so as to display the white collar, if not of a blameless life, at least of a business that did not call for concealment.

"About four hundred yards of the distance had been covered when a frantic challenge in Turkish brought us to a standstill, and five armed and agitated figures sprang forward in the starlight and began to interrogate us at a distance, which they seemed disinclined to lessen. As five triggers had clicked and five rifles were covering us we dropped our valises and 'uphanded,' but without reassuring our questioners, who seemed to be possessed of a panic which might more reasonably have been displayed on our part."

Neither reporter knew a word of Turkish. Hector had been studying Bulgarian but since that was the language of the rebels he felt it would be inappropriate. Still, every time he tried to phrase a sentence in French, Bulgarian words sprang to mind. He ended up saying nothing.

"The men had reached a point whence they were unwilling to approach nearer, and for a minute or two they took deliberate aim from a ridiculously easy range in a state of excitement which was unpleasant to witness from our end of the barrels.

"At last two lowered their rifles, and after stalking round us with elaborate caution managed to secure our hands with a rope or sash-cord which was hurriedly produced from somewhere. The operation would have been shorter if they had not tried to hold their rifles at our heads at the same time. When it was safely accomplished the statement that I was 'Inglesi effendi' and the demand for our Consuls allayed their suspicions to a certain extent, but nothing would induce them to pick up my valise until the light of day should show its real nature, and it is still lying out on the waste land, where, if it explodes violently, no great harm will be done."

Inside the railway waiting room, Hector and the American joined trainloads of other passengers, and there horrified officials "flocked to release us with a haste which made the untying process almost as long as the binding." Once freed, Hector was inquisitive. Why, he asked his captors, didn't you shoot us? It was their trick with the collars, one guard said. Turned down that way, they did not look like those of Bulgarian desperados.

Little more than a week later, Hector was writing to Ethel with his usual aplomb about a young man he had met who was part of the movement to reform Turkey's government and restore the nation to its former grandeur. "There is a 'Young Turk,' if you know what that means, staying in this hotel, very interesting and amusing. He has learnt and forgotten a little English but the other day in the midst of a political discussion in French he took our breath away by starting off at a great rate 'Twinkle, twinkle, little star,' and went on with more of it than I had ever heard before. It's a funny world."

Knowing Ethel's dedication to all things furry and four-legged, Hector told her with obvious satisfaction of having rescued a tiny kitten that might otherwise have been trampled when the rebels made a raid on the telegraph office. And just as he had deprecated but mentioned all the same the description of him in print as an attractive figure in Burma, he told Ethel, who could pass it along to the Gov, that his adventures at the railway station had been written up in the *Neue Freie Presse*. "A highly coloured account," Hector called it happily.

In his *Morning Post* report about the assault on the telegraph office, Hector did not mention his ministrations to the kitten and he described the carnage more graphically. "In company with other correspondents, I was taking luncheon in a restaurant opposite the Hôtel d'Angleterre, when two reports sent everyone to his feet.

"On getting into the street I saw a young Bulgar lying in the roadway outside the telegraph office, apparently not quite dead, but no one venturing very close to his body in fear of the possible explosion of a bomb.

"In another minute several soldiers had run in and extinguished any spark of life that might have been in him, and an officer with difficulty thrust them aside and searched the body for explosives. A bomb and two bars of dynamite were found on him."

A curfew was causing the correspondents some inconvenience, and when he wrote about it, he mentioned the succor that had been extended to him at the highest level. "The prohibition to go through the streets after sundown is still enforced, and it cannot be disregarded without considerable personal danger.

"The hotel in which I am staying does not include a dining department and the problem of feeding at another hotel without having to fix the dinner hour inconveniently early is difficult of solution in present circumstances. Rather than give me and a brother correspondent authority to migrate nightly from our feeding ground to our hotel his Excellency Hassan Bey, Vali of Salonica, offered us with charming Turkish courtesy to supply us every evening with whatever we desired—a responsibility which we did not feel justified in adding to the many cares which at present beset the Administration."

If Hector had a complaint about the way the Turks were responding to the crisis—and, on the whole, he continued to praise the government's vigor and judgment—it was a demurrer as to its choice of troops. In Burma, so far as his health had permitted, Hector had assumed the burden of empire; now, seven years later, he indicated that nothing in those months in the Orient had made him question the assumption. It was a mistake on the Turks' part, he said, to guard Salonica with Asiatic battalions. "Possibly they possess the virtue of being the most handy which, with Governments that choose to be taken unawares, is always a consideration; but they are composed of men who are naturally more excitable, more ignorant, and more terrified of the unknown than their Western brothers, and if the trouble grew to more serious proportions the presence of a steadier military element would be desirable."

Along with Henry Brailsford and his wife, the British colony in Salonica included a noted journalist of the day,

H. W. Nevinson. An old Balkans hand, Nevinson described the peculiar allure of the land: stretches of open marsh and lake between the mountain ridges, valleys brilliant with the plumage of fruit trees, wild swans, gulls that had learned to catch and feed on flies. From Byzantine Salonica he could look past the intensely blue bay to the snow on Mount Olympus. A tireless reformer, Nevinson had come to Macedonia primarily to aid in the relief effort, and he was drawn to the Brailsfords—young, attractive and imbued with the same Samaritan spirit. Despite the disturbing misery on every side and the daily perils, the three of them went through their time together laughing and joking. Afterward, Nevinson looked back with a quizzical nostalgia at the incongruous joy of those days. Was it the danger, he wondered, that had made those hours so abandoned? Nevinson also knew Hector during that period, but he gave no sign that the clever young man had contributed to the prevailing mirth. Once in a while, among his closest friends, Hector could caper and sing. More of the time, he was amiable, alert and very reserved. It seems to have taken a friend who understood his sexual tastes to know Hector well, and an introduction to such a friend among the press corps lay two years away in St. Petersburg.

In the aftermath of the Bulgarian bombings, Hector put forward an estimate, which he had checked with the British consul, that fewer than a hundred people had been killed; other estimates had run to the thousands and Hector dismissed them as "fantastic." Since he continued to praise the resourcefulness of the Vali in putting down the insurrection, it was no wonder that the Turk, if he kept abreast of the outgoing dispatches, extended offers of lavish courtesy to him.

Hector went to Monastir and found that town in a state of panic over reports of more Bulgarian bombs. After a brief review of the rumors, Hector violated a prime editorial rule by complaining in print about how hard his job had become. "It is difficult to get news out of the town, but I am making private arrangements to get this hurried dispatch through."

These reports were now taking a week to make their

way from Macedonia to the *Morning Post,* but the paper was giving Hector ample space—almost two full columns in the issue of May 15, 1903. He had at last found a Vali he did not like, a Turk named Ali Riza, whom Hector considered too lax in putting out the sparks of revolt. When he proposed his own solution, it sounded as though Aunt Augusta would have made the perfect Vali. "If a permanent beating tribunal, armed with sticks of appreciable thickness, was set up to chastise without mercy or favour all Bashi Bazouks and citizens guilty of breaking or attempting to break the peace, and if a general confiscation of weapons was carried into practice, both the desire and the means for disturbance would be restricted within manageable limits."

Hector described arriving on the train from Monastir on May 6, with a colleague, the two of them the only correspondents in town and, with the trouble underway, "not as welcome as the flowers in the spring." He fancied that the Vali would not have minded if Kismet had dynamited the tracks from Salonica, since he was one of those Turkish leaders who stood well with Russia and could see these Western arrivals only as an intrusion.

As a shirttail to his dispatch, the *Morning Post* printed Hector's response to a reader who had protested his antipathy toward the Serbs and his low estimate of their population in Macedonia. Hector defended himself by explaining his polling techniques. "When I have made inquiry among the peasants as to their racial affinities I have been careful to do so without the least suggestion as to which answer would be more acceptable."

He added, "Since I last wrote on this subject several amusing instances have come under my notice of peasants who naively admit to having become Serb for a monetary consideration, and I have been tempted to invent the term 'Serbo-plated' for Bulgarians who come under this heading."

Hector warned that the situation in Macedonia was fast becoming intolerable, "while statesmen and politicians have been earnestly inquiring after reforms, as one might ask tidings of the health of a sick and interesting baby . . ."

From Salonica a few days later, Hector was able to supply details about the bombing of the Ottoman Bank. A tunnel, it turned out, had been dug from a small shop across from the bank. "As the earth under the roadway was dug out (a process which was in operation for several months) it was transferred into barrels of portable size, which ostensibly contained petroleum. These barrels were purchased from time to time by confederates who came in the guise of customers, and in this way the earth was safely carried off the premises without arousing suspicion."

When Hector filed his next report, it betrayed his own impatience more than that of the population. Then as now correspondents preferred to witness a climactic moment and they could agitate for a cataclysm rather than admit that they had come late to the entertainment or had been called away before it began. "War between Turkey and Bulgaria may not be exactly imminent at the moment," Hector wrote, "but it is certainly uppermost in the thoughts and desires of the Turkish authorities and of their well-wishers in foreign political circles, as well as among the cosmopolitan trading-folk, who find the present state of alarm and insecurity playing havoc with their affairs."

Yet even as he was welcoming a conflagration, Hector was dismayed by its likely consequences. Turkey might be able to win against Bulgaria but only at immense cost, and throughout Macedonia the Slavs would turn in despair to Russia for deliverance. "Sofia would simply become, as it had nearly been on one or two previous occasions in its history, an advanced telegraph post of the Russian Empire." Hector finished his cheerless analysis by admitting that it was easier to criticize than to suggest a promising alternative. "For the second time within a quarter of a century of Balkan history the cards seem all in the hands of Russia."

On May 19, 1903, Hector was badly scooped, and permeating his dispatch of that day was a tempered indignation together with a rather feline dismissal of his competition. "I have telegraphic information that the representative of a Danish newspaper has been permitted to travel across country from Monastir to Okbrida. On the

7th of May a request on my part to make the same journey was refused by the Vali (Ali Riza Pasha) with some vehemence, and I was assured that no foreign correspondents would be allowed to journey into the interior of the country.

"Three weeks ago, when the prohibition on upcountry expeditions was first announced, I expressed the opinion that a special relaxation would be made in favour of this particular correspondent, as he has considerable Russian influence at his back, and the Turkish authorities will refuse nothing to the Russians.

"I have, of course, entered a protest against this discrimination, and the matter has been taken up by the British consular authorities. The incident is chiefly interesting to me as confirming the impressions which I have already recorded of the diplomatic undercurrents in this country."

The resentment showed throughout the story, honing the correspondent's pen. Of overblown reports of battling between Turkish troops and the Albanians, he noted, "A statement is current that the entire Turkish Army has fallen back on Prizend. I think it is more likely that, in the absence of trustworthy information, someone has fallen back on his imagination."

As Hector was becoming more deeply immersed in the conflict, he was forgoing praise for Turkey's handling of the uprising and focusing instead on its mistakes. He had taken the reporter's first step toward disillusionment with a war: he did not oppose the war itself, only the way in which it was being waged. He was convinced, for example, that the Turks had erred by rounding up more Bulgarians as terrorist suspects than they intended to prosecute. When the government released those prisoners on the same vast scale, it would surely mean an increase in rebel activity. "You cannot permanently imprison the population of an entire district," Hector observed with a new asperity.

On May 23, Hector was in Sofia, where he was granted an interview with the new Bulgarian premier, General Petroff. Hector was impressed with the general's air of quiet determination, and despite his own disposition toward the Turks he found Petroff several moves ahead of his political opponents. The general demanded reforms from the Turks and a release of his countrymen from their mass imprisonment. Hector was gratified to hear the Bulgarian leader analyze the problems in Macedonia in almost the language of his own dispatches; that is, that Turkey and Bulgaria had congruent interests if only they could see it. To help his readers understand the mistaken tactics of the Turks, Hector suggested a parallel: What if, during troubles with the Irish independents, the British government had imprisoned every prominent Irish citizen in Liverpool and Glasgow?

Summing up, Hector praised the general as mildly Turkophile and he only regretted that Petroff had not come to power five months earlier, in place of the Daneff government, which favored the Russians. Now it might be too late. "Poverty and panic are the two least desirable conditions in a land when a revolutionary spirit is abroad," Hector wrote, and he saw them both stalking Macedonia.

What Hector did not do for the *Morning Post* reader was to portray vividly the poverty to which he alluded. On ceremonial occasions he could render a fête or parade with a wealth of details, particularly the satirical ones. But Nevinson conveyed better the reality of guerrilla war—the head of a Bulgarian chieftain, murdered by a gang in the pay of a Greek archbishop, severed at the neck, bullet through the jaw and dripping blood. And among the peasantry, the hunger and smallpox, the rape of women and the desecration of churches, the human dead devoured by dogs. Nevinson's rage flared across his pages and what he saw left him repelled ever after by Turkish soldiers. Hector avoided such emotional reporting. His sympathies lay with the Turkish government, but most of all, since his Russian history, he had forsworn the style. Once, sounding like Anatole France, Reginald had silenced the Duchess when she boasted of England's generosity in alleviating misery around the world. " 'I wonder,' said Reginald, 'if you have ever walked down the Embankment on a winter night?'

" 'Gracious, no, child! Why do you ask?'

" 'I didn't; I only wondered.' "

It is Reginald's one recorded expression of sympathy

for the poor, and, if such expressions were at a premium in heaven, Hector would score no higher.

By the end of May, Hector was christening the martial element in Turkey "the War-at-Any-Price Party," and he had found evidence of the same thinking in Bulgaria. To prove that such a bellicose spirit could prevail even though it was held by a minority faction, Hector drew on his own experiences in Burma. "Ten years ago we did not succeed in preventing a serious Mussulman-Hindu outbreak in Rangoon. Though both parties to the disturbance only represented a comparatively small fraction of the population." If that comparison struck no response, there was a more recent parallel. The Bulgarian government was trying to stop raiding parties from entering Macedonia, Hector wrote, the British reader might recall how hard it had been to avoid unauthorized forays in South Africa.

Meanwhile, a list had been released of the Bulgarians taken into custody in the sweep after the dynamiting at Salonica, and Hector could condemn afresh those indiscriminate arrests when he found among the imprisoned men more than fifty "merchants and traders, some of them of considerable standing." It does not seem to have occurred to Hector that prominent and wealthy men might join a nationalist movement.

The tone of his dispatches lightened whenever Hector could introduce a public figure. He presented such men as almost fictional characters, replete with dialogue and stage directions; one example was an interview he conducted with one of those Bulgarian politicians who saw Russia as an ally. The man, a M. Ludskanoff, explained that although Russia's proposals to Turkey for reforms in Macedonia were obviously inadequate, their very shortcomings would compel Russia to offer more in the future. In one thrust, Hector not only pricked that bubble but Britain's torpor over Macedonia as well. "The policy of asking for less than you want in the hope of getting more is not a very usual or promising method in Eastern statescraft, and M. Ludskanoff's high opinion of Russian benevolence towards Bulgarian interests was not particularly infectious.

" 'France,' he observed, 'seems to have started out on the road towards being our good friend, and then to have stopped short . . . and the policy of Great Britain in the Balkan question'—but there I stopped his criticism. Of the moribund speak nothing but good."

Beginning to appear in Hector's dispatches by early summer were his own ideas for resolving the Macedonian crisis. He had been covering the battlefield for nine months, and very few reporters, after similar periods of gestation, have not felt obliged to offer their solutions to whatever puzzle they were sent to describe. When a foreign correspondent learns, as Hector would, that, although he is better informed than the statesmen he interviews, his proposals will be ignored, his chagrin sometimes sends him home. In Hector's case, he tendered his proposal with the diffidence appropriate to a student of Darwin:

"I do not invoke the name of humanity on behalf of any remedial scheme I have to suggest, because nature, which after all is the final arranger of these matters, uses as a rule the most heartless methods to attain its ends. I simply offer a political solution of a political problem.

"In looking over the map of Macedonia it is possible to put one's finger on certain districts which are preponderatingly Bulgar, others which are more distinctly Greek, Ottoman, Wallach, or Serb, others—inconveniently many —where the inhabitants are mixed in an ethnographic medley, which must have suggested the culinary term of a 'blending of fruits.' The existing vilayets in no way correspond with any of these folk-groupings; in fact it would be impossible for them to do so.

"My suggestion is the creation of smaller political districts, carved out as skilfully as possible with no particular standard of size but simply with the view of making each district as exclusively a one-race unit as could be contrived. Having secured this end, or, rather, this beginning, the various districts, which might range in extent from the old English 'hundred' to a large-sized country, would be handed over to the administration of a satrap, who would be responsible for the payment of a fixed contribution to the central Government and for the order and well-being of his province, and who would have under him a gendarmery and civil and judicial staff (with purely local powers) of his own appointing."

In the reports that followed, Hector was all the more inclined to blame Russia for blocking any recommendations for peace, his own included. But he could point out that a Bulgarian envoy arriving in Constantinople intended to put forth a scheme for redistributing Macedonian districts on an ethnographic basis.

Some idea of Hector's daily rounds came in his report published on June 9. After analyzing the character of the Bulgarian envoy, he told of visiting the Aleksandrovski Hospital in Sofia to talk with Macedonian fugitives wounded by Turkish forces. "The most picturesque and interesting figure among them was a veteran of sixty-two years, by name Simon Neneskoff, who is familiarly known in revolutionary circles as 'Dyedo (Grandfather) Simon.' " By birth a Macedonian, in his leisure moments a builder, Simon seemed to have adopted irregular warfare as an alternative profession, and in his youth he had fought as a volunteer under Garibaldi and saw service in France.

"Of the little French which he picked up in those days he has forgotten everything except the words of an old camp song, which he suddenly trilled out for my benefit," Hector wrote, and the episode recalled the Young Turk with his inexhaustible verses of "Twinkle, Twinkle." Hector repeated to his readers that story, which he had confided to Ethel the previous month. It is a measure of Hector's attractiveness as a foreign correspondent and his elusiveness as a brother or friend that the language of the two accounts differed hardly at all.

On June 10, Hector was handed his most sensational story so far. Early in the morning hours, army officers in Belgrade overthrew King Alexander and his unpopular queen, Draga—dynamited their bedchambers, in a regicide that was energetic, if redundant. The rebels shot them and, to be certain, threw their bodies down to the street. Hector heard the news that afternoon in Sofia when the Bulgarians lowered the flag over Prince Ferdinand's palace to half-mast out of sympathy for its neighboring dynasty.

Hector got on the evening train for Belgrade, looking out at station after station across the Serbian lowlands for signs of lamentation. There were none. There was not even evidence of any unusual stirring. When he reached Belgrade before dawn, he looked instinctively to the rear of the railway restaurant for the huge portraits of Alexander and Draga that had always struck him as depressing. He found only a blank wall with telltale squares of brighter paint.

The *Morning Post* led its compilation of reports and speculation with Hector's dispatch. Just as the newspaper characterized most uprisings as "Troubles," so were attempts on royalty headed either "Outrages" if they failed, or "Tragedy" if they succeeded. Hector's first brief report ran under the heading "The Servian Tragedy." He told of a short burial ceremony followed by no visible signs of mourning throughout Belgrade. "The buildings are, indeed, gaily decorated with flags.

"The Army is acclaimed everywhere.

"The soldiers have torn from their helmets the cockades bearing the initial 'A' and have replaced them by sprigs of roses." Details of the murders came by way of Vienna from reporters with better sources within the army than Hector's. He could only go to the palace, shuttered except for the two windows from which the bodies of Obrenovitch and his queen had been hurled. Symbolically, those windows had been left open.

"History will concern itself with the yea and nay of the fallen dynasty, with its hapless marriages and its coups d'etat, and sentiment will be busy with the contemplation of its vicissitudes and its fatal catastrophe.

"Here, face to face with the tragedy, it behooves neither to blame nor to pity. The issue was a domestic one, and lay between the Servian people and the Servian ruling family.

"But above all other reflections stands the horror of that final loneliness in the dark Palace, when amid the crashing uproar of forced-in doors the hunted couple sought in room after room for succor or safety and found only desertion and enemies.

" 'It was dreadful, was it not?' a Servian will ask you half-anxiously when going over the pitiful details.

"And you can truthfully make answer, 'It was intensely dramatic.' "

By the following day, Hector was congratulating himself on having been present at so historic an occasion and admitting that he had found a certain glamor in the week's events. But with a new king installed, Hector had little to do except wander the streets, noting that the gas lamps burned long into the night at the ministries and admiring the mounted patrols in blue-and-scarlet trappings that gave them the look of a child's lead horsemen. There were also flirtations of the moment, which Hector could describe, assured that his readers would take them as innocent. "Wandering boys from Tzigane orchestras made their way to their night lodging, hunting as they went for cigarette ends under the outdoor tables of the restaurants, and grasping joyfully at the cigarette silently and unexpectedly offered."

But finally Hector was disheartened by the lack of public response to the murder of the king. He complained that scarcely more people than would have lined a London sidewalk to watch a fallen horse struggle to its feet had gathered to observe the restoration of a dynasty. "I had seen a King-choosing, a *Königswahl*—one must put the word in German to get its fullest effect—and it had not come up to expectation."

Recovering his equanimity Hector soon produced an essay on one of his favorite themes, the traits that distinguish one nation from another. The people of the Balkans fascinated him, with their physical vitality, their garrulousness and—a trait he indulged in himself but disapproved in others—their indifference to commerce. Of course, he wrote, their boundless curiosity had to lead to political instability. "The Kingdom of Servia may be likened to a grain of mustard seed which fell among peasant politicians and would have thriven better if they had not pulled it up by the roots from time to time to see if it was growing."

He described his own experiences as a shopper in Belgrade. "The business that takes you into a Belgrade shop is of faint interest to the proprietor, if he should be a native: that you wish to buy a particular quality of notepaper is a weakness which he does not feel bound to encourage.

"The paper is there somewhere no doubt, but don't you want more urgently a picture of the new King? Why don't you want it, and why have you left London, and what do you think of Belgrade? Why did you make war on the Transvaal, and where is President Kruger now, and why are you clean shaven, and why are most Americans and British clean shaven?

"While his questions run on it saves time to hunt for the paper yourself; when it is found the shopman will obligingly wrap it up for you, but he will declare that for any ordinary purpose the thick, ruled sheets he first showed you were quite as good—in his opinion better . . ."

Hector remarked later in a story that the people of Crete "make more history than they can consume locally." But throughout the summer of 1903, the people of the Balkans were not producing enough news for a diligent reporter to export. Hector, who had been analyzing the situation exhaustively for months, fell back on metaphors that came as quickly to his mind as they passed from the reader's. "The Eastern Balkans at the present juncture resemble a 'danger building' in which shells are being handled with a certain degree of carelessness; and as, furthermore, one of the rooms is well alight, and the efforts used to stamp out the flames are shaking the whole building, the situation is disquieting even to those whose political nerves have been made in Austria, where there is a State bounty on optimism."

On other occasions, Hector took a seat across from a diplomat and with the savoir-faire of a veteran correspondent allowed himself to be interviewed. "You think there will be a war?" a Turkish dignitary asked on a sweltering summer day. "I expressed a hope that there would be none while this weather lasted."

When every other device failed, he could return to travel writing. It was the era before filmed travelogues, cheap cameras and packaged tours, and many writers journeyed abroad to set exotic sights before the chair-bound at home. While Henry James was sketching Italy, Hector, painting in more primary colors, was sending back a picture of Sofia for readers who would never cross the Thames. He made his investigatory rounds atop a roan mare so overstrung that he named her Paula Tanqueray, after the heroine of the play he had missed during his stint in Burma. Together they cantered across the rolling landscape of wheat, barley and maize in search of peasant life. Few farmers crossed their path, but Hector took delight in the Balkan buffalo, hairy and uncouth, and in crowds of solemn-gaited storks. Young boys tended flocks of sheep, and brown-skinned peasants, women working alongside the men, harvested their crops into sheaves bulkier than those of an English cornfield. These were casual excursions, and Hector did not try to trick them up as anything else. But set among the smudged gray columns of the *Morning Post,* they stood out as sharp and vivid as picture postcards.

Another day, Hector lectured the British exporter on why his products were losing out to Austrian goods in eastern European markets. Too expensive was one complaint he had heard, and Hector lamented that "the peasant, all the world over, buys cheap. It is his one extravagance." Then, too, that class just above the peasantry had slender means. Economic stories of this kind usually focused on the problems of a housewife feeding her family. Hector's used the example of economies forced on a young shop assistant.

No matter how he padded and chuffed, the Macedonian troubles seemed to be clearly on the wane. Hector filed one last dispatch and then headed back for leave in London. That was July 31, a Friday. On August 2, the Macedonian Revolutionary Committee issued a call to arms, and two days later that opening salvo was followed by fierce skirmishing, which went on into the month. Hector's remarkably poor timing suggests that while he talked with a number of youths on many subjects, he had never penetrated the revolutionary councils.

From Macedonia, Hector had sent back to London two more Reginald stories, which had been published in March and April. Now, sojourning in London between foreign assignments, he could again take up the incorrigible young man, who had particular reason to be pleased with himself these days. While Hector was being earnest in the Balkans, Reginald had delivered a sally that had proved enduring. It had come during his recital of the misadventures of a woman who had fallen into the habit of always telling the truth. The resulting indiscretions had already cost her most of her friends and her dressmaker. Then one morning she upbraided her cook for drinking, a home truth she had immediate cause to regret: "The cook was a good cook, as cooks go; and as cooks go, she went."

Catching up on plays around the West End, Hector took along Reginald to ridicule those dramas written in the manner of Ibsen. "Reginald closed his eyes with the elaborate weariness of one who has rather nice eyelashes and thinks it useless to conceal the fact. 'One of these days,' he said, 'I shall write a really great drama. No one will understand the drift of it, but everyone will go back to their homes with a vague feeling of dissatisfaction with their lives and surroundings. Then they will put up new wall-papers and forget.' "

Reginald, who shared his creator's passion for wolves, said he intended to have them skulking outside the window, "and whenever the characters could think of nothing brilliant to say about marriage or the War Office, they could open a window and listen to the howling of wolves. But that would be very seldom."

Even more stimulating to Hector than nightly theatre were the politics of the day. He submitted to the *Morning Post* occasional essays on those politicians whose Liberal views most offended him. The paper printed one in the fall, "Crumbs From the Big Loaf," which lampooned the Free Traders in Parliament. Another meditation, on tariffs, was ascribed to Reginald by the simple device of adding the words "said Reginald" in parentheses. "Talking about tariffs, the liftboy, who reads extensively between the landings, says it won't do to tax raw commodities. What, exactly, is a raw commodity? Mrs. Van Challaby says men are raw commodities till you marry them."

The Reginald stories could survive occasional descents into the topical. Two other political parables that Hector wrote in November sank of their own weight. "Spadework Out of Monmouth" presented unemployed workers being confronted by their Liberal leaders. ("I cannot indeed find evidence that you really exist. In the worst of times you are only 4 per cent. I've seen that in statistics.") Hector's heart was clearly less with the poor than in puncturing what he saw as Liberal inanities. Two weeks later, "The Angel and His Lost Michael" reminded readers even more forcefully how important the drawings of Carruthers Gould had been to the success of Hector's sketches. He then tried another Jungle Story without Gould, who remained loyal to the *Westminster;* the *Morning Post* editors buried it on page nine. In it, Hector's disdain for democracy was not cloaked by the fable: "Every now and again the folk of some township or district hold a choosing; not one-tenth of them could give you a guess at the different races inhabiting Asia and where each fitted in. It is an unwritten book to them. But they are busy putting little crosses against the names of the candidates, and when those little crosses are counted that is the supreme thing in all our political purpose."

Hector was no more diverting when, a few days before Christmas, he sent St. Nicholas driving his reindeer through the Balkans and encountering the Great Powers in their predictable animal form—the Russian Bear, the British Lion. But as his holiday gift a day later, Hector produced a Reginald story that denounced Christmas house parties. Reginald lamented that his last hosts on such an occasion had been his distant cousins. "Mrs. Babwold wears a rather solemn personality, and has never been known to smile, even when saying disagreeable things to her friends . . . Her husband gardens in all weathers. When a man goes out in the pouring rain to brush caterpillars off rose trees, I generally imagine his life indoors leaves something to be desired."

8

The Byzantine
Omelette
(1904-1907)

At the beginning of 1904, Hector took up a habit most unlike him: he began a diary. It was not, to be sure, much of a diary; probably it had been a gift. Called De La Rue's "Fingershape," the little book measured only one inch wide by three inches in length, but that proved ample for a man of crabbed writing and unconfiding disposition. On January 7, Hector left London for Brussels to resume his career as a foreign correspondent. On the 8th, a Friday, he traveled through Köln to Passau, on Saturday through Vienna to Pest. On Sunday he arrived in Belgrade.

Apparently Hector suffered the pang that can afflict even the most exhilarated traveler in the first days of a new excursion, for he wrote a large number of letters. In just one day, Monday, January 11, he wrote to persons he listed as "Vates, M., B., V. and Dunn." On Tuesday he wrote to a man named Eric. It was Dunn, however, with whom he stayed most closely in touch, and Dunn was very possibly his editor at the *Morning Post;* the scant records and recollections from that era do not identify him.

For the first weeks, Hector kept his diary in purple ink, and in the left-hand column he ran a tally of the number of articles and short squibs, which he called "Notes" and "Notelets," that he sent to his paper. In the last two weeks of January, there were eighteen. One, for example, was entered in the diary for Friday, January 15, as "gip ball" and on January 26 the paper published "At a Gypsy Ball. Written by H. H. Munro." Usually Hector's notations were straightforward. He told when it was wet and when there was frost. He observed that on Saturday, January 16, he rode and on Monday, January 25, he sent "islam Reg FCG." That would have been "Reginald's Rubaiyat," which was sent to Carruthers Gould and published about a week later: "The other day (confided Reginald), when I was killing time in the bathroom and making bad resolutions for the New Year, it occurred to me that I would like to be a poet." Several examples of assertedly comic verse followed.

The most intriguing of Hector's notations were not words at all but squiggles in the diary's right margin. The first appeared on the line for Tuesday, January 19. "Wr E," Hector wrote, "art. M. P. Snow." All quite plain: he had written to Ethel; sent an article to the *Morning Post;* observed that it had snowed. Then, at the margin, ~.

The following day it appeared again. "Wr B-l-k, card to Den Wr Steed ~." Two days passed with the margin bare. Hector wrote, "Bern, Paul, Note MP Meth. Moore." No squiggle. Nearer the end of the month, the marks began to show up again—one each on January 28, 29, 30. By mid-February he had started to put in a line (—) on any day when the ~ was not appropriate. There are, of course, several acts of daily life that a reticent man might prefer to code in a diary that could fall at any time into hostile hands. Given Hector's past ailments, he might have wanted to keep an accurate record of his health. But there are lengthy lacunae between the squiggles, sometimes as much as seven days, and if he had been recording, for instance, exercises, swimming, or bowel movements, a week of immobility would suggest a debility he does not seem to have experienced.

Another possibility presents itself. Even in more sexually candid times, men and women have taken care to disguise the diary entries referring to their lovemaking on the principle that no one has ever had to apologize for excessive discretion. If Hector took pains not to offend the prudery of his time—and, it should be remembered, risk disgrace and imprisonment—his diary should not be exploited in our day for prurient reasons. But, having paid homage to that lofty principle, what do we find when we pry? If every squiggle did represent a conquest, Hector found six occasions in January to gratify himself and apparently, given his wide correspondence, others. If this surmise is correct, Hector's average in his best months was an encounter every second day; when he was busy or traveling, every third day. On a few occasions he would let his diary lapse and then catch it up at one sitting. When that happened, he sometimes made one symbol and then had to correct it. Does it speak of a certain wistfulness that Hector more often drew the squiggle and then, perhaps reluctantly, drew through it the straight line of abstinence?

Time—past time—to put aside such speculations. Yet they crop up repeatedly as one reads Hector's dispatches over that year. For instance, his amusing description of the gypsy ball has an unmistakable undertow:

"A payment of two dinars (two francs) gave one the right of admission, though it requires some physical manoeuvering to get through the throng that hung about at the first entry. After one had got accustomed to being addressed as 'Molly' (*molí*—'If you please') by everyone who wanted to squeeze past, and had unwedged oneself from the tangle of loiterers, it was possible to take stock of the revellers . . . Some of the Gypsy boys were clad, mountaineer fashion, in short black embroidered jackets and white kilted skirts, and moved about with an unconscious grace suggestive of black panthers . . . it was noticeable that the Romany lass did not invariably pair off with the Romany lad, but chose the most glittering partner she could get in the way of cavalry officer."

After that, it is almost obligatory to turn to the diary to learn whether Hector left the ball by himself. But if he did try to console one of those spurned Romany panthers, on the evidence of his diary he did not immediately succeed. The first squiggle of 1904 came five days later.

Throughout the early months of the year, the mix for Hector was as before. He lingered in Belgrade, filing lengthy reports on Balkan unrest. His life was leisurely, and sometimes he claimed to see advantages in the formalities of reporting that were being imposed on him. When, for example, the Minister of Foreign Affairs demanded that all questions be submitted in writing, Hector told his readers that the method insured that the answers he would later receive had been considered carefully. On February 1, Hector noted in his diary that he had been paid, an occurrence he stopped recording when it became routine.

Later that week Hector had a cabinet reshuffling to report, for which he sounded grateful. "After hanging fire for a few days the ministerial crisis has at length come to pass. For a while it had almost seemed as if the Ministry did not possess sufficient strength to fall to pieces." By mid-February, Hector was offering more predictions about the fighting that was expected to break out in the spring, but there was a perfunctory tone to his reports. Although he could now contrast authoritatively the current Balkan troubles with the level of the year before, it does not seem to have been an expertise that gave him much satisfaction. And the weather was cold, snowing and sleeting. On March 12, Hector escaped to Vienna, a city so stimulating to him that even a funeral procession with its white trotting horses, he confessed, came dangerously close to exciting him.

After a week of lunching with friends, Hector moved on to his last assignment, Warsaw. On March 28, he took rooms, and the next day he sent Gould the last of his Reginald series, "The Innocence of Reginald." The species "brilliant young man" was by now familiar enough in London society to be a target for other writers besides Hector. A woman columnist defined it as "young (at present); he has good digestion (as yet); the sufferings of hu-

manity cause him no trouble and no heart-searchings."
She concluded, "May Heaven preserve me from this kind
of 'brilliant young man.' " To which Reginald might well
have replied, "And vice versa."

In the tale of his innocence, Reginald considers writing
a book of personal reminiscence that would leave out
nothing.

The Other is properly appalled. "Reginald!"

"Exactly what the Duchess said when I mentioned it to
her. I was provoking and said nothing, and the next thing,
of course, was that everyone heard that I'd written the
book and got it in the press. After that, I might have been
a goldfish in a glass bowl for all the privacy I got." Encountered at the theatre, Miriam Klopstock had taken the
proposed indiscretion especially poorly. "I saw her tearing
little bits out of her programme for a minute or two, and
then she leaned back and snorted, 'You're not the boy I
took you for,' as though she were an eagle arriving at
Olympus with the wrong Ganymede."

The *Westminster Alice* had now sold more than 25,000
copies. With the appearance of the fifteenth Reginald,
publishers began to consider collecting his adventures between hard covers, and Hector wired his agreement that
the firm of Metheun bring them out in the fall. Meanwhile, there was a living to make, and a little more than a
week after his arrival in Warsaw, Hector was sending back
his impressions. The tramway system was inferior to
those of Sofia and Belgrade; the streets could scarcely have
been worse paved in the Middle Ages; the gilded towers
of a Russian church may at first seem impressive but then
in an unfortunate moment one sees them as inverted onions and after that can see them in no other way. He noted
that, despite anti-Semitic passport regulations, trade was
largely in the hands of Jews. And the new industrial class
that Hector saw rising was not likely to be conservative.
Already one-third of the German Reichstag was socialist.
Would it be different in Warsaw or in Russia's industrial
centers?

April 3, Easter Sunday, Hector was on the street to see
how the Poles observed it. Some solitary men respond to
holidays by committing suicide; others, like Hector,

greatly value and anticipate the celebrations. The avenues fill with bodies and create for a moment an illusion of intimacy. For this one day, when people expect to smile and exchange greetings, there is no danger of being thought forward. Best of all, it is an exemption from drab daily life, and since that break in the routine can enliven even a cheerful temperament, to the reserved man or the mildly glum, it is better than drink.

On this occasion, Hector listed the richness of the traditional Polish Easter feast—suckling pig, boar's head, roasted duck, Paschal lambs molded from sugar or marzipan, a three-foot column of sponge cake—and pointed out the irony in such a repast celebrating a religion that stressed denial, moderation and abstemiousness. "It is as though the races of Europe turned back on this special festival to do honour to the old gods and myths of nature and the human passions." Hector never said it, but perhaps one grievance against Christianity that he shared with other homosexuals was a conviction that the prohibitions against them sprang from the Bible, from the Old Testament prophets and from St. Paul. In other men, that sentiment provoked regret for the passing of the Greek age; in Hector, for the banishment of woodland spirits from the environs of Devon, where they could have nurtured his childhood.

On May Day there was another kind of activity. Expecting a demonstration, Hector invited himself to tea at a house that fronted the Ujazdowska Allée, where Cossacks and police were sure to be quartered. Crowds began to gather. The extent of the rebellion turned out to be one or two youths and a few older persons sporting red in their buttonholes. But the police charged all the same. When a demonstrator was hauled into the yard, Hector went around to the side window, "which gave me a view of the more private proceedings. My vantage ground had not been ill-chosen, and the police, on getting their man into a quiet corner, were not quite aware that their position had been outflanked. One seized the prisoner by the hair and held him while four others kicked him and beat him with their scabbarded swords and thick sticks. This went on for about two minutes."

More arrests and beatings ensued. "A touch of comedy was given to the proceedings when three tall policemen marched into the yard with a small newsboy of about ten years old, but the comedy evaporated when they began the same process of beating and kicking him, thrusting him in among the dismounted Cossacks so that they might lend a hand. Though big enough to be battered he apparently did not reach the size limit for detention and was allowed to escape." Beneath Hector's detachment, he wanted his readers to take away three facts: that these were Russian policemen, that they were attacking innocuous civilians, and that if the Turks had put down a genuine riot with the same brutality, the outcry in Europe would have been prolonged. "But," he concluded, "a political conscience has its watertight compartments."

While Hector was observing those Polish rituals, a celebration of equal anthropological interest was taking place at home without him. When his brother Charlie left the Burmese police, their father got him a post in Ireland, first at Castlebar Prison and then, less than a year later, as governor of His Majesty's Prison at Londonderry. Charlie, who had become an imposing man of hearty good humor, found in Londonderry a bride, Inez Mary Muriel Chambers, daughter of Sir Newman and Lady Chambers of Donegal.

Her parents provided a fashionable wedding for Muriel, a sweet-faced young woman with reddish gold hair and an expression that suggested a faint and indefinable anxiety. As the organist played the grand march from *Lohengrin*, the bride appeared in a dress of ivory crêpe de Chine set off by a necklace of pearls and turquoise, a gift from the groom. Ethel was one of the five bridesmaids, and no doubt the calmest among them since she had little reason to wonder when her day might come. Family legend later accorded her the courtesy of one beau but had to acknowledge that it had come to nothing. Colonel Munro and Aunt Tom were on hand for the wedding, and the *Londonderry Sentinel* listed them with the dozens of other guests and recorded their gifts among the hundreds received. The Colonel had given a piano and a service of old china. Aunt Tom produced a brooch, brought back from India by some military Munro and set, depending on the appraiser's eye, with an exquisite or minuscule emerald, ruby and bit of turquoise. Ethel contributed a dessert set of old Spode and a book, which the *Sentinel* recorded as "Omar Khazzam." From Warsaw, possibly with Omar in mind, Hector had sent a decanter and a dozen long-stemmed goblets, ornate with gold leaf and of a delicacy that indicated elaborate packing and special instructions at the dock.

Because of the *Sentinel*'s industry, we also know the number of silver cream jugs the young couple received (three) and that three guests sent checks, although their amounts were not divulged. At the end of the newspaper's account of the prodigal outpouring of silver and hand-painted Belleek china, Charlie made an asterisk and added in a satisfied hand, "A good many other presents besides above."

Although Hector still kept in regular touch with Ethel, he now tended to write once a month rather than once a week, as he had done during his lonely rustication in Burma. As ever, he seems to have withheld little from her, telling her about swimming every day with the schoolboy nephew of the American consul in Warsaw and about a fourteen-year-old Polish boy who not only shopped for Hector but on hot days sprayed siphons of soda water between his shoulder blades.

As for most of the Polish young men, Hector found them pleasant but lethargic. "He could not get them to be energetic" was the way Ethel phrased it in her memoir, and she quoted from a letter to demonstrate Hector's frustration. "On the most scorching days nothing will induce them to join my amphibious afternoons in the Vistula; they agree to come, with every sign of nervous depression, but return presently beaming to say they have remembered they have got a cold and it would be dangerous, etc. . . ." Hector described these men as being Poles of his own age but he may have meant merely closer to his own age than the teenage boys who were his companions. At thirty-three, Hector saw himself as young rather than merely youthful.

"The amateur valet continues to be amusing," he informed Ethel six weeks later. The boy had quarreled with his mother and had gone to live with an aunt. He was avoiding a reconciliation because his mother gave him only tea in the mornings while his aunt gave him chocolate. "What is home and a mother where no chocolate is?" asked Hector, who had been denied both.

He had expanded a collection of old Russian and Polish coins, some going back to 1300, buying them from a man whom Hector dazzled with his minute knowledge of east European princes: "—an Englishman is expected to be profoundly ignorant of such things."

Ethel's little dog had lately disappeared, and Hector, who joined in the mourning, was indignant when a female acquaintance wrote to him blithely without understanding the depth of their loss. "I keep dreaming that he is found," Hector wrote, "and then comes the waking disappointment. Of course it's worse for you because he was always with you." He wondered whether Ethel might consider getting a wolf instead. There would be no license to buy; it could feed on the smaller offspring of a fertile family in her neighborhood; and its presence would guarantee that Ethel could do her marketing in comfort. "Think it over," he advised.

Between bathing and playing tennis, Hector was filing regularly for his newspaper, and his emphasis on the Russian character suggests that he knew already that Warsaw was only a way station on the road to St. Petersburg. Commenting on the Russo-Japanese War, he wrote, "It is not a question of white or yellow skin that is to be decided. The governing factor of the struggle will be the gray matter that men call brain," and he suggested that in that competition Russia was stagnating under a burden of superstition and philosophical mediocrity. In Warsaw certainly, Hector saw the stagnation everywhere. Interminable holy days disrupted education and commerce; a university course took two years longer to complete than in the West. Policemen chased away poorly clad boys trying to make an honest living by selling newspapers while they overlooked the swarms of professional beggars.

As the Japanese scored victories during May 1904, Hector was warning the British not to sell the Russians short. Russia might attempt to save face by drawing in the European powers as peacemakers. Recovering her prestige was an even more urgent goal for Russia than securing a warm-water coastline, he contended.

The *Morning Post* was giving no prominence to these dispatches, using them as little more than sidebars to the day's main reports of the Russo-Japanese engagements around Port Arthur. There was a consolation: his stories might begin low on the page, but the paper had begun running at the end of each notelet the parenthetical line, "Copyright in Great Britain and the United States." Even functioning at something less than his top form, Hector was offering a perspective that the *Morning Post* wanted to protect.

Hector corrected the proofs of the Reginald stories and sent them back to Methuen. As he read them over, he had also been compiling a short history of the Chunchuses tribesmen of Manchuria, a plundering band that had taken up arms against the Russians. For all the critical abuse he had endured, Hector could not surmount his pedantry about Slavic names, and before he analyzed the group's tribal character he first informed readers that the word should be rendered "Khunguz."

Hector had not met a single Chunchu, whereas several young men around London fancied that they were the prototype for Reginald. If it pleased them, Hector saw no harm in it. But Reginald was most truly he, and as Hector envisioned the Chunchu, that warrior was a part of him, too; not perhaps as he was at the moment but as, given the chance, he could still become:

"Cruel, but brave, steadfast and enduring, he has a high regard for his plighted word, and for those to whom he is attached he is ready to face torment and death."

With its huge ghetto population, Warsaw exposed Hector to more Jews than he had ever known, and his reflections on the subject of anti-Semitism showed that he had not resolved his ambiguity. Everything in his experience with Jews seems to have been positive, yet he could never overcome the ingrained suspicions of his time, country and social class. "To the Jew in Warsaw is meted out a wealth of disfavour and contempt that is hardly pleasant to witness. The British stranger, however, who normally lives far from any personal contact with these huge Jewish populations, is not altogether in a position to pass judgment on this deeply-seated Anti-Semitic rancour. It pervades all classes of Polish society, and finds expression in a variety of ways. The youth who obligingly performs my minor marketing for me, in return for a tolerant attitude on my part on the subject of small change, was interested in the fate of an egg which I had pronounced to have passed the age limit of culinary usefulness.

" 'Don't throw it away,' he begged; 'give it to me.'
" 'What do you want it for?'
" 'Oh, it will do to throw at a Jew.'

"Personally I have found the Jew in several Slav-inhabited countries easier to deal with than some of his Christian neighbours. He understands that it takes two to make a bargain, and if he haggles it is always with the view of doing business; with the Slav haggling seems often to be carried out on the principle of art for art's sake. For that reason the Russians will never rid themselves of the economic pressure of the Jews, and if they absorb any considerable mass of Chinese subjects these, too, will soon have a tenacious grip on the trade affairs of the Empire."

On September 7, 1904, Hector packed up his belongings, bade farewell to his ragamuffin of a servant and departed Warsaw. He reached St. Petersburg the following day and took rooms the day after that. Men of Hector's disposition make exemplary foreign correspondents. They have no households to disrupt when a change of posting arises, and their pleasures are simple and easily gratified. Within an hour of arriving in a strange city, such a man knows where the story is unfolding—be it war, election or murder trial—and how he can most reliably convey his observations to his headquarters. Within two hours he knows the location of the three best restaurants and where the nightly card game will be staged. Sexual leads may take an hour longer, depending on how freely he feels he may speak with his colleagues. In St. Petersburg, Hector finally met a colleague with whom he could be candid.

A. Rothay Reynolds, named for a river in Scotland, was another gentleman journalist, a small man with a youthful manner, rosy cheeks and an alert expression. He too had had autocratic aunts; his own would send her maid running ahead to hold up her hand at intersections and stop traffic until her mistress was safely across. Reynolds' father had once owned a large interest in the London Electric Company, and he had sent his sons to Cambridge. There Rothay, whom the family called Roy, trained for the Anglican priesthood. But the fortune dissolved and so did Roy's calling. He left the clergy, taking away a taste for suits made by Kilgour and French, tailors to the Prince of Wales, and shirts from Dacre and Dare—with only the prospects of an overeducated reporter on which to indulge such pleasures. Reynolds' enthusiasm for tennis and bathing matched Hector's, and he danced extremely well. He was a good talker and a discriminating gourmet. Had he not remained a devout Christian, converting later to Catholicism, he might have become a snob. Instead, his parties were known for their easy hospitality and the range of his guests; it was rumored that once he had invited his dentist.

Reynolds had also reported from Warsaw, a city he admired for its millinery, gloves and hosiery, and he believed that, like the French, the Poles possessed innate good taste. He shared traces of Hector's pedantry—he spelled Warsaw "Varsharva"—and Hector's bemusement with the role of the Jew in that city. "They remain a race apart," Reynolds wrote, "having an eye to the main chance, and, as a rule, showing little sympathy with the Poles." Unlike Hector, however, Reynolds lived to see the day when Max Reinhardt was banished from the Berlin theatre and Bruno Walter barred from conducting at Leipzig, and he came to have great sympathy with the people he had once treated offhandedly. When he died of pneumonia in Palestine in 1940, he was buried in a Franciscan graveyard in Jerusalem.

Possibly inspired by his friendship with Hector, Reynolds produced a bit of fiction of his own. One story, set at a cafe concert in Warsaw, turned on the revelation that the featured entertainer was a female impersonator. Its climactic line was " 'Good Heavens!' cried Wladislaw. 'She's a man!' " In the opening chapters of his novel, *The Gondola,* Reynolds revealed the technique for recruiting those lithe young servants that both he and Hector preferred. His hero, Richard Venning, maintains an extended affair with a contessa but his ardor for her never matches the interest he takes in a boy he meets on the train and engages for his household. " 'You are Italian, aren't you,' said the young man to the peasant-boy. 'Yes, I am Italian,' answered the boy, 'but how did Monsieur guess it?' 'You have the dark eyes and the clear skin of the South,' said the other . . ." Venning invites the boy to luncheon at the next stop. Only after a glacial reception by the waiter does Venning realize "that it was unconventional to take decorative, but unwashed, peasant boys into the coffee-rooms of fashionable hotels." The boy himself is less innocent. "In my business one always gets a place when one is good looking." And about that happy truth he has no doubt: "I have the face of a Madonna, only my eyes are wicked." Venning has recently received twenty pounds—something over a hundred dollars—for a magazine article, and he can think of no more pleasurable way of spending it than by engaging this young Italian. "Luigi is a beautiful name," says Venning, and the contract is struck.

Near the end of the novel, Reynolds introduces a second English correspondent, Hugh Blair, who resembles in many respects his friend Hector Hugh Munro. Blair drinks absinthe at the Hôtel de France in St. Petersburg, a gathering spot for foreign correspondents and a particular favorite of Hector's. "Give me the old days of bombs and assassinations," says Blair at one point. "I haven't sent a wire for three days." Later, hearing a scrap of gossip, Blair says, "I think I can fake something from that." It is an affectionate caricature of the way Hector presented himself. "He's a reporter, I believe," says a Russian baron, "but his manners are quite good." And as a practitioner himself, Reynolds got the journalistic details right—the abbreviated language that the wire rate of twenty kopeks per word forced upon a report ("course conversation me safternoon Baron von Geck") and the cynicism about editors. "They like a little stodge occasionally," Blair remarks. "It makes the public think they're serious."

If that quotation was accurate, Hector seldom heeded his own counsel. More often in place of stodge he gave his editors light essays, such as the one on the immense labor and patience required to get a parcel through Russian customs. He granted that the Byzantine process had a certain humor, but he also saw in it a caution for those Britons who were inclined to admire all things Russian:

"If three-fourths of these wearisome trivialities were thrown aside, and those useless reams of solemn nonsense wiped out of the day's work, not only in the postal department but in many others, a much smaller staff would be required and a higher scale of pay could be afforded, and incidentally Russia would be a pleasanter country to live in. But there is not the faintest sign on the horizon of a man who could carry out such a reform."

Ethel said that Hector was very happy in St. Petersburg, and there is every reason to believe it. We know from a memoir that his new friend Reynolds found it a magnificent city—beguiling in spring, magical in winter. The broad streets and the sheer size of the public buildings made up for stretches of undistinguished architecture. In late afternoon, the tapering pillar of the Fortress of St. Peter and St. Paul, where political prisoners were lodged with dead tsars, caught the sun's last rays and looked to Reynolds like a shaft of flame. Better still was the hour after midnight in the month of the white nights, when, standing on the quay, one did not know whether the crimson light beyond the Neva was the end of the sunset or the first of the dawn.

Best of all, an Englishman found freedom from the hundred inflexible laws of the British middle class. He could go unshaved or attend the theatre in a checkered jacket. "The peccadilloes he concealed from all but kindred spirits when he was in England," Reynolds wrote, "he need make no further effort to hide," adding that Russians knew Cupid to be an unaccountable boy. Russian youths, fourteen to seventeen years old, were already jaded by sexual conquest, Reynolds reported, sounding a little put off but considerably intrigued. He quoted an English friend as saying that he had never determined which was the greater bar to human happiness, religion or the family. If that friend was Hector, he was living within a stratum of Russian society that put no faith in either.

In September, Methuen brought out *Reginald* to reviews that were generally favorable though not extensive. The *Athenaeum* called Hector "one of the brightest hands of the *Westminster Gazette*," but then went on to suggest that *Reginald* owed a debt to the hero of G. S. Street's *Autobiography of a Boy,* a certain "Tubby," who had been sent down from Oxford in his third year. To a reader today the comparison seems insulting to Hector. Tubby shared with Reginald only the appearance of languor, and even that, given his energy at affronting his elders, was as illusory in Reginald's case as in Balfour's. The review did grant Hector's book a "sustained brilliance," and the notice concluded with one of those disclaimers that would turn up repeatedly in criticism of Saki, a nervous apology for having responded so enthusiastically. "We fear, however, that the jaded literary appetite after such an orgie of *hors-d'oeuvres* will be less disposed than ever to be satisfied with simpler and possibly more wholesome fare."

Ethel sent Hector the *Athenaeum* review along with others, and he replied that Aunt Tom had already rendered her verdict. "The *Athenaeum*," Hector wrote, "consoled me for Aunt Tom's remark that it was a pity the book had been published as, after the 'Alice,' people would expect it to be clever and of course be disappointed. The 'of course' was terribly crushing but I am able to sit up now and take a little light nourishment."

Reginald was adding more to Hector's reputation than to his bank account. At most, each story had fetched from the *Westminster Gazette* three pounds—about fifteen dollars—and Methuen made no effort to promote the collection. Hector would go on being a journalist.

One fall morning, Hector rose early to attend a demonstration protesting the death of a student, a political prisoner who the police claimed had killed himself in jail. His story is a classic account of the timeless ritual of demonstrators and police. At the Nevski Prospect, the police marshaled their forces behind the cathedral and stationed their reserves in the yards of the neighboring houses.

The students began appearing from the Technical School, the Imperial University, and the Forestry School. Hector thought the women students' faces were set in particularly combative expressions, and he noticed small touches of mourning worked into their dress. As they assembled he sought a vantage point. By now, one knows two things about a morning like this for Hector: he was exhilarated by the promise of violence, although he would take care to mute that note of expectation in his coverage. And when the scuffle had ended, he would find it wanting. "As the crowd is becoming uncomfortably dense on the pavements the windows of a conveniently-situated restaurant offer a more agreeable vantage ground, and one seizes the opportunity to combine the functions of taking luncheon with sightseeing . . . At one window sits a gentleman of obvious Teutonic origin, the points of whose moustache stand stiffly upward, recalling the twin spires of Cologne Cathedral . . . Then a narrow lane is made by common agreement, and a little group on foot following a one-horse hearse makes its way through the police cordon. It is a forlorn little procession that hurries across the great empty square and vanishes in the chill and gloom of the cathedral, round whose frieze, in gilded old Russian lettering, run the high-sounding phrases, ending with "and on earth peace," and below a clatter of hoofs and a rattle of accoutrements sweep round and round the structure like the skirl of a driven storm, while beyond the cordon surge restlessly some thousands of those who are debarred from taking a nearer part in the service for the dead . . . Little by little the human tide on the Nevski ebbs away, the demonstration ceases to be interesting, and the gentleman with the Gothic moustache once more turns his undivided attention to the serious business of the midday meal."

There would be many riots during Hector's stay in St. Petersburg, and while he analyzed each of them carefully, he never succeeded in finding a pattern or an underlying cause that would unite all his superficial explanations. When Russia called up military reserves from the provinces, Hector predicted that those raw youths would be ripe for socialist propaganda. Then, when a riot did occur among the reservists, he ascribed it to a lack of food and the closing of the vodka shops. In one area only had Hector's early years given him surer ground for prophecy. Growing up in Devon, he had learned about farming, and as the mobilization of reservists increased to meet the Japanese threat, Hector, in town, was alert to the problems facing the farms. With ten percent of the population gone to war in a country where farming still took heavy muscle, the price of field labor was soaring. To meet it, farmers were selling cows, pigs, everything they had, with the result that fallow strips and patches were replacing the wheat fields. Hector warned that the effect on the next year's harvest would be considerable.

At about this same time, late December 1904, the *Morning Post* stopped running Hector's byline and substituted "From Our Correspondent." Because the society of diplomats and reporters in St. Petersburg was so ingrown, the editors could not have expected that somehow, against the upheaval that seemed to be taking shape, Hector would be better protected by the anonymity. Rather, it looks like the whim of an editor who believed that the impersonal style imparted greater authority to a dispatch. In Hector's case, the change was irrelevant. He wrote like no one else on the newspaper, and when at last he left Russia the shift between his style and his successor's was so extreme that the *Morning Post* might as well have run an advertisement about his departure.

When Port Arthur fell finally to the Japanese, Hector reported that the citizens of St. Petersburg were too busy preparing for their Orthodox Christmas to pay attention. He was becoming aware, moreover, that the battle against Japan was less vital to Russia's future than the internal clashes of its own people. "The cleavage between Russian and Russian today," he reported early in January 1905, "is not merely a cleavage of political schools. It is a personal hatred, a memory of humiliations and vexations and disadvantages, a measure pressed down and welcoming an opportunity for running over." That realization had tempered Hector's disdain for liberals; he acknowledged that, at least in Russia, their ranks included capable and public-spirited men. But would an uprising bring them to the forefront? Hector thought not. "There is no force in the land that could permanently stand between the extremes of autocracy and Agrarian communism." He granted that greater individual liberties were a pressing need; he was less prepared than his friend Reynolds to enjoy the sexual license of St. Petersburg and call it freedom. But Hector was convinced that lasting reform could only come from a conservative—the work of an autocrat, as he phrased it, rather than of a demagogue. After all, what would these liberals, idealists though they might be, substitute for the admittedly archaic institutions they wished to destroy?

In January 1905, Ethel decided to join Hector in St. Petersburg for a winter holiday. She was nearing forty, handsome but unmarriageable, fiercely devoted to animals in a way that suggested that, if justice were done, it would be humans who would be spayed, kept on a short leash, and taken at any provocation to the pound. That she idolized her brother there is no doubt, but his feelings are more equivocal. Once, when she urged him to write a story about Aunt Tom, he replied, "I shall write about her some day but not until after her death." And those who saw Hector with his aunt remember the faint look in his eye that seemed to say, Yes, of course she's outrageous, but— In his behavior toward Ethel, there may have been a similar forbearance. If nothing else, the contrast between his unfettered life as a journalist and hers at home, tending to their father and fending off Aunt Tom, would have played enough on his sense of justice that he would not have begrudged her a treat. Ethel arrived in St. Petersburg ready to be amused, and Father Gapon obliged her with his march on the Winter Palace.

Georgy Apollonovich Gapon, child of the Ukraine, had been born ten months before Hector, also to a military father, a Cossack. His mother, who was illiterate, bore nineteen children, of whom ten lived. Georgy, subjected to hours of stories from the lives of the saints, grew up sensitive and good-hearted, given to weeping in front of the icons and praying for forgiveness of his childish sins. In the Russia of the late nineteenth century, to become a priest gave a man a good living on earth and salvation in the afterlife. Georgy's mother struck that bargain on behalf of her son. The boy was small, very dark-skinned and lively—in all, the companion of Hector's boyhood fancies, except that he too, while strong for his size, was inclined toward ill health. But blood and martyrdom—the saints and heroic tales of the Cossacks—were mingled in Georgy's fevered imagination.

He married and had children; a Russian Orthodox priest could also be a husband and father. Then, on the death of his wife, with whom he had been happy, life for Gapon lost its meaning. Until he found Socialism.

He considered leaving the church but, as he told Lenin's wife, he could not bring that disgrace on his old parents in their village. At the beginning of 1905, after travels through Europe to promote labor's cause, Father Gapon was back in St. Petersburg. Standing before a hall of factory workers, he urged them to strike for an eight-hour day, a one-third raise in their wages, more sanitary conditions and free medical aid. His eloquence had moved parishioners to tears during mass, and it did not fail him at the Putilov Ironworks. The vote to strike was unanimous.

The ranks of strikers continued to grow until 140,000 men and women had left their jobs. Having demonstrated their power, they would now take their message to the Tsar. Surely, Nicholas would appreciate the truth to their grievances and he would act. Trotsky, who knew better, considered the idea of Gapon's march fantastical. But he believed that the priest was doing the revolutionaries a service by sanctioning their strike with his religious authority. After that, according to Trotsky, it would be up to history to deal with Gapon.

The letter that the priest sent to the Tsar was in turns humble and contemptuous. By meeting their demands, Nicholas could imprint his name eternally on his people's hearts. But if he refused them, "we shall die here, in this square in front of your Palace . . . Before us lie only two paths: to freedom and happiness, or to the grave." They would march to the Palace at two o'clock on the afternoon of Sunday, January 9, to receive his answer. It was as though the signers of the Declaration of Independence had decided to serve it personally on George III.

Hector, with his own instinct for *lèse-majesté*, recognized arrogance when he saw it, and he understood that the Tsar was no duchess in the stalls to be insulted with impunity. He hurried Ethel down to the Hôtel de France before noon that Sunday morning—by the Western calendar it was January 22—so they would have a front-row seat. En route, he was struck by a look of sullen determination on every face, yet the mood did not seem truly threatening. Until the last moment he kept thinking that the day might end as one more disappointment. At the hotel, they were joined by a Polish friend of Hector's. Ethel was never good about supplying the names of these friends, perhaps because she resented them, or because she took no interest in any man but her brother, or simply because when she came to write her memoirs she was looking back across two decades.

The hotel's food was usually worth lingering over, but on this day the three wolfed down their luncheons. Hector deposited Ethel in the smoking room with a view of the street that led to the Winter Palace, while he and the Pole went out to reconnoiter. Very shortly, Ethel saw them come running back amid a crowd of onlookers with the cavalry, swords drawn, at their backs. Swaddled in a heavy overcoat, Hector was winded from moving fast across the slippery snow.

Not all the demonstrators had been intimidated. Hector watched a well-dressed woman strike a young officer of the Horse Grenadiers in his sleigh. The crowd took heart from her example and dragged him from his perch, tore off his saber and cloak, and beat him badly. The young man barely escaped alive, and Hector watched him as he ran away.

The Tsar's troops had sealed off the palace square and were allowing no one to enter. Since the Nevski Prospect was a popular promenade on Sunday, much of the crowd was more curious than politically committed. As people pressed closer to see what was happening, the Cossacks drove them back, lashing them with their whips.

Hector and the Pole knew another exit from the hotel and went to the nearby Moïke Embankment. Finding it a good vantage point, Hector sent back a page to fetch Ethel so that she shouldn't miss the fun. But when nothing could be seen, Ethel, avid for excitement and no doubt cold as well, returned to her window inside the hotel. As soon as she had left Hector and the Pole on the Embankment, soldiers from a guard regiment fired three volleys at the spot where the three of them had been standing. (Hector made a note that they were from the Ismailoffski Guards; even under fire, such distinctions mattered.) He and his friend pressed themselves as flat as possible against a doorway. One bullet whizzed past Hector's head and embedded itself in the wall a foot away. He watched as sleigh drivers jumped from their seats to lie pressed down behind their sleighs. Nearby, a man and woman had been wounded and a horse killed. People were beating wildly on the closed doors along the street, trying to escape death. From the lavish splashing of blood across the snow, Hector judged that the military was assailing the throng with some form of jagged bullet.

By ten minutes to three, the battle was done and the corpses and wounded were being dragged from the Palace square. The next day, the *Morning Post* prefaced Hector's dispatch with a leader more emotional than anything he had filed—"Russia's dark day came yesterday."

With some difficulty, Hector persuaded a sleigh driver who was timid about venturing out to convey him to the suburb of Vassili Ostroff, so he could confirm for himself the enormous casualties reportedly suffered there. When he returned, he wired his story to the *Morning Post* and then collected Ethel for dinner at another hotel. They were joined by a reporter for Reuter's Telegrams who assured them that the Revolution so long predicted had at last begun.

The next morning, Hector and Ethel hired a sleigh to inspect the carnage. Many corpses were still lying unclaimed in the outlying streets, and in Nevski Prospect sightseers were surveying the public buildings for bullet traces. Everywhere the Cossacks were on patrol, men whom Hector found savage-looking, unmistakably Mongolian. It was clear today how freely the cavalry had used its sabers. To Hector the cloven skulls of the bodies were a terrible sight, and as their sleigh glided past Cossack sentries, Hector scowled so disapprovingly that Ethel tried to distract him, afraid that disdain so insolent would provoke retaliation. For her it was all most exciting, one of those unsuitable history books from Devon brought to life.

For all of the control in his dispatches, the massacre had left Hector's loyalties torn. He had been a police officer in a land where a mob could constitute a threat to his life. Yet he had never been compelled to fire into a crowd and certainly not into a crowd of his own countrymen. He believed deeply in law and in the orderly redress of grievances, even when that process might seem for the moment hopeless. What was he to make of men who were "well-dressed"—his usual adjective to denote respectability—shouting out to Russian officers in cafes, "You cannot beat the Japanese, but we are weak enough for you"? Or women, whom he always called "ladies," joining in the imprecations? He had seen the wounds that provoked these jeers and deplored them. All the same, he considered the civilians "almost demented" and their protests fell on his ears as "shrieks."

For two nights, Hector and Ethel had to cut short their rides through the city at dusk and return to Hector's rooms. The electricians had gone on strike and it was not safe for them to travel the dark streets. Since Hector's was one of many households left without bread, he had slipped away one evening to hunt for food when he heard an officer shout that in two minutes his men would shoot anyone found on the street. Breathlessly, Hector ran to local shops and snatched up eggs, tongue, sweet biscuits and Bessarabian wine just as the frightened merchants were locking their doors. Ethel admitted that Hector was the only member of the family with any palate for food, and yet she swore that she had never dined better than at that makeshift meal, "with excitement as a sauce."

She was not the only one exhilarated by the week's

events. Hector detected an air of gaiety on the streets, the Russian way of responding to tension with hilarity. Then, speaking of the shootings, a Russian's demeanor would change and he would choke with rage. That at least was the reaction among Hector's acquaintances as they dashed into his flat to report the latest Cossack atrocities. Watching them pace the room, Ethel pronounced their performance better than any play. There was even a note of comedy: After telling of searching from hospital to hospital for a friend whom he at last found dead, a Russian in the next breath invited Hector and Ethel to accompany him to the opera. Between Hector, who was shaking his head no behind the man's back, and the sheer incongruity of the invitation, Ethel could hardly keep from laughing. She wrote her account long after the Revolution, aborted in 1905, had subsequently succeeded and spread its consequences for the world to judge, but there is little in her pages to suggest that she had been touched by anything beyond the excitement. Father Gapon had simply organized a "Push," more elaborate if less cunning than those of Hector in Davos. When a Push was done and the red paint, or blood, spattered over the walls, there were snug rooms in which to gloat over its success. So long as Hector was not caught or killed, there could be no tragedy for Ethel. To the end of her life, she pronounced her holiday in St. Petersburg the most perfect time abroad, except for Davos, that she had ever spent with her brother.

In the aftermath of the rioting, General Trépoff, a former Minister of Police, was named Governor General of the city. Hector could scarcely believe the appointment, given the general's limited political background. But it was true, and the general vowed an unflinching suppression of any further demonstrations. The Orthodox Holy Synod denounced the strikes and claimed that the workers had been led astray by a criminal priest. Father Gapon was variously reported as arrested, wounded or escaped in disguise to Moscow. A month later, he appeared in Paris.

Hector's reporting had been so circumspect that when the autocratic Trépoff called in foreign correspondents to complain about their coverage of the massacre, Hector was the only one he did not demand to see. In his usual cautious and deflationary way, Hector had estimated the dead and wounded at fifteen hundred; the estimates of his colleagues went much higher. Ethel took it as a compliment to Hector that he should have stayed in the general's favor. Perhaps it was. But later histories put the casualties of the day at a thousand killed and many more than that wounded.

As a fretful calm returned to the city, Hector could take Ethel sightseeing and to cafes where the orchestra played a medley of the cakewalk and Viennese waltzes. Sunday night was the ballet. Hector had engaged what Ethel described as a "very good little servant," and Hector dispatched him to buy tickets to the ballet for the one evening all of fashionable St. Petersburg turned out. On Sundays, scalpers sold the three-and-a-half-ruble seats in the stalls —already more than five times the daily wage of a factory worker—for ten rubles. The rule at the opera was third row for Italian composers, sixth or seventh for Wagner. Russian aristocracy did not entertain performers in their homes, but neither Hector nor Roy Reynolds shared that prejudice, and after Ethel returned to England they came to know Fokine, the choreographer, and heard about a beautiful young student at the Imperial Dancing School, Vaslav Nijinsky.

Although Hector continued to enjoy its amusements, St. Petersburg after the massacre and the moment's nervous excitement had become a dispirited place. People from every social class agreed that the situation had become intolerable but they could not agree on a remedy. Had Voltaire lived now, Hector wrote, he would have found a court society that regarded everything as being for the worst in the best of possible worlds.

The tensions in St. Petersburg provided Hector with daily opportunities to dissect at length Russian history, society and temperament. One day he amused himself by paraphrasing a line from the *Athenaeum*'s review of Reginald: Were these events, he asked, "the *hors-d'oeuvres* of an orgie of revolution . . . ?" Then spring arrived, and despite a severe Russian loss to the Japanese at Mukden, St. Petersburg sprang back to life. "Parisian toilettes in the various hues of a tulip bulb," Hector observed, "uniformed youths of the School of Nobles in their naval-looking cocked hats, laced and cockaded in gold and green and silver," heavy, hearse-looking horses interspersed with a motor carriage or two or "the recurring 'chug-chug' of a motor bicycle, displayed to more than its full advantage by some irrepressible youth."

By May, the Russian government was trying to win support with religious concessions that would eliminate discrimination against Roman Catholics, Mohammedans, every sect but the Jews. "Any relaxation of anti-Jew restrictions would be extremely unpopular in the country districts," Hector wrote. But there was a subdued trace of gratification two weeks later when he reported that the Jews of Little Russia were organizing armed resistance to threats of attacks by Christians: "A militantly defensive Jewish organisation will involve considerable additional embarrassment to the Government, which has hitherto been able to rely on the Jews not hitting back." Hector's attitude toward Jews was undergoing an evolution. As recently as Warsaw, he had been inclined to think the Poles were justified in resenting the sure business instincts of the Jewish minority. Now, in St. Petersburg, he was wondering whether the real problem was not more basic. Perhaps Jews were simply smarter than their neighbors, and if so, what could be done about that?

The Russian moves in a narrow world, he noted, its horizon bounded by the most minute interests. "Incessantly sipping syrup-sweetened tea, munching sunflower seeds, smoking cigarettes, chatting and chaffing endlessly with his neighbors, or, if he be a boy or lad, frolicking in mild horse-play which never attains the pitch of blows given in earnest; if he be a soldier or sailor, lolling aimlessly in shady avenues or public gardens, wearing for ten months out of the twelve a heavy flapping overcoat, and suggesting an invalid pacing the hospital grounds rather than a son of Mars; if he be a kerb-side merchant, solicitously dusting and rearranging the apples or envelopes which comprise his wares, but never seeming to bother about pushing their sale."

This laggard, this dullard, could hardly claim that his intellect or his future was straitened: ". . . nothing could be in more marked contrast than the alert and keenly-trained brainpower which makes the Jew such an awesome competitor in the Russian world. With the same, or perhaps fewer, possibilities and with many disadvantages added to those under which the youthful Russian labours, the Jewish working-class lad begets himself an education which seems to leave very little out of its purview."

When Russia made military moves along the border of Afghanistan, Hector took the occasion to lecture his readers once more on Russia's imperial aims. "In British political circles there are two sharply-defined schools of thought with regard to Central Asian affairs: one which declares with comfortable conviction that Russia would not dream of doing this or that, the other which is less concerned with what Russia is dreaming than with what she is doing and why she is doing it." Far from leaving Russia disillusioned and exhausted, Hector thought its Japanese misadventure could have the opposite effect. "The more formidable and distasteful the military problem becomes in Manchuria the more naturally will baffled energies turn towards the Persian borders and the passes of Afghanistan."

While Hector was turning out sober essays from St. Petersburg, an odd trial was coming to an end in London. His colleague of the Macedonian troubles, Henry Brailsford, was charged, together with an actor, with obtaining a false passport that was later used by a man killed as he planted a bomb in the Hotel Bristol in St. Petersburg. Brailsford had obtained the passport on behalf of the actor, who did not use it to travel to Russia. How it had come into the hands of a dynamiter was not established. Even the prosecution, secure in its charge that Brailsford had misled the Foreign Office, did not try to implicate him directly in the explosion. The jury took a quarter of an hour to find both men guilty. The episode was more evidence of how sharply Hector's antipathy for the revolutionaries had separated him from some of his colleagues in the British press corps.

Yet his long exposure to the Russians was tempering Hector's original suspicions, and after nine months in St.

Petersburg he was advising the Foreign Office that an alliance between Britain and Russia would neutralize Germany, then as later his chief villain. "If a good understanding with Russia is a door to which our diplomats can find no key, there are enterprising locksmiths in Berlin who are ready if necessary to remove the hinges."

Back in Devon, Ethel was now a veteran of the Russian Revolution and she rose to a new appreciation for Hector's insights. She too had noticed the slackness and inertia of the Russian male, and she cut from the *Morning Post* one of Hector's meditations on the want of vigor among even the military class. Admittedly the Russian officer was brave, charming and good-natured. But how to account for this? "A young officer stationed in a town drives from his quarters to his club, from his club to his restaurant, back to his club and so forth, and that represents about the sum of his non-professional exertions . . . The daily routine of an old lady at Bath with a taste for cards would not be very widely different, except that she would perhaps go less often to church and never to parade or café chantant . . .

"Probably the custom of dressing nearly every male civilian, from small errand-boys to postmen and such minor officials, in high military boots is responsible for many of our earliest notions of the Russians as a stern, truculent warrior breed. An army, it has been said, marches on its stomach; the Russians for several generations have lived on their boots. If an average British boy were put at an early age into such boots he would become a swashbuckling terror to his family and neighborhood, and in due course would rove abroad and found an Empire, or at any rate die of a tropical disease. A Russian would not feel impelled by the same influence further than the nearest summer garden."

It was as though, having once been sickly himself, Hector set an abnormally high value on the rude dash and swagger of health, the sheer jump of life. There is also to his recriminations the note of having been somehow cheated. Perhaps their lassitude in some way diminished the attraction he had found in vital gypsy boys but not in their Russian counterparts. Languid exquisiteness, as exemplified by Reginald, was a subject fit for fun but not desire. When Reginald flirted, it was with his reflection on the back of his silver hairbrushes. There was an element of that in Hector, too—the determination not to be seen unless one is perfectly turned out—but it was not a trait in which he took pride.

Hector did find an ethnic strain that met his standard. The men of Baku, on the Caspian Sea, struck at the oil refineries, and the Russian government's response was predictably quick and brutal. This time Hector's sympathies were wholeheartedly with the demonstrators— "lithe, athletic specimens, they have an eye for a sight and a finger for a trigger." Had the protesters always embodied Hector's ideal of manhood—and in his view being led by a priest could not have been an asset—he might have warmed gradually to their cause. As it was, he ended his first year in St. Petersburg as opposed to revolution as when he arrived, though he had come to understand its roots, and he could congratulate General Trépoff on an unbending attitude that had spared the city "anything savouring of serious bloodshed." After all, "the 'red' Socialists, however harmless in reality, have themselves invoked the disorder and have not hesitated to preach methods of violence."

Deplore the violence as he might, it was increasing on all sides. Hooligans prowled the streets, beating up Jews and any passerby better dressed then they were, and on New Year's Eve, Hector witnessed a shooting that affected him strongly. He was dining at the Medvied Restaurant, where Russian society and the diplomatic corps saw in the New Year. At midnight, when the orchestra played the Imperial Hymn, it was soundly cheered except by one student sitting a few tables from Hector. The boy refused to stand. A quarrel broke out, and a civilian man fired five shots into the boy's chest. A few other men broke champagne bottles over the assailant's head, but he was allowed to escape. There is no doubt that Hector was genuinely appalled by the event, even though, in reconstructing it, he could not resist the ironic detail:

"Nearly every woman in the room had fainted . . . Although the restaurant is in the centre of the city 70 minutes elapsed before the police appeared, during which time several parties resumed their supper within a few feet of the weltering corpse.

"The melodramatic nature of the scene was heightened by the intermittent arrival of groups of the victim's friends, who exchanged furious denunciations across his body with equally vociferous partisans of the assassin who indecently gloated over the tragedy.

"Naturally the superstitious Russians regard the episode as a terrible portent for the New Year and doubly deplorable from the fact of its being enacted before a large assembly of foreign witnesses."

The next day, Hector was still troubled by the incident, and, repeating again that several well-connected Russians had not only applauded the murder but continued carousing a few paces from the body, he asked: "What particular stage of civilisation has Russian society reached?" It was as though, like Ethel, he had found the tableau of demonstrators against Cossacks merely part of the inevitable workings of history, too impersonal to stir the heart. But to see a boy killed at short range in a fashionable restaurant, where such things should not happen, aroused his pity.

Hector could not forget the episode. Days later, he began a piece on political thuggery by alluding to the murder before he continued, "An individual who is a bully and a nuisance has in this country an enormous extension of license, because public opinion, however strongly against him, seldom develops into public action. Able-bodied men, adequately armed and perhaps enjoying ample authority of position, will sit watching a scene of unwarranted and disgraceful aggression with no further active expression of disapproval than the ejaculation of the useful word 'skandál' (which includes anything from regicide to the scolding of a waiter) under their breath; and this national tendency to treat an emergency as a spoilt child is one reason why emergencies are so plentiful in the land."

As in Macedonia, the heavy-handed official response to civil disorder, combined now with the pain of having watched a boy murdered, was driving Hector from his instinctive support for the government. As his loyalties wavered, he felt obliged to spell out his credo in more personal terms than most news columns today would accommodate. "The police have unlimited powers, and all the methods of the old régime are flourishing once more. I do not believe, as is sure to be objected, that the action of the revolutionaries has rendered this necessary. I do not believe that the best way to fight revolution is by lawless and arbitrary repression." Then, more to assure himself than the reader, Hector tacked on the qualification of every man whose view of himself as toughly realistic has been shaken by a twinge of compassion: "Lastly, and most important, it is not the immorality or the illegality of the methods that I find reprehensible, but their stupidity and ineffectiveness."

Although Hector was meeting performers from the ballet, he did not seek out Russian writers, whether from diffidence or a lack of enthusiasm for their work. Language was not the problem; he spoke Russian quite well. At the time of the march on the Winter Palace, he filed a brief note that Maxim Gorky had apparently been released from detention. But when Count Leo Tolstoy supported a landlord who had given away his holdings to the peasants who farmed them, Tolstoy's statement came to the *Morning Post* by way of the Central News Wire. Hector that day was lamenting the barbarous treatment of animals by marauding peasants. Bundles of kerosene-soaked rags had reportedly been fastened to the manes and tails of yearlings and then set ablaze. Horses were strapped to the sails of windmills and then dashed to earth. The stories came to Hector secondhand, from a reporter for a progovernment newspaper, but they incited him to new levels of indignation—"devilish," he called the behavior, and "fiendishly ingenious." For the moment, he was back solidly in the antirevolutionary camp. "This picture of the South Russian peasants' methods of conducting an economic agitation may supply material for reflection to those who glibly propose to bestow a wide measure of suffrage on 90,000,000 Russian peasants."

Attempting to defuse the prevailing explosiveness, the Tsar had called for a convening of the Imperial Duma, a parliament whose deliberations might give a patina of democracy to his autocratic rule. For Hector, throughout the spring of 1906 there was little to do but wait for the gathering of this body, in which—correctly, as it turned out—he put little faith. As he waited, he spun out a theory to establish a connection between hair and politics. That his own hair, fine but never luxuriant, was receding regularly before the aggressive advance of his brow may have alerted him to the subject. In any case, he observed that during the Stuart period in England "a flowing and elaborate coiffure marked allegiance to the old order of things, and the more uncompromising and violent a man became in the opposite direction, the closer he clipped his locks." In the Russia of 1906, it was different. "One accurately judges the lengths a man is ready to go in revolutionary legislation by the length and studied disorder in which he wears his hair, and it is not unusual to see such individuals enter a restaurant proudly displaying a chevelure which could only be worn in England by a character in a stage production of a farcical nature. A merciful provision of nature has endowed these men with conscientious scruples against occupying the more expensive seats in theatres, otherwise one might be doomed to sit behind a frizzled halo as obstructive to one's range of vision as the most pitiless matinee hat . . . The tendency to wear one's hair like an Angora kitten becomes fainter and fainter as one approaches the reactionary circles of society, and by the time one has reached the Imperial Corps of Pages one has caught up with the sleek-headed, cleanly-shaven fashions of the Twentieth Century and the West."

When the Duma opened at last on May 10, Hector sent to London paragraphs of his most relentless "color"—"the scarlet pennons of the Lancers, the equally brilliant tunics of the Cossacks of the escort, and the orange saddlecloths of the Dragoons made a gorgeous foreground to the dark-red Palace"—along with an ironic observation at the expense of the clergy and a tribute to one of his particular delights. "Monsignor Ropp was planted immediately opposite to a row of stiff cloth of gold figures with flowing white beards which almost looked like some special effort at upholstery, but really represented the Orthodox Metropolitan Prelates and Archimandrites waiting to commence the initiatory religious ceremony. The Nubian pages, who have been a Court institution since the time of Peter III., in imitation of the fashion then prevalent in Western Europe, were mistaken by many of the foreign onlookers for Deputies from some outlandish province."

The *Morning Post* ran Hector's reports of four and five paragraphs as its lead for the continuing Russian story, but the Reuter's correspondent was sending back more sympathetic views of the reform faction, particularly of its demands for amnesty for political prisoners, for woman's suffrage and for the abolition of the death penalty; the *Morning Post* appended those reports to Hector's.

Debate intensified over the agrarian question—the demand by peasants for their own land to till—and Hector took a stance of pained reasonableness. Where was the land to come from? "Of the combined total acreage of the Imperial and State domains more than 73 percent is situated in the three extreme northern Governments of Vologda, Olonetz, and Archangel, where you would not send a peasant to farm unless you hated him; of the remainder of these lands more than three-fourths is occupied by forest or otherwise unsuitable for agriculture." And if one took the private lands, what about the grooms, gardeners, nurserymen and the rest who made their living there? Public ownership would also mean a drop in productivity; the moujik was "a poor husbandman and a careless stock-keeper."

But since it was the will of most of the political parties to experiment with land reform, Hector resigned himself to the prospect that it would be sweeping, inconsistent and ill thought out. "Russia is unmistakably on the eve of a very acute period of disorder, and no one can foresee with certainty what shape those disorders may take or to what intensity they may attain. Before flinging oneself into a breach one likes to know that it really is a breach and not an abyss."

After less than two months, the Tsar, even more annoyed with the Duma than Hector was, ordered it dissolved. Hector expected British opinion to condemn the move, but he believed that the liberal majority of the Constitutional Democrats, called the Cadets, had brought the end on themselves. "Russia demanded statesmanship; the Duma responded with a rechauffé of ultra-Radical doctrines of which Western democracies have long since become tired." The Emperor called for a new session of the Duma to be convened in March, 1907, but Hector would not be present to chronicle its opening. After another six months of general strikes, political assassinations, and mutinies among the military, Hector left Russia for France. Roy Reynolds claimed that St. Petersburg could ruin forever afterward any British correspondent forced to return to the moral and gastronomic austerity of London. To cushion him, Hector had the prospect of a tour of duty in Paris before he would confront that adjustment.

9

The Unkindest Blow (1907-1909)

In Paris, the first task Hector set for himself after finding a flat was, as ever, engaging a servant. He went to the registry office and inspected many young men but none had the quality he sought; none was—as Ethel, for lack of a more precise word, put it—"original." At last he found a man who looked possible. His name was Marcellin and he turned out to be a good cook who was not perturbed by the nature of Hector's household.

The Paris of 1907 necessarily struck Hector as St. Petersburg with a Gallic accent. On one of the first Sundays of the year, demonstrators singing the *Internationale* surged through the boulevards while the cavalry trotted alongside and police agents knocked off a few hats. Hector found the casualties "comparatively trifling." Besides keeping watch over the boulevards, Hector strolled to the French Chamber, where he was oppressed by the untrammeled debate and the stuffy air. When he suffered attacks of an undiagnosable malady, Ethel blamed the close atmosphere of the Senate's galleries. Hector's acquaintances insisted that these intermittent spells were influenza. But he observed that, since all the symptoms of influenza were absent, it might equally well have been snakebite.

One marked advantage to being in Paris was the demand from the *Morning Post* for reviews of French theatre and galleries. Readers who were unlikely to travel to St. Petersburg were apt to cross the Channel looking for diversion, and Hector, whose French was even better than his Russian, could serve as their guide. He inspected *Electra* at the Comédie Française, where he admired the very literal stage settings and the performance of Madame Louise Silvain, who conveyed "a dry, burning, consuming passion, asking only one thing of fate, and asking it with all of its life, implacable and unperishing, and very human, as the clear-eyed Greeks saw humanity." In case that was a bit rich for the English breakfast table, Hector, by the review's end, had recovered himself: "Described on the programme as a tragedy in three acts, the piece was really presented in two, the curtain only coming down between the second and third acts. The audience took some time to grasp the fact that the final curtain had descended, and uncertain groups waited about in the corridors and cloak-rooms vainly endeavoring to get some official intimation as to whether the drama had really terminated."

Of *La Française,* a new comedy at the Odéon, Hector was blunt about his own effort to be diplomatic. "The purpose is to present to a French audience the author's opinion that Frenchwomen in general are more careful of the conventionalities and more loyal to their marriage obligations than certain simple-minded and not very experienced foreigners have been given to suppose. 'La Française' is a play that doubtless reads better than it acts, which is a tactful way of hinting that it does not act very well." When a troupe at the same theatre set a Zola novel to music, Hector took refuge in reviewing the audience: "The first-night audience suffered considerably between conflicting desires to applaud at the conclusion of effective pieces of acting and reluctance to drown the opening notes of incidental music, and the result was an intermittent conflict of tempestuous clapping with little storms of sibilant protest."

The Palais de Glace in the Champs Élysées presented a showing of comic art, and Hector went along to pay tribute—albeit anonymously; there were to be no bylines in Paris, either—to his patron on the *Westminster Gazette*. The German artists on display evinced genuine humor, Hector reported, sounding surprised. The French were inclined to be too brutal. But Carruthers Gould hit precisely the right note by dealing with an issue rather than with setting out solely to give offense; despite their Liberal viewpoint, "they could be found not only in any drawing-room but in any Tory drawing-room."

The more leisurely pace of his new assignment gave Hector a chance to file those brief items, hardly more than fillers, that amused the British reader by proving that, past the Channel, the world took on a ridiculous tilt: "Madame Liane de Pougy was slightly injured last October in a motor-car smash, and the chauffeur was to-day arraigned for alleged careless driving. The chauffeur was, however, acquitted of carelessness, but Madame Liane de Pougy, who is not present in Paris, was fined 25fr. for not attending as a witness."

Street criminals drew Hector's attention, particularly the Parisian Apaches, who had not yet been domesticated into modern dancers but were still genuine robbers and assassins. To stop the wave of crime, Hector put forth his all-purpose remedy. "There are, of course, excellent folk who assert that flogging would brutalise these murderous footpads, but I think that they are rather optimistic. The brutes of Paris, the horses, dogs, cats, not to mention the wolves and bears that appear on the music hall stage, are so amiable and well behaved, that if a mere whipping could bring the prowling night ruffian up to their level, the experiment might well be accorded a patient trial. But in Paris one scarcely looks for such virile measures."

In May 1907, at the age of thirty-six, Hector was confronted by the last death in his family that would matter to him. His mother's death, when he was little more than an infant, had helped to shape what he had become. Now his father's death would help to determine what he was to write. The circumstances of the Gov's death aroused in Hector a Celtic mysticism that was always threatening to erupt through his cultivated urbanity. Ethel had written to him that the Colonel was ailing but there seemed to be no cause for special concern. Hector went about his rounds, which included a night out playing bridge. All at once, as he related the episode to Ethel, he had a visitation. Five years later he used the incident in his first novel to portend, as it had for his father, impending death.

"As the ladies rose to leave the table Comus crossed over to pick up one of Lady Veula's gloves that had fallen to the floor.

" 'I did not know you kept a dog,' said Lady Veula.

" 'We don't,' said Comus. 'There isn't one in the house.'

" 'I could have sworn I saw one follow you across the hall this evening,' she said.

" 'A small black dog, something like a schipperke?' asked Comus in a low voice.

" 'Yes, that was it.'

" 'I saw it myself tonight; it ran from behind my chair just as I was sitting down. Don't say anything to the others about it; it would frighten my mother.'

" 'Have you ever seen it before?' Lady Veula asked quickly.

" 'Once, when I was six years old. It followed my father downstairs.'

" 'Lady Veula said nothing. She knew that Comus had lost his father at the age of six.' "

The morning after he saw the black dog, Hector got Ethel's wire telling him to come home. Two days after he arrived, his father died. Once one has established the conviction of the person telling the story, there is little to be said about such apparitions. Hector might have stretched a point to give Ethel gooseflesh; it was almost a younger brother's obligation. But the episode rings so false in his novel that we can be reasonably certain he yielded to that worst reason for including an event in fiction—that it had happened that way in life.

In the South of France, labor agitation erupted in the wine-producing area around Narbonne, but Hector elected to remain in Paris to report on the rioting which threatened momentarily to bring down the government of Premier Clemenceau. As a result, his readers got an idea of the skirmishing but no clear idea of what had provoked the outbreak. The judgment would have annoyed Hector, but as a correspondent he had often shown himself to be a brilliant observer and less often a penetrating thinker. When he could not mix directly in the action, he had little success in conveying coherently the issues at stake. He was not the first sensual man to fancy himself cerebral, just as he was not the first romantic to reach middle age convinced of his own cynicism.

Through July, Hector turned up all around Paris, writing with a range and restlessness he had not often shown in Russia. At the French Department of Interior, he unearthed a report that claimed that insanity occurred more often from drinking too much brandy than from overindulging in absinthe, and he professed pleasure at clearing the reputation of what he called the "maligned green Muse." On the Fourteenth of July, Hector could write a column about the day's festivities and not once fall into banality, or encourage Republican sentiments, by mentioning the Bastille. During the celebration, a steerable balloon named the *Patrie* loomed suddenly in the sky, looking to Hector like a gigantic shark. A Frenchman near him remarked, "It will be most useful for dropping explosives in wartime." Hector's response was smug. "I had not the heart to tell him that the first Hague Conference had foreseen and forbidden that interesting possibility."

In August, Hector followed local custom and went on holiday. Believing perhaps that Ethel needed a change of scene after their father's death, he invited her to join him in Pourville on the Normandy coast. There Hector found rooms in a small and newly opened hotel run by a woman who, according to Ethel, "possessed a temperament." She admired her brother's unerring instinct for places a little out of the ordinary.

In the morning, they went to the beach; in the afternoon, they walked or rode across the countryside. In the evening, they sometimes watched the gambling at the casino. And with brother and sister reunited, there were hoaxes. One day Ethel entered a small shop next to the hotel to buy picture postcards. When she asked how much they were, the clerk behind the counter proved to be Hector, who stayed on, with the owner's amused approval, hawking wares to the other shoppers.

Ethel found the impersonation great fun, the more proof of Hector's irrepressible spirit. But he understood that by itself the joke fell somewhat short of hilarity, and when he used his prank in fiction he dressed it up accordingly. In one story, a young man mistaken for a department-store clerk marks everything on sale and puts the proceeds in his pocket. In another, "Quail Seed," Hector heightens the drama still further. An honest shopkeeper is complaining that the larger shopping chains are drawing away his trade. Listening to him are an artist and his sister, and the artist hits upon a trick to win back the patrons. He sends his handsome young male model to the market to play out a charade that leads other customers to conclude that the merchant is selling opium under the guise of quail seed. The intrigue packs the store with shoppers, illustrating Hector's theory that the only thing people want more than to save money is to find relief from their boredom. When the women shoppers hie from a new and thrilling installment of the artist's invention to a nearby drawing room to talk it over, Hector remarks that "to go directly from a shopping expedition to a tea-party was what was known locally as 'living in a whirl.' "

In Pourville, Hector and Ethel met a man who was well-off but unforgivably stingy. Two years later, Hector recreated him as Laploshka, who, besides being mean, "said horrid things about other people in such a charming way that one forgave him for the equally horrid things he said about oneself behind one's back. Hating anything in the way of ill-natured gossip ourselves, we are always grateful to those who do it for us and do it well." In the story, a friend borrows two francs from Laploshka, and when he evades repaying them, Laploshka dies of grief. Hector in life also scored off the man, but Ethel did not recall the less lethal joke he concocted.

The holiday ended, Hector returned to Paris. But with the death of his father, much of the satisfaction had gone out of journalism. He had been deprived, he told Ethel, of his most appreciative reader. But lost, too, was a father to judge his sons and conclude that being a gentleman journalist in distant capitals was almost as manly a calling as being a gentleman police officer or a prison warden. And from his father's estate Hector would receive one-third, or twenty-three hundred pounds. He stayed on in Paris another eighteen months, but he was going through the motions, preparing for the day that he would leave journalism.

Once in a while, an event could still stir Hector's curiosity sufficiently for him to venture out with some minimal expectations. When Zola's body was conveyed to the Panthéon, for example, there was a gratifying struggle between those shouting, "À bas!" and those shouting, "Vive!" In the fray, Alfred Dreyfus was slightly wounded by revolver shots from an otherwise respectable old partisan. Hector blamed the incident on the haste with which Zola was being made immortal. "Hawkers did a thriving trade in postcards, which were the reverse of complimentary to the hero of to-day's ceremony, and the walls of Paris were covered with broad-sheets of an even unkinder nature. All these derogatory manifestations, or most of them, it is held, might have been avoided if the transfer to the Panthéon had been held over for at least another ten years."

The question of taxation in Indochina was occupying the French public, and it also piqued Hector's interest since he had known life in neighboring Burma. He much endorsed a form of sales tax over the poll taxes and land taxes imposed by the Mandarins, which were responsible, in Hector's view, for much of the rebellion in Annam. "Indirect taxes amounting to 1 fr. 88c. per head are by no means onerous, and the native who goes each week to market for tea, alcohol, and opium does not notice that each time he has paid rather more than 3c. to the State. On the other hand, the burden of direct taxation is heavy, cruel and inhuman."

When Bulgaria at last declared its countrymen in Macedonia independent of Turkey, Hector sent an unexpected endorsement to the *Westminster Gazette,* which had been supporting that cause while Hector was still praising the restraint of Turkish beys. He had come around to a simple truth: "The Macedonian of Bulgar blood will prefer to prosper in a progressive Bulgaria rather than in a reformed Turkey."

It was while Hector was based in Paris that Wilbur Wright came to France to test his airplane at Le Mans. The *Morning Post* assigned another correspondent to cover the flights, a man who could write knowledgeably about pulleys, rudders and air inlet pipes. Hector stayed with what he knew and what he thought he knew. Idly, he had continued to draw. On a Parisian telegraph form, he might sketch the face of a pretty boy in a cap, or a sly charging boar, or dogs so feral they were one leap away from becoming wolves. At the galleries, sophisticated Parisians were admiring the work of painters whom Roger Fry and Desmond MacCarthy would introduce to London two years later as "Post-Impressionists." If in his role as critic Hector sought out Cézanne, Gauguin or Matisse, he did not write about them. His taste ran instead to the clever, the literal and the macabre.

"A large painting by Charles Cottet, 'Au pays de la mer: Douleur,' successfully records a sea-tragedy in some Breton fishing village. A stark drowned corpse lies in the centre of a wonderfully rendered group of wailing and peering fisherfolk, and in the background are uneven cottage roofs and the stiff red sails of anchored boats."

"Georges Rötig has hit on a good subject in his gruesome scene 'The destruction of wolves by poison.' The bleak, snow-covered waste under a wintry sky, where a pack of wary, half-frightened wolves watch in silence while two of their fellows lie in their death agonies over the remains of a devoured sheep, makes an impressive study of the wild. The dying wolves in the foreground are, however, not painted with his usual accuracy, and there is little that is distinctively wolfish in their appearance."

"The marble group 'Baiser à la Source,' of Henri

Coutheillas, represents an exquisitely posed nude youth leaning at full-length over a shelving rock in the act of kissing a gracefully recumbent water-nymph."

At the theatre, Hector's taste was somewhat surer, although his reviews of Madame Sarah Bernhardt extended no critical boundaries. He found her "superb" in a benefit performance of *Adrienne Lecouvreur;* "wonderfully well-suited" to her role in *La Courtisane de Corinthe;* and wearing "the magic of her own personality" in a revival of a *Sleeping Beauty* in which the actress played both the prince and his reincarnation a hundred years later. In London, Bernard Shaw was offering *Man and Superman* at the Court Theatre in Sloane Square, but Paris was just becoming acquainted with him. "The playwright's reputation," Hector explained to his readers, "had arrived in advance of his play, consequently 'Candida' presented itself to a French audience much as Westminster Abbey did to the fair American who had 'heard it very highly spoken of.' " Hector preferred to let the French critics speak about the performance, quoting at length from *Le Temps,* which found Shaw's comedy "gross, puerile and labored."

Only a French rendering of *Peter Pan* prompted Hector to attempt a criticism beyond the bestowing of a few favorable adjectives. The play was certain to intrigue a man who had also resisted, past the last permissible moment, society's injunction to grow up. But where Barrie eulogized the child, Hector's fascination lay with the adolescent. As he would later suggest very obliquely, the difference to him was sexual and, therefore, crucial. The French audience did not warm to Barrie's fantasy, but Hector did not blame the play. "To understand 'Peter Pan' one must have read and enjoyed Lewis Carroll's best work; and the French have never had a Lewis Carroll. Outside the fairy story and the nursery rhyme the French child has but a scant choice of literature, and he has hardly ever been exploited for the amusement of his elders. The average Frenchman and French woman undoubtedly display the greatest affection for their children and the greatest interest in their development, but their interest is essentially practical—for the French are a practical nation—and they have little sympathy for those fancies and dreams which are childhood's 'clouds of glory.' If the French parent loses by this attitude perhaps the French child gains, since it to a great extent is saved from the besetting sin of the modern child, self-consciousness."

In a review of a light French comedy, Hector had complained that although the play had been bright and unflagging for the first two acts and part of the third, "Life is largely made up of unnecessary fourth acts, and in this respect no doubt M. Gavault's play is true to life."

So far, Hector's own life had fallen into two acts, a childhood upon which he could draw sometimes for a charming sense of freedom, sometimes for an overpowering rage; and an adolescence that, helped along by an indulgent father and a career so emotionally feckless as that of foreign correspondent, he had managed to prolong almost to the age of forty. Now Hector was returning to London and staking everything on his ability to make his third act brilliant.

10

On Approval
(1909-1911)

For an employed journalist to trade regular pay and the daily satisfaction of seeing his words in print for a precarious life writing fiction involves no small risk. In making the change, Hector had several assets to draw upon: *Reginald* had proved that he could write fiction and *Alice* suggested that his writing might sell. Between the inheritance from his father and his own savings, he had enough money to buy a cottage in the Surrey hills, twenty-three miles from London, which had the twin advantage of giving Ethel an agreeable place to live and one that was not with him. Although he preferred to dress well—which required, in 1909, a herringbone tweed overcoat, plain jacket and striped worsted trousers, light-colored gloves and bowler—a man might make the investment to be properly fitted out and then dismiss the subject. Roy Reynolds had lamented that coming back to London meant eating at a Lyons bread-house, but Hector liked the bland fare, cheap prices and unpretentious atmosphere. Best of all, and a requisite for success as a free lance, Hector wrote quickly. Reynolds said that his hand moved so swiftly across a page that he might have been sketching.

The first pieces he turned out that spring were, in fact, sketches: Laploshka; Aunt Tom delineated as "The Sex That Doesn't Shop"; and Reginald, who turned out to travel badly, sent to St. Petersburg for "Reginald in Russia." The *Westminster Gazette* seems to have been pleased by the prodigal's return. The stories were prominently featured and printed within a week after submission. That promptness allows us to estimate that it was mid-May 1909 when Hector took his first large step as an artist. The experiment ran a bit longer than Hector's previous pieces, and it swept up into one neat package almost all of his creative concerns. Critics unfamiliar with his life would sometimes call Saki an impersonal artist, but they were misled by the distancing of himself behind his careful prose. Very few writers return as often as Hector, or as ingeniously, to tap again a few lifelong obsessions. The new story was called "Gabriel-Ernest," and it began, " 'There is a wild beast in your woods,' said the artist Cunningham, as he was being driven to the station."

Van Cheele, the protagonist, brushes aside Cunningham's alarm; what he saw was either a stray fox or resident weasel, and the matter is dropped. Van Cheele lives with his aunt and shares some of Hector's own interests but not his reticence about them. "It was his custom to take mental notes of everything he saw during his walks, not so much for the purpose of assisting contemporary science as to provide topics for conversation afterwards. When the bluebells began to show themselves in flower he made a point of informing every one of the fact; the season of the year might have warned his hearers of the likelihood of such an occurrence, but at least they felt that he was being absolutely frank with them."

On this day he comes upon an apparition, a boy of about sixteen, sprawled naked by a pool, letting the sun dry his brown limbs. "His wet hair, parted by a recent dive, lay close to his head, and his light-brown eyes, so light that there was almost a tigerish gleam in them, were turned toward Van Cheele with a certain lazy watchfulness."

Van Cheele and the boy talk at cross-purposes. Van Cheele believes he is being chaffed. " 'What do you feed on?' he asked.

" 'Flesh,' said the boy, and he pronounced the word with slow relish, as though he was tasting it.

" 'Flesh! What flesh?'

" 'Since it interests you, rabbits, wild-fowl, hares, poultry, lambs in their season, children when I can get any; they're usually too well locked in at night, when I do most of my hunting. It's quite two months since I tasted child-flesh.' "

The vision darts away and Van Cheele, puzzling over the dialogue, remembers that about two months ago a child had disappeared from a family at the mill. He wishes the boy had not made his uncanny remark. "Such dreadful things should not be said even in fun." The next day the boy appears in Van Cheele's morning room, drier but no better dressed. " 'Suppose my aunt should see you!'

"And with a view to minimizing that catastrophe Van Cheele hastily obscured as much of his unwelcome guest as possible under the folds of a *Morning Post*. At that moment his aunt entered the room."

The boy is introduced as an amnesiac, which the aunt finds touching. She dresses him, names him Gabriel-Ernest, and arranges that he should help her entertain the infant members of her Sunday-school class at tea. Van Cheele hurries away to consult with the artist who first alerted him to the wild presence in the woods. After a bit of persuasion, Cunningham agrees to tell what he saw and, appalled, Van Cheele rushes back to his house. But his aunt has sent Gabriel-Ernest to escort the little Toop child home. " 'It was getting so late, I thought it wasn't safe to let it go back alone. What a lovely sunset, isn't it?' "

A scream is heard, and when Gabriel-Ernest's clothes are found by a pool, the villagers assume that the child fell into the water and that Gabriel-Ernest was lost, too, after plunging in to save him. Miss Van Cheele proposes a memorial brass to the brave unknown youth who sacrificed his life for another. The story ends, "Van Cheele gave way to his aunt in most things, but he flatly refused to subscribe to the Gabriel-Ernest memorial."

Confronted with a story like that one, the American writer Christopher Morley suggested that Saki was beyond criticism, that he was unique, and any attempt to dissect him would only expose the critic's solemnity. Morley was right that an analysis is almost certain to be less subtle than the original. But it is no greater an affront to explore Saki's secrets than to visit the kitchen in the hope of picking up pointers from the chef.

There are three elements to "Gabriel-Ernest"—the erotic, the horrible and the comic—and it is proof of the author's mastery that the comic element prevails. Given the times in which he wrote, the erotic may have been obvious only to those who shared Hector's enthusiasm for his portrait of a naked brown-skinned boy. Nearly fifty years later, in a frank and beautifully written examination of his own homosexuality, J. R. Ackerley announced that men of his own background had never excited him, only workingclass men who held that promise of sexual vigor assumed by writers as different as E. M. Forster and D. H. Lawrence. Hector took that longing further and made it more fastidious. Better that the boy be unbred than ill bred; better naked than wearing stained and baggy trousers. For a different audience, Hector's story could have been equally erotic, and even more chilling, had the poacher been Gabriella, a young woman. But that change might have made the story too shocking for its day, conjuring up more widespread pornographic fantasies and undermining the traditional view of women as gentle and maternal. In this instance, Hector's sort of eroticism helped to make his story marketable.

As he mutes the erotic side of his tale, Hector gives the horrific full measure. Cunningham may describe what he saw in the language of melodrama but it is not the language of parody. If the reader consents to be frightened, Hector is willing to do his part:

" 'What I thought I saw was something so extraordinary that no really sane man could dignify it with the credit of having actually happened. I was standing, the last evening I was with you, half-hidden in the hedgegrowth by the orchard gate, watching the dying glow of the sunset. Suddenly I became aware of a naked boy, a bather from some neighbouring pool, I took him to be, who was standing out on the bare hillside also watching the sunset. His pose was so suggestive of some wild faun of Pagan myth that I instantly wanted to engage him as a model, and in another moment I think I should have hailed him. But just then the sun dipped out of view, and all the orange and pink slid out of the landscape, leaving it cold and grey. And at the same moment an astounding thing happened—the boy vanished too!'

" 'What! Vanished away into nothing?' asked Van Cheele excitedly.

" 'No; that is the dreadful part of it,' answered the artist; 'on the open hillside where the boy had been standing a second ago, stood a large wolf, blackish in colour, with gleaming fangs and cruel, yellow eyes.' "

How does Hector keep so grisly a story funny? The answer rests mainly with Van Cheele. First there is, as there would always be with Hector, the rightness of his name. Inane but not preposterous, it defines him, just as, in choosing a name for his victim, Hector offers the consolation that at least the child has escaped going through life as "Toop." Then there is Van Cheele's character. A bachelor, he lives with his aunt, and Hector, having escaped from Devon, is ready to endorse the convention that such men are figures of fun. Van Cheele is an incurable chatterer, and he is very dense, even though we must admit that given the incredibility of what he is asked to believe, some of his thickness is forgivable. The scene in which Van Cheele tries to wrap his werewolf in newspaper is unashamed farce. Van Cheele's practical aunt hears that the boy has lost his memory and suggests that his underclothes may be marked. " 'He seems to have lost most of that, too,' said Van Cheele, making frantic little grabs at the *Morning Post* to keep it in place." And when the truth at last overcomes Van Cheele's incredulity, and he must take action, his responses remain silly: "He dismissed the idea of a telegram. 'Gabriel-Ernest is a werewolf' was a hopelessly inadequate effort at conveying the situation, and his aunt would think it was a code message to which he had omitted to give her the key." Instead, Van Cheele hustles home and arrives too late.

Since the story is seen entirely through his eyes, and since he is a goose, nothing truly serious can befall him. Van Cheele stands within a charmed circle of ineptitude. When Hector makes one last attempt to lull the reader still further, the device betrays a deep prejudice of his own: "Mrs. Toop, who had eleven other children, was decently resigned to her bereavement." It was the judgment of a social class for whom three children represented a seemly regard for posterity but eight or ten convicted a mother of ruttishness or popery. Finally, what has come of the tragedy? By not subscribing to the memorial, the worm, while hardly turning, has swerved a few degrees. Because it ends on that mild triumph, the story ends cheerfully.

When "Gabriel-Ernest" was published the following year as part of the next Saki collection, it preceded a story called "The Saint and the Goblin," a trifle that Hector had published seven years earlier, before he went abroad as a reporter. The sequence of stories could only puzzle an attentive reader; the tale of a stone saint in a cathedral who debates theology with a goblin in the opposite niche is predictable in its iconoclasm and in its final twist. The stories of O. Henry had reached London as Hector was making his own first efforts, and young writers tend to breathe deeply whatever is filling the air. Hector admired Kipling, but robust vitality was nothing he could imitate; with Mark Twain, there was the same admiration and incompatibility. But he could invent surprises as ingenious as any by William Sydney Porter, and for a while that seemed to him worth doing. Before the spell broke, Hector added a dozen exemplary models to the genre.

O. Henry defined a good story as a "bitter pill with the coating inside." Hector might have agreed so long as the core had no trace of sugar, either. "The Reticence of Lady Anne," the tale of a man trying desperately to patch up a quarrel with his silent and unyielding wife, is worked out with enough parenthetical wit that it avoids the fault of most stories with trick endings: that they are unreadable once one knows the surprise. Getting to that surprise,

Hector reveals so much about the joyless nature of the marriage between Egbert and Lady Anne that the horror at the ending produces at best a very mild shudder but vast admiration at the way Hector has baited his trap. "Lady Anne was not drinking her tea. Perhaps she was feeling unwell. But when Lady Anne felt unwell she was not wont to be reticent on the subject. 'No one knows what I suffer from indigestion' was one of her favourite statements; but the lack of knowledge can only have been caused by defective listening; the amount of information available on the subject would have supplied material for a monograph." To mend the argument, Egbert swears forlornly to lead a better life. "He wondered vaguely how it would be possible. Temptations came to him, in middle age, tentatively and without insistence, like a neglected butcher-boy who asks for a Christmas box in February for no more hopeful reason than that he didn't get one in December."

As he wrote those early stories, Hector was settling into a routine that would allow him five remarkably productive years. His rooms at 97 Mortimer Street were within a brisk walk of the British Museum and only fifty paces from the tempting shops of Regent Street, at that place where the peaked roof of the Church of All Souls rises like a witch's hat. Bachelor's suites in the neighborhood rented for thirty-five shillings a week; for that Hector got large and well-proportioned rooms in the plainest red-brick building on the street. During his earlier stay in London, he had joined a club, and now, when he did not take his lunch at Lyons, he ate there.

For a Tory, the choice of club often fell between Ozinda's or the Cocoa Tree, which had been named in the days when it had been a public chocolate house. Each member financed his club by purchasing an annual share of stock. Hector bought two shares at a pound each and later, as dues went up, a third share. The Cocoa Tree, at 64 St. James Street, was not quite of the first rank; at White's, a member was given his change in washed silver coins. But it was eminently respectable, having lived down the era when it had been popular with high-plunging sportsmen. Hector may never have felt with Sam

Johnson that "the great chair of a full and pleasant town club is, perhaps, the throne of human felicity," but he made regular use of his membership in the Cocoa Tree. Often, he spent his evenings at its bridge tables. And he probably endorsed the sentiment of another man about town that "a club is a weapon used by savages to keep the white woman at a distance."

Past members of the Cocoa Tree had seldom been rich, which made the club's history of high stakes at faro and hazard somewhat scandalous. In Hector's time, however, most members had an income of four hundred to eight hundred pounds a year, and they could expect the club table, in season, to provide caviar, plover's eggs and asparagus, the three staples in Hector's stories when he wanted to suggest epicurean abandon. On Ethel's visits to London, Hector took her to Italian restaurants for her favorite food, a consolation for having to leave behind in Surrey her animals—Logie, Dandy and Ho, the black Persian. The Gourmets was one regular stop, and after the theatre the Café Royal off Piccadilly. When Hector visited his sister at the cottage for a weekend, he sometimes brought a friend from town. Ethel liked to regard the young men as charity cases. "Lame dogs," she called them, and she admired the practical ways in which Hector helped them in their struggle to get on.

Hector shared Ethel's delight in the beds of flowers and vegetables she was cultivating—a garden, after all, is supposed to provide an Englishman with the repose and sensual satisfaction the French traditionally seek in the salon of a mistress. Both Hector and Ethel loved tulips, and one night he was called upon to prove how much. At supper, Ethel swung a lamp impatiently to release its oil and it burst into flame instead. It is hard to picture Ethel being domestic or reacting decisively in a crisis. In this instance, she regarded the fire and wondered how to put it out.

"Earth is the best thing," said Hector, and he ran to the garden.

Meantime, a friend on the scene responded even more practically. Seizing the hearth rug, he smothered the flames. Quite a time passed before Hector returned; when he did, Ethel taxed him with the delay. (A year after their wedding, Charlie's wife, Muriel, had borne a daughter, giving Ethel a niece. But long before that, she had set on the path to becoming an Aunt in the Munro tradition.) "You've been a long time fetching that earth," she scolded Hector.

"Well," he answered, "the tulip bed came first, and of course I couldn't disturb *that,* so I had to go farther on to the cabbage plot."

After he left Russia, Hector stayed in touch with Roy Reynolds, and Reynolds had sent to Charlie and Muriel's little girl, Felicia, a handsome volume of Polish fairy tales. But Muriel, when she met Reynolds later, let friends know that she did not care much for him; possibly there was to Roy Reynolds a shade too much of a quality that the family preferred to overlook in Hector. And away from the tolerant society of St. Petersburg, Hector may have thought so too. When Reynolds sent him a postcard from Russia with a greeting that began, "In memory of . . ." Hector snipped off the rest of the message and used the unrevealing remnant as a book marker.

Methuen wanted to publish a volume called *Reginald in Russia.* It was a misleading title; there would be only one Reginald story in the book and that a weak one. But by the end of 1909, writing a story a month and exhuming his early work, Hector had fifteen pieces ready for the volume. Even his most negligible of those items included well-turned lines, which, while not epigrammatic, said something ill-natured about humanity with admirable grace: "She had a strong natural bias towards respectability, though she would have preferred to have been respectable in smarter surroundings, where her example would have done more good. To be beyond reproach was one thing, but it would have been nicer to have been nearer to the Park." Or the man who "spoke of several duchesses as if he knew them—in his more inspired moments almost as if they knew him." Or "Thank you for your sympathy all the same. I daresay it was well meant. Impertinence often is."

As the final entry in the collection, Hector wrote "The Mouse," another of his stories that depended on one stroke of invention. A young man on a train feels a mouse in his clothes. Across the aisle, a young woman is sleeping. With a modesty remarkable even in the last year of Edward's reign, he manages to get himself and the mouse out of his clothes only to learn that his contortions have been unnecessary. The young woman is blind. But after Lady Anne, whose reticence resulted from being dead, the surprise Hector provides on this occasion is even more modest than his hero.

Accepting the truth that a free lance cannot always choose his showcase, Hector sent another effort, a playlet called "The Baker's Dozen," to one of his army friends, who bought the piece for the *Journal of the Leinster Regiment*. The magazine not only published the piece but later gave *Reginald in Russia* one of its very few reviews. The reviewer, an army captain, displayed a good-natured tolerance to Hector's creation. "Admirers of a pretty wit will learn with much satisfaction that Mr. H. H. Munro has written a further series in the career of that adorably decadent being, Reginald."

Hector's experience with Methuen had proved unrewarding, and what little money he extracted from the company was slow in coming. At one point, a Methuen clerk wrote that since a royalty check of slightly more than four pounds—twenty dollars—seemed to have been lost in the mail, the publisher would issue a new check. Hector waited a few days and then, barely masking his suspicions, wrote again. "The fresh cheque for £4.1.1 of which you speak in your letter of the 4th instant appears to have had no better luck than its predecessor." A year and a half passed after *Reginald in Russia* had sunk from sight before an editor at Methuen wrote again to Hector, and his note was insulting in its brevity and insensitive in its praise. "We write to inquire if you are likely to have another volume of stories ready before long. We like your stories very much, and we should be glad to make them better known."

With noticeable restraint, or with the free lance's recognition that bridges may be singed but must never be burned, Hector replied, "Thank you very much for your letter of the 22nd. I did not submit my last batch of stories to you (since published as *The Chronicles of Clovis*) as the previous book, *Reginald in Russia,* had a very limited sale and I feared you would not consider the game worth the candle. My next 2 books are bespoke but at some future time I may again have the pleasure of submitting a book to you."

Hector's defection to his new publisher, John Lane, in a sense represented a homecoming. Reginald had been shaped by the sensibilities of *The Yellow Book* of the 1890s and Lane had published that epoch-making periodical. Lane, like Hector's first patron, Carruthers Gould, was from Devon, where his family had been yeomen for centuries. They boasted that the first pipe ever lighted in England had been smoked by a Lane on Putford Bridge. Small and springy, gray-bearded, John Lane had shown a hunger for talent even more rapacious than his taste for profit, and in the brief life of his *Yellow Book* he had brought together some remarkably disparate styles. Henry James published "The Death of the Lion" there and Yeats "The Blessed." The elusive Baron Corvo was represented by "Stories Toto Told Me" and by the vermin he carried into the office; after he called, the arm chair in which he sat had to be sprayed with insecticide. Max Beerbohm, in an essay on cosmetics, had written the publication's manifesto: "For behold! The Victorian era comes to its end and the day of *sancta simplicitis* is quite ended . . . Artifice, that fair exile, has returned."

But the work that set an enduring stamp on the *Yellow Book* was the art of Aubrey Beardsley. He was a young man when the journal first appeared in 1894, and Lane, enthralled by his gifts and never quite believing in his depravity, treated him like a mischievous child. Whenever Beardsley submitted a drawing, Lane held it sideways and upside down to be sure that Beardsley had not slipped in an impertinent anatomical detail. Then, in one day, Lane's airy and prestigious enterprise crashed to earth on a misunderstanding. Lane was in New York when Oscar Wilde lost his libel action against the Marquess of Queensberry and was taken under arrest. In bold type, the Sunday newspapers proclaimed variations on the headline, "Arrest of Oscar Wilde, Yellow Book Under His Arm." The report was, as it turned out, true yellow journalism. The book Wilde was carrying as he drove grandly off to court was no publication of Lane's but rather a copy of Pierre Louÿs' *Aphrodite,* which chanced to be bound in yellow. "It killed the 'Yellow Book,' " Lane said afterward, "and it nearly killed me."

No correction caught up with the error. Outraged moralists gathered outside Lane's offices on Vigo Street and threw stones at the windows. That display was followed by thuggery of a worse kind. Six of his prominent writers joined together to send a cable to Lane threatening to withdraw their work from his list unless he took Wilde's name from his catalogue and Beardsley's art from a forthcoming volume of the *Yellow Book.* Lane, still in America, passed the decision on to his staff, and they agreed to meet the writers' demands. The notoriety distressed Lane terribly; only after it ended did he confide to associates that the ultimatum had been poorly drawn, since Beardsley, who had quarreled with Wilde during their collaboration on *Salomé,* had made it a condition for joining the *Yellow Book* that nothing of Wilde's appear there. The scandal also touched the Lane office more personally. One of his office boys, a young man named Shelley, was named in court as a willing participant in Wilde's revels. From that time on, Lane became suspicious of every new acquaintance, sure he was concealing perversions that would be Lane's ruin.

At the outset, John Lane had no such fears about Hector. By now Wilde had been dead ten years, and Hector's stories were appearing in the *Westminster Gazette,* a journal so resolutely high-minded that it had not even covered the Wilde trial. For a royalty of ten percent on the first two thousand copies and fifteen on all subsequent sales, John Lane became Hector's publisher, with a right to his next three books except for a proposed novel titled *The Vandermeulen,* which Hector had promised elsewhere. As it turned out, by the time that book was ready for publication as *The Unbearable Bassington,* John Lane could have it, too.

After his disappointment with Methuen, Hector may have thought he would be better treated by his West County compatriot. But Lane, though his eyes tended to blur as though with uncontrollable fellow feeling, was a sharp trader, and after he had made the fame of H. G. Wells and then Arnold Bennett, neither man hesitated to take their work where they would be better paid for it. Still, besides being a Quaker, Lane regarded disputes and squabbles as a waste of time, and his former writers might treat him coolly but seldom with rancor. Hector summed up their attitude when he was walking one day with his cousin, Willie Mercer, and they encountered Lane. After he had passed, Hector said quietly, "Good fellow, Lane. Just don't let him publish your books."

At about the time Hector brought his first stories to Lane's office, a young clerk came to work there, and the author took an avuncular interest in the robust and unavailable youth. In the course of his three years with Lane, young Ben Travers met some of the era's famous men— few bulked larger in his memory than G. K. Chesterton —but it was with Hector and with a Canadian humorist, Stephen Leacock, that he became best acquainted. The two authors were very different in manner as well as in humor, and Leacock was much the easier to know. A bear with a ginger mustache, he embraced experience as resolutely as Hector held it at arm's length. Yet Hector had his own quiet appeal. For one thing, Travers found him very handsome, the slight crimp to Hector's face not marring good looks that were set off by clothes, often a blue suit, cut to perfection. Without a trace of dandyism or foppery, Hector was absolutely the cleanest-looking and best-dressed man Travers had ever seen. He was reserved, nothing like Leacock spewing his dogmatic opinions everywhere with the smoke from his pipe. Hector was observant, however, and generous. When he saw this newcomer bent over a desk, correcting the proofs of *The Chronicles of Clovis,* he invited the young man to lunch at the Cocoa Tree. Travers went and enjoyed the afternoon greatly. He had no idea that Hector was homosexual, and such was the mood in 1911 that, had he suspected it, he would have refused the invitation.

The deadline for including stories in *Reginald in Russia* excluded a story that Hector had written in November

1909 about a remarkable cat. That meant that his next collection, the *Clovis,* could offer "Tobermory." But to make it qualify as a story told by Clovis Sangrail took more extensive editing than Hector usually spent on a piece when it went from newspaper to hard covers. Most of his stories could be reprinted exactly as they had first appeared, but to give *The Chronicles of Clovis* some slight continuity, Hector went over all the published work and interjected a word or two from his new narrator. In the *Westminster Gazette,* the story of Tobermory—the cat got his name, like Rothay Reynolds, from a map of Scotland —involved a young man named Bertie van Tahn, who was not exactly Reginald and not exactly Clovis. Reginald had been, like Tinkerbell, little more than a flash of light or an Elizabethan humour. Both Bertie and Clovis had progressed near enough to Restoration comedy that at least they were given last names. If there is a distinction between them, it is that Bertie is more heartless than Clovis. Neither young man would qualify for a humanitarian award, but Bertie raises hell as though it were a cash crop. Looking for virtues in him, Hector found only one: Bertie "was so depraved at seventeen that he had long ago given up trying to be any worse." Clovis is less the delinquent and more the hanging judge, paying off scores against the stingy and the pretentious. Clovis, too, is the better friend to those distraught matrons who act as his hostess. Once a woman in distress takes Clovis into her confidence, his enterprise and ingenuity will be set exclusively at her service. Though he shares Bertie's rebelliousness, Clovis channels it into the rescue of social occasions. To put it baldly, one can imagine having Clovis as a friend; one cannot imagine Bertie having any friends or wanting any.

Evelyn Waugh's austere appreciation of Saki in the late 1920s was all Hector might have wished, and Waugh's was the most unerring instinct of any of the notables who wrote about Hector after his death—Graham Greene, Chesterton, A. A. Milne, Noël Coward. Waugh observed that when, almost by chance, Hector's themes exactly fitted their prescribed dimension in a newspaper, the result could be a masterpiece. "Tobermory" is one of those masterpieces.

Ancient Highland legends teemed with wolves and ravens, but it was cats and their mysterious nature that had cast a particular spell over Hector's ancestors, and he was not immune to it. By the end of her long life, Ethel Munro had worn out any number of cats, and on her deathbed she demanded that her final cat, a big male named Tommy, be killed so that he would be waiting to meet her on the Other Side. The family did not grant her request, and since Ethel knew the lesson of "Tobermory" very well, it is hard to understand just what conviviality she had hoped to find there.

The story opens with nondescript Cornelius Appin invited to Lady Blemley's house party because he has a vague reputation for cleverness, which he partly redeems with his claim that he can teach intelligent cats to talk. The Blemleys' Tobermory, he reports, is a "Beyond-cat" of extraordinary talent; in Ethel Munro's parlance, he would be an original cat, an unconventional cat. Appin's claim proves true. Tobermory saunters into the drawing room and, to an offer of milk, responds clearly, "I don't mind if I do."

Conversation thereafter tends to lag. The guests are a typical weekend gathering, not really up to the demand of being interesting to a superior cat. But social amenity triumphs and one woman is rash enough to risk a question. " 'What do you think of human intelligence?' asked Mavis Pellington lamely.

" 'Of whose intelligence in particular?' asked Tobermory coldly.

" 'Oh, well, mine for instance,' said Mavis, with a feeble laugh.

" 'You put me in an embarrassing position,' said Tobermory, whose tone and attitude certainly did not suggest a shred of embarrassment.

" 'When your inclusion in this house-party was suggested Sir Wilfred protested that you were the most brainless woman of his acquaintance, and that there was a wide distinction between hospitality and the care of the feeble-minded. Lady Blemley replied that your lack of brain-power was the precise quality which had earned you your invitation, as you were the only person she could think of who might be idiotic enough to buy their old car. You know, the one they call 'The Envy of Sisyphus,' because it goes quite nicely up-hill if you push it.'

"Lady Blemley's protestations would have had greater effect if she had not casually suggested to Mavis only that morning that the car in question would be just the thing for her down at her Devonshire home.

"Major Barfield plunged in heavily to effect a diversion.

" 'How about your carryings-on with the tortoise-shell puss up at the stables, eh?'

"The moment he had said it every one realized the blunder.

" 'One does not usually discuss these matters in public,' said Tobermory frigidly. 'From a slight observation of your ways since you've been in this house I should imagine you'd find it inconvenient if I were to shift the conversation on to your own little affairs.'

"The panic which ensued was not confined to the Major.

" 'Would you like to go and see if cook has got your dinner ready?' suggested Lady Blemley hurriedly, affecting to ignore the fact that it wanted at least two hours to Tobermory's dinner-time.

" 'Thanks,' said Tobermory, 'not quite so soon after my tea. I don't want to die of indigestion.'

" 'Cats have nine lives, you know,' said Sir Wilfred heartily.

" 'Possibly,' answered Tobermory; 'but only one liver.' "

The solution is obvious: Tobermory must die. And here Hector's touch is characteristically deft. The cat eludes the strychnine left out for him and falls instead in combat with a big yellow Tom from the rectory. Not a hero's death but an honorable one, and comedy depends heavily on a sense of honor. Cornelius Appin is chagrined at the hostility to his breakthrough—"an archangel ecstatically pro-claiming the Millennium, and then finding that it clashed unpardonably with Henley and would have to be indefinitely postponed, could hardly have been more crest-fallen." When word comes weeks afterward that Appin has been trampled to death by an elephant in the Dresden Zoological Garden, Clovis remarks that if he was trying German irregular verbs on the beast then he deserved all he got. On this day, her sullen guests departed, Lady Blemley "sufficiently recovered her spirits to write an extremely nasty letter to the Rectory about the loss of her valuable pet."

It is a remarkable performance by Saki, the supernatural presented with so little flourish that the story is done before logic has recovered itself enough to protest. By now Hector was carving his stories with a keen blade, suffering no extraneous word or commonplace phrase. He had reached that degree of proficiency where the humor came less from his jokes than from the precision of each sentence. The reader laughs with delight at the absolute rightness to his language.

A. A. Milne, who early in his career took Saki as his favorite author, went through *The Chronicles of Clovis* to illustrate with examples that instinct for the irreplaceable word. Milne quoted this description of the way diners in a restaurant cope with choosing a wine: "The wine lists had been consulted, by some with the blank embarrassment of a school-boy suddenly called upon to locate a Minor Prophet in the tangled hinterland of the Old Testament, by others with the serene scrutiny which suggests that they have visited most of the higher-priced wines in their homes and probed their family weaknesses." Milne added, " 'Locate' is the pleasant word here." But such pleasant words abound on every page. A certain royal duchess "nursed a violent but perfectly respectable passion for beef olives." And even earlier, when Van Cheele is trying to explain away the wolf-boy to his aunt, he glances "apprehensively at the waif's face to see whether he was going to add inconvenient candour to his other savage propensities."

Wit may be rebellious in its intent but in its perfection of expression it upholds a universal order.

Not surprisingly, given Hector's sexual foraging, a number of his stories turn, like "Tobermory," on a threat of blackmail. His own life had a few protections: He had lived for years in foreign countries where any young native had more to fear from a scandal than he did. In London, with his instinct for self-preservation sharpened, he had no single employer who could dismiss him, no fame so large that notoriety could damage it, no family whose collective heart could be broken. Throughout his life, he remained on excellent terms with Charles, who was far away in Ireland, and as for Ethel, the young cad who showed up at her door peddling tales about her brother would have emerged worse scarred than Tobermory at the mercy of the rectory cat. Still, even for Hector there was the possibility of exposure and prison, a reminder that the Victorian Age had bequeathed secrets that no amount of Edwardian emancipation could tempt to light. As Clovis waits with the other guests for Tobermory's return, he cheers them with, "He won't turn up tonight. He's probably in the local newspaper office at the present moment, dictating the first installment of his reminiscences."

Blackmail turned up as well in childish forms—Nicholas in "The Lumber Room" bargaining for strawberry jam with the Evil One; Mathilda in "The Boar-Pig" demanding money to free two women from a garden where she has trapped them with a huge white Yorkshire pig; the three children of "The Penance," who threaten to smother a man's two-year-old daughter unless he performs an elaborate rite of repentance for killing their kitten. In each case the adult is caught in a ludicrous or menacing situation that a child exploits to get his way. Even without Ethel's memoir, we could deduce from the stories that while visions of sugarplums danced in other children's heads, Hector's throbbed with visions of muddy revenge.

Those instances constituted a child's blackmail against respectability. When the weapon was used by one adult against another, Hector threatened the victim with psychological, not physical, reprisals. Sometimes, as in "The Treasure-Ship," the story winds down to a flat, predictable ending. But in "Mrs. Packletide's Tiger," Hector found a proper framework for this particular obsession. Mrs. Packletide was one of Hector's small stock company,

which included Clovis Sangrail; his aunt, Mrs. Thacken-
bury; Bertie van Tahn; Vera Durmot; and Agnes, who is
ever gluttonous, whether she is the Agnes Blaik of "The
Strategist" or the Agnes Resker of "Tobermory." Mrs.
Packletide lives for her social competition with a matron
named Loona Bimberton. In "The Recessional," the Bimberton woman steals a march at the time of Edward's
death by getting into a newspaper a coronation ode for the
new King George.

But when La Bimberton goes riding for eleven miles in
an airplane, Mrs. Packletide knows it will require heroic
measures to regain social supremacy. She decides to re-
coup by going to India and shooting a tiger. "Mrs. Packletide had already arranged in her mind the lunch she
would give at her house in Curzon Street, ostensibly in
Loona Bimberton's honor, with a tiger-skin rug occupying most of the foreground and all of the conversation.
She had also already designed in her mind the tiger-claw
brooch that she was going to give Loona Bimberton on
her next birthday."

Off to India goes Mrs. Packletide with her paid companion, a Miss Louisa Mebbin. For a thousand rupees a
hunt is arranged and a goat is tethered in moonlight to
tempt the village's aging and half-deaf tiger. The bait
works. A rifle flashes; there is a loud report. The tiger falls
dead.

"It was Louisa Mebbin who drew attention to the fact
that the goat was in death-throes from a mortal bullet-
wound, while no trace of the rifle's deadly work could be
found on the tiger. Evidently the wrong animal had been
hit, and the beast of prey had succumbed to heart-failure,
caused by the sudden report of the rifle, accelerated by
senile decay. Mrs. Packletide was pardonably annoyed at
the discovery; but, at any rate, she was the possessor of a
dead tiger, and the villagers, anxious for their thousand
rupees, gladly connived at the fiction that she had shot the
beast. And Miss Mebbin was a paid companion. Therefore
did Mrs. Packletide face the cameras with a light heart,
and her pictured fame reached from the pages of the *Texas
Weekly Snapshot* to the illustrated Monday supplement of
the *Novoe Vremya*. As for Loona Bimberton, she refused

to look at an illustrated paper for weeks, and her letter of thanks for the gift of a tiger-claw brooch was a model of repressed emotions. The luncheon-party she declined; there are limits beyond which repressed emotions become dangerous."

Everything had turned out perfectly. Mrs. Packletide even goes to the County Costume Ball in the character of Diana. Then: " 'How amused everyone would be if they knew what really happened,' said Louisa Mebbin a few days after the ball."

Hastily, an agreement is struck that permits Miss Mebbin to retire to Dorking and a cottage that was a bargain at six hundred and eight, freehold. Mrs. Packletide gives up big-game hunting; the incidental expenses are so heavy.

In his later work, Hector sometimes expressed a reverence for the hunt, more because it was a noble English tradition than because of any obvious appeal to him. The earlier stories, however, treated hunting as "Mrs. Packletide's Tiger" did, as proof of a desperate need to impress others. Hector did not take his theme as far as other opponents of hunting have done; he did not suggest that Mrs. Packletide was driven to shoot because of doubts about her masculinity. Mrs. Packletide merely wanted to get her picture in the paper, to have a trophy for her drawing room, and to make an enemy envious. Hector's story reminds us that until the day women began to write fiction as women and not as men called George, the homosexual's was one of the few voices in literature to point out when the effort to be male had passed over into foolishness.

Another theme, entirely frivolous, could also rouse Hector to a splendid performance. Perhaps it, too, involves revenge. At least, in each case an unprepossessing man, ill treated by the world, wins success by virtue of a thoroughly silly talent. Hector may have been mocking himself when he wrote the stories, especially "Cousin Teresa," which dealt with the rivalry between one brother pursuing, like Charlie, a solid career in government service and another who is an artist of sorts. In the three best pieces, Hector proved something else: that other, more lucrative careers had been open to him besides short-story writer. Not that of poet; when he asked either Reginald or Clovis to compose poetry, their doggerel was worse even than the occasion demanded. But when Hector was being playful, he often concocted the sort of loony nonsense that can overpower the mass taste. For "Cousin Teresa" he devised a vaudeville sketch; for "The Secret Sin of Septimus Brope," he furnished persuasive examples of popular lyrics: "Dainty little girlie Mavis / She is such a rara avis / All the money I can save is / All to be for Mavis mine." And for "Filboid Studge, the Story of a Mouse That Helped," he demonstrated that as an advertising man he might have had the whole town splurging.

Mark Spayley of "Filboid Studge" is a poor artist in love with the daughter of a business tycoon who is about to lose his fortune because he has invested in a breakfast food called Pipenta. "It could scarcely be called a drug in the market; people bought drugs but no one bought Pipenta." (Doomed projects played on Hector's sympathies. In another story, "Fate," he told of hapless Rex Dillot: "For a few months he had been assistant editor and business manager of a paper devoted to fancy mice, but the devotion had all been on one side, and the paper disappeared.") The businessman agrees to the wedding, knowing that in a brief time his daughter will be penniless. Spayley would like to show his gratitude, but he feels like a mouse proposing to help a lion. Says his future father-in-law, "Get people to buy that beastly muck."

"Three weeks later the world was advised of the coming of a new breakfast food, heralded under the resounding name of 'Filboid Studge.' Spayley put forth no pictures of massive babies springing up with fungus-like rapidity under its forcing influence, or of representatives of the leading nations of the world scrambling with fatuous eagerness for its possession. One huge sombre poster depicted the Damned in Hell suffering a new torment from their inability to get at the Filboid Studge which elegant young fiends held in transparent bowls just beyond their reach. The scene was rendered even more gruesome by a subtle suggestion of the features of leading men and women of the day in the portrayal of the Lost Souls;

prominent individuals of both political parties, Society hostesses, well-known dramatic authors and novelists, and distinguished aeroplanists were dimly recognizable in that doomed throng; noted lights of the musical-comedy stage flickered wanly in the shades of the Inferno, smiling still from force of habit, but with the fearsome smiling rage of baffled effort. The poster bore no fulsome allusions to the merits of the new breakfast food, but a single grim statement ran in bold letters along its base: 'They cannot buy it now.'

"Spayley had grasped the fact that people will do things from a sense of duty which they would never attempt as a pleasure."

The new campaign was—and who is to say that it might not yet be?—a sensation. "On the breakfast-tables of cheerless parlours it was partaken of in silence. Once the womenfolk discovered that it was thoroughly unpalatable, their zeal in forcing it on their households knew no bounds. 'You haven't eaten your Filboid Studge!' would be screamed at the appetiteless clerk as he hurried weariedly from the breakfast-table, and his evening meal would be prefaced by a warmed-up mess which would be explained as 'your Filboid Studge that you didn't eat this morning.' Those strange fanatics who ostentatiously mortify themselves, inwardly and outwardly, with health biscuits and health garments, battened aggressively on the new food. Earnest spectacled young men devoured it on the steps of the National Liberal Club. A bishop who did not believe in a future state preached against the poster, and a peer's daughter died from eating too much of the compound. A further advertisement was obtained when an infantry regiment mutinied and shot its officers rather than eat the nauseous mess; fortunately, Lord Birrell of Blatherstone, who was War Minister at the moment, saved the situation by his happy epigram, that "Discipline to be effective must be optional."

The financier makes a colossal fortune on the product and finds his daughter something more appropriate than a two-hundred-a-year poster designer. But Hector's brainstorms were not always fated to end unhappily. Septimus Brope, prodded by Clovis, reverses the sentiment of his trite little songs and enjoys another great popular success with "How you bore me, Florrie / With those eyes of vacant blue . . . / I'll throw you down a quarry, Florrie / If I marry you." And Lucas Harrowcluff, whose brother has rendered stout diplomatic service to the crown, is the one who gets knighted for a vaudeville sketch that sweeps London: "It's just a couplet; of course there will be other words, but they won't matter. Listen:

Cousin Teresa takes out Caesar,
Fido, Jock, and the big borzoi.

A lilting, catchy sort of refrain, you see, and big-drum business on the two syllables of bor-zoi. It's immense. And I've thought out all the business of it; the singer will sing the first verse alone, then during the second verse Cousin Teresa will walk through, followed by four wooden dogs on wheels; Caesar will be an Irish terrier, Fido a black poodle, Jock a fox-terrier, and the borzoi, of course, will be a borzoi. During the third verse Cousin Teresa will come on alone, and the dogs will be drawn across by themselves from the opposite wing; then Cousin Teresa will catch on to the singer and go off-stage in one direction, while dogs' procession goes off in the other, crossing *en route,* which is always very effective. There'll be a lot of applause there, and for the fourth verse Cousin Teresa will come on in sables and the dogs will all have coats on."

Hector's reputation, while spreading discreetly, was not of a sort to get him knighted, but it did increase his invitations to mildly fashionable houses. Max Beerbohm, in a position to know, had once said of Winston Churchill that he had obtained the one thing in life worth having—success when success is sweet, in youth. Despite his determined rear-guard battle against growing up, Hector was no youth when the first small success warmed his life. He had become known, slightly, for *Alice in Westminster,* but parody had to it a touch of the parasitical, and the work had struck its author as so flimsy he had not at first wanted his name on it. Then he had gone to the Balkans. One disadvantage in the life of a foreign correspondent, especially for a man seeking fame, is that he is abroad while his reputation grows, among foreigners who will never hear of him and fellow correspondents eager to shelter him from celebrity. Back in London, Hector again wrote his stories as Saki for the *Westminster Gazette,* that being the publication in which he had first come to public notice. But late in 1911, Hector began sending stories to the *Morning Post,* where they would reach a wider readership. There he signed them, as he had his dispatches from the Balkans, H. H. Munro. It was then that a few ladies began the attempt to lure him to their drawing rooms. On occasion, Hector even gave a party himself.

Whatever diminution of the intimacy with Roy Reynolds that had occurred when Hector left Russia was repaired when Reynolds came home on leave to London. Together they decided to give a reception for Sergei Diaghilev's ballet troupe during its first tour of England. The Russian ballet at the moment was enjoying that advantageous degree of scandal that kept away only those people who would never have gone. After its uproarious debut in Paris in 1909, Lady de Grey had written to entreat Diaghilev to add London to his tour. The following year the ballet was engaged for the Aldwych Theatre, but then King Edward died and the performances were canceled. At the urging of Sir Thomas Beecham, the troupe was finally lured to London in 1911, to appear at Covent Garden for the coronation of King George. The premiere was not a success. The dancers were nervous and neither Karsavina's variations nor Nijinsky in *Armide* received the slightest applause. Then, at the end of the evening, the troupe heard a sound they could not at first identify. It was an audience tepidly applauding through kid gloves.

The next night was the true opening. During the Prince Igor dances, the theatre's business manager ran up to Diaghilev crying, "It isn't dancing—it's just savage prancing about." At least a hundred elderly and diamond-laden women walked out. As Reginald, foreseeing such a protest, had remarked, "It requires a great deal of moral courage to leave in a marked manner in the middle of the second act, when your carriage isn't ordered till twelve."

All in all, it was a scandal of the dimension and pedigree to appeal to Hector, and he and Reynolds drew on friendships from St. Petersburg to produce the troupe at their party. They were risking no opprobrium where it mattered. Beecham was already acknowledged to be the ballet's patron, and Lady de Grey, a lady in waiting to the Queen, had scheduled a supper for Diaghilev. All the same, it was Hector's most ambitious social undertaking, and since neither his rooms in Mortimer Street nor Reynolds' temporary lodgings would do, they staged their "at home" at a friend's studio. They set one criterion for invitations, one at least that they disclosed to Ethel: Every guest had to speak French, since that was the only foreign language the dancers understood. The troupe enjoyed the evening. They were not being widely feted, and Nijinsky for all his gifts was a simple young man with little knowledge of the world. All that has survived of the evening is one brief exchange between the two guests at first glance the least kindred in spirit. Nijinsky chatted with Ethel about animals, the dancer expressing surprise at seeing so few of the English national mascot. "In Russia," he said, "we heard that every Englishman walks out accompanied by a bulldog."

Later, Ethel found Nijinsky and another man peering intently under a table.

"What is it?" she asked.

"It is the devil!" Nijinsky said.

It was an Aberdeen terrier, a breed Nijinsky had never seen.

To add body to his concoctions, Hector had often folded in a duchess or a peer's daughter, until it appeared that he traveled widely in titled sets. But what puzzled critics later on was how little Hector had ventured into society. Somerset Maugham recalled seeing him at a party or two, nothing more than that. When his cousin, Willie Mercer, was in his middle twenties, Hector sometimes invited him to the Cocoa Tree or to a dinner party at a Soho restaurant. Mercer found, as others did, that while Hector was always amiable, always interesting, going through the evening with a smile playing over his face, he never laughed and he rarely said anything to match the brilliance of his work. In that Hector resembled Pope and Sydney Smith, two wits who saved their inspiration for the printer. Mercer could never remember Hector speaking sharply to anyone, but then Hector did not take him among people who might have provoked a quick retort. Indeed, Mercer puzzled over why Hector's friends were so ordinary. Willie always seemed to find himself seated between precious women given to talking about "values"; he even wondered whether the invitations were a hoax, whether Hector was sitting back enjoying the discomfort of a hearty young man in such pinched company. Another oddity: Among Hector's friends, male or female, Mercer did not find a single one of them physically attractive. It did not occur to him that the friends who were useful for entertaining one's young relations, the high-minded and respectable friends, did not necessarily constitute Hector's entire circle.

In England as in Russia, except for the men he met through journalism, Hector did not seek out other writers. It may have been a matter of pride. By now, he knew what he was accomplishing, and yet officially he was only a comic writer. In the business of literature, comic writers ranked with haberdashers and florists; they provided the equivalent of a pocket handkerchief or a boutonniere. One youth who knew better was apprenticing himself to the same career. Noël Coward, a teenage actor, went around to John Lane when a new book by Saki was announced; he wanted to be the first man in his set to have read it. More typically, however, Hector would have agreed with the sentiment of Oliver Wendell Holmes: "The wit knows that his place is at the tail of the procession."

When John Lane gave a banquet for Anatole France, the guest list suggested a literary command performance: Kipling, Barrie, Shaw, Pinero, Conan Doyle, Arnold Bennett. Mr. Thomas Hardy, O. M., president of the Society of Authors, sent regrets. Ben Travers was not surprised to see that Hector's name had been omitted from the guest list. Saki was not considered serious, Travers reflected; the humorist was not even at the tail of the procession. That place was occupied by the successful hack. The wit went ignored. There was another reason for Hector's exclusion that would not have occurred to Travers until later. Very softly, in the most subterranean ways, word had begun to circulate that Hector was homosexual. When anyone raised the topic around Lane, he put his hands over his ears and pretended not to hear. It was enough that he, a Liberal, was publishing the work of the Conservatives' wittiest writer. That tolerance fell within the broad protection of free speech; besides, Lane had never been able to resist wit. But to seat Hector at a public table, even below the salt, might revive unfortunate memories of Sodom and its notorious ambassador, Oscar Wilde, also a John Lane author.

In Hector's day, perhaps in any day, the arbiters of society were three or four women who had reached their position through birth or marriage or both. The three great ladies of London when Hector first arrived there had been the Duchess of Manchester, later the Duchess of Devonshire; Lady Londonderry; and Lady de Grey, the balletomane, who became Lady Ripon. That they had all been noted beauties was their only bond.

The Duchess of Devonshire, a German countess by birth, had lofty ambitions for the Duke, her second husband. But he reserved his enthusiasm for his livestock and he was happiest when one of his pigs took first place at an agricultural show. The Duchess survived, a bewigged crone, to a vast age but her strivings never galvanized the Duke. Once, forced into making a public appearance, he yawned widely and explained it by saying that his speech was so damned dull.

Lady Londonderry, a marchioness, was known to enjoy manipulating people; her friends claimed that she was good-hearted and only wanted to gratify their desires. The best example her biographer could summon, however, was a time when the King left her house and she called in her maid to sit on the cushion he had vacated. Lady Ripon, six feet tall, used her height to make other women feel stunted. Her finest days had come in the 1890s, when she filled her house in Bruton Street with faintly Bohemian guests.

Except for the Duchess of Devonshire, ranking hostesses made no effort to be grand; their eminence went before them. True, Lady Londonderry wore her diamond crown to parties, but she dismissed it as "the family fender." Lady Ripon, for all her avowed love of music and her allusions to "my beloved Melba," principally enjoyed the opera's social aspect. It was said that she could have sat through a Beethoven symphony only if she had been a personal friend of the composer.

Such were the women Hector knew by sight and reputation. His own circle, considerably less exalted, included Lady St. Helier, the widow of Sir Francis Jeune. Jeune had been a judge in the Admiralty Division of the High Court of Justice. He was created a baron in February 1905 and died the following April, leaving his wife to the life of a hostess. Willy Mercer thought that she was much taken with Hector, although her waved white hair proclaimed her old enough to be his mother. At the least, she found him a dependable and entertaining extra man. As conservative in his politics as Hector, Lady St. Helier was more inclined to charity and better able to afford it. Among her causes was the Factory Girl's Country Health Fund, which sent poor young women for a fortnight at a fresh-air camp. Hector's view of such enterprises was more like that of Reginald, who spoke of a woman who "went in for slumming quite as seriously as if it were a sport.

"She belonged to the Guild of the Poor Dear Souls, and they hold the record for having nearly reformed a washerwoman. No one has ever really reformed a washerwoman, and that is why the competition is so keen. You can rescue charwomen by the fifties with a little tea and personal magnetism, but with washerwomen it's different; wages are too high."

When she published her memoirs in 1909, Lady St. Helier gave readers immediately to understand that there would be no reason to read them: "One is confronted at every moment with the fact that what would most surely tend to make it amusing and interesting is exactly what cannot be published." Nonetheless, she gave a more detailed accounting than anything in Hector's stories of life among the upper classes. "We lived more simply in those days," she wrote, with a sigh for the days of her first marriage to a Colonel Stanley in the 1870s. "A cook, a house-maid, a parlour-maid, with a between-maid, sufficed for our wants."

Since Lady St. Helier had known many literary men before Hector, when she came to write her autobiography she had more illustrious names to drop than his, and Hector went unmentioned. She considered her intimate moments with Tennyson among the proudest of her life. She had treasured his letters, and she shared one with her readers:

"Dear Mrs. Stanley,

"Those were pleasant days at Naworth Castle, and not forgotten; but I cannot dine with you on Saturday. I will, if possible, look in on you in the evening. Yours truly, A. Tennyson."

Her guilelessness carried over to Lady St. Helier's description of her success with guests less elusive than the poet laureate. "Once, indeed, I heard a guest say coming upstairs she felt rather like a herring packed in a barrel, and some of my friends pleasantly described my parties as being like the day of judgement." Those were the "at homes" and formal parties that Hector frequented, where he acquired the fund of fashionable talk he returned home to parody.

A more important titled family in Hector's life was the Charnwoods. In 1911, Godfrey Rathbone Benson, formerly a Member of Parliament and a lecturer at Balliol, received a created baronetcy that made him the Baron Charnwood, and Hector became a regular guest at Lady Charnwood's afternoons. Although he was not the sort to make in person the quotable judgments he gave to his characters ("Constance—one of those strapping florid girls that go so well with autumn scenery or Christmas decorations in Church"), Hector paid his way at social events in other valued coin. Thomas Guthrie, who wrote as Francis Anstey, recalled meeting him at the Ladies' Park Club, where Hector told a brief tale the other man never forgot. It seemed that a fellow was out from home when he was seized by a sudden and violent hunger. In his pocket he had only a penny. Fortunately, however, outside a shop he came upon an automatic chocolate machine. Eagerly, he put in his penny. And got in return a box of matches.

After Hector's death, the absence of a young woman in his life would trouble Ethel. It was solely a concern for his posthumous reputation, not for what he might have missed in life. While Hector lived, Ethel seems to have been happy to have had his attentions to herself. But as keeper of his memory, she became increasingly disturbed by the glaring lack. When Rex Harrison applied to the estate, which Ethel controlled, to make a film version of Hector's first novel, Ethel wanted to check on his suitability and she took her niece to attend a matinee of the play in which Harrison was then performing. It was Noël Coward's *Design For Living,* which resolves a romantic triangle by two men agreeing to live with one woman. Ethel was appalled by that hint of homosexuality, and, although her niece tried to remind her that it was only a play and that Mr. Harrison in private life was probably nothing like the role he played, Ethel could not be budged and the project was dropped.

It was in this same spirit that Ethel once floated a suggestion that Hector had come close to making a match with Rosalind, eldest daughter of the Earl of Iddesleigh. Had the story been true, it would have been a match as brilliant, and fantastical, as anything in Hector's stories. Lady Rosalind's family could be traced reliably to 1103, the third year of the reign of King Henry I. The family baronetcy was no twentieth-century invention; it dated from 1641, though the earldom was of more recent creation. *A Genealogical and Heraldic History of the Peerage and Baronetage, the Privy Council, Knightage and Companionage,* the book usually referred to by its authors' names as *Burke's Peerage,* listed Lady Rosalind's precedence in the realm as 13,203, which meant that her place in court functions was 198 positions ahead of Hector's new friend, Charnwood.

If common interests alone could assure a happy marriage, Hector and Lady Rosalind might have been well suited. She was also a writer. Her books about the Devon countryside were thorough and precise, genteel and pallid

(Barnstaple wore "an air of peaceful contentedness"). But however many evenings Hector made himself agreeable to Rosalind, there was no romance. When Willie Mercer —then called Dornford Yates—learned of Ethel's attempt to caulk this crack in Hector's façade, he offered an explanation that would have outraged Ethel more than the gossip she was trying to quash. On Colonel Munro's death, he said, Hector probably put aside all thoughts of marriage because he knew he would have the lifelong responsibility of an increasingly eccentric sister.

If Hector was deprived of close friendships with writers and young women, he found consolation elsewhere. Several times he sent Clovis and other young men to the Turkish baths on Jermyn Street, which he described with unmistakable first-hand knowledge. Until they closed in the 1970s, the baths represented a rosy twilight arena for elderly men who came to sweat poisons from their systems and youths who came to strike beguiling poses in Turkish towels. Such baths had been a venerable institution from the time of the Roman occupation, and although they were closely overseen by attendants they provided a discreet place to inspect a young man before offering him a cup of tea at Lyons. Hector's protagonists flaunted their enthusiasm for the baths. In his playlet, "The Baker's Dozen," even middle-aged Major Dumbarton, father of five or four children, makes a mildly risqué allusion to them:

"Mrs. Paly-Paget: 'I was dining with Lord and Lady Slugford. Charming people but so mean. They took us afterwards to the Velodrome to see some dancer interpreting Mendelssohn's Songs Without Clothes. We were all packed in a little box near the roof, and you may imagine how hot it was. It was like a Turkish bath. And, of course, one couldn't see anything.'

"Major: 'Then it was not like a Turkish bath.'

"Mrs. Paly-Paget: 'Major!' "

Besides these occasional youths, at least one man, who may have begun their affair casually, stayed on to allow a deeper feeling to develop. In Paris, Hector had received the gift of a small gold locket. It was fashioned in the shape of a heart, with a round turquoise embedded at its center. When the tiny hinges were prized apart, there were spaces inside for two photographs. Instead, the donor had written "8th May 1908" on one half of the divided heart and on the other, "Hector With best love Cyril."

Hector was not given to ornaments. Ethel had given him a gold tie pin, a duplicate of her own, with the Munro eagle and "Dread God" worked into its design. But she fastened hers to her jabot more faithfully than he wore his. Even had Hector been inclined to jewelry, a small gold heart would scarcely have suited his style or his era. But Cyril—who may have been an actor, a military officer or a man about town; Hector knew one of each named Cyril —must have understood his friend's tastes, and it is possible that while Willie Mercer and Ben Travers were admiring the chaste fastidiousness of Hector's appearance, he had concealed beneath his crisp shirt front a secret emblem of his affections.

Hector's dedication page in *The Chronicles of Clovis,* published in August 1911, may well have served that same hidden purpose, allowing him to appear blameless in the world's eyes while paying tribute to a hidden love. Hector wrote, "To the Lynx Kitten, with His Reluctantly Given Consent, This Book Is Affectionately Dedicated. H. H. M." By now Ethel was dotty enough about cats to have dedicated an encyclopedia to them. But Hector had maintained a better balance, and given an inclination to see young men as untamed creatures of nature, the dedication may have been his way of repaying Cyril or Cyril's successor. Hector did not wish us to know, and we don't.

The reviews for *The Chronicles of Clovis* were of a kind that may seem favorable to the critic who writes them but are gall to an author because they compare him to other writers. The *Saturday Review* managed it twice in one sentence: "Mr. [W. W.] Jacobs never wrote so gruesome as Sredni Vashtar while Tobermory is worthy of F. Anstey." The *Daily Chronicle* was cryptic: "Mr. Munro is more than clever." All in all, sales were not so great that any editor at Methuen had to reproach himself for letting Hector slip away.

At about this time Hector sat for two portraits, one by the eminent photographer E. O. Hoppé, which showed him fine-boned and vulnerable with an air of doomed romance that foreshadowed photographs of another student of manners, Scott Fitzgerald. The second sketch was verbal. Hector called at the studio of Arthur Minton, where the painter was engaged on a miniature of Miss Irene Vanbrugh and where Hector was to meet an employee of John Lane's publicity magazine, the *Bodleian*. The writer described Hector smoking a cigarette in the leisurely way of one who is performing one of life's great functions; and it seems that the two men had met before and were treating the interview as their joke.

"To look at, Mr. Munro is what nice old ladies would call 'interesting.' He is very slim and straight, and well-groomed; his eyes are shadowed mysteriously; his mouth has ironic curves, and there is a delicate lack of energy about his movements that is rather charming. He does not upset chairs, talk in a loud voice, drink excessively, or get on one's nerves. So he is an excellently worthy companion; withal, studiously and unobtrusively observant. But the personality of the man is frankly baffling, and he declines to talk about himself."

As though to contradict that judgment, Hector proved to be a model of forthcoming helpfulness. "My favourite flower is the periwinkle; my favourite animal is the kingfisher, my favourite bird is the hedge-sparrow, and I like oysters, asparagus and politics. Also the theatre." Was Hector satisfied by the reception of *The Chronicles of Clovis?* Hector said he was. The critics had been kind, the booksellers had done well with it and his friends had promised to read it if he would send them copies. The interviewer volunteered that he liked Hector's methods of mixing his stories, "the weird with the winsome."

"Do you?" asked Hector, in that disconcerting way of some Englishmen, who can sound disputatious even as they agree. "I was a little surprised to see how well it has come off. Many of my critics want me to devote a whole book to tragic stuff."

"It is very unusual—and exceptionally a compliment—

for a man whose wit is admired to be asked to do purely serious work."

"Yes," said Hector, "a humorist is almost invariably expected to be funny for life."

11

The Image of the Lost Soul (1911-1912)

In the history of letters, there may have been a short-story writer who was never pressed to write a novel, but if so his name has been lost to us. The demand, of course, ignores the different ways in which the imagination works on a writer's mind. Some impulses can only form a story, others must be worked out at length. The difference is nothing a writer can will for himself. But those who continue to insist—grasping publishers, vainglorious friends—go on believing that if a man can father a child, with a little more discipline he could produce triplets.

Although the writer should remain deaf to these pleas, he is often won over by them, and occasionally his imagination will be obliging and fertile and he will write *Fathers and Sons*. Hector, more than most short-story writers, had reason to yield to temptation. *The Chronicles of Clovis,* though it won praise from lesser journals, had not even been reviewed by the *Times Literary Supplement*. If he wished to be included at dinner the next time a French eminence crossed the Channel, he had better write a novel and it had better not be too funny. Hector half succeeded and called the half-success *The Unbearable Bassington.*

The book has been a trial to critics since its publication in 1912. Evelyn Waugh may never have reached the pinnacle of Hector at his best but Waugh was the better craftsman, and he took *Bassington* apart with a pained precision, concluding that as a work of art it was inferior to the finest of Hector's short stories. The serious intent to which writing a novel attested did force the *Times Literary Supplement* to take notice, and the journal gave a review of fifty approving words, among them these: "Mr. Munro, who is a real humorist, shows that he has other gifts as well." The book, then, served one purpose. Hector was acknowledged to be more than a comic writer by those persons who believe there is something more to be.

The plot is not complicated. A woman as attached to her surroundings as Mrs. Gereth in Henry James's *The Spoils of Poynton,* must choose between her son and her comforts, and she sacrifices her son. Hector told a friend that he drew on his own feelings about going to Burma when he sent his hero to exile in West Africa, and that confession has led to a critical tendency to treat the novel as Hector's reliving an episode from his youth. But it is more accurate to see the book as treating a far graver crisis, one that was occurring in Hector's life as he wrote it.

The advent of middle age, a cruel visitation in many lives, is said to strike most mercilessly at the homosexual. Not only must he watch helplessly as his youthful appeal drains away, but he is denied the consolations of other men: the secure love of a wife, the regeneration represented by children. It is a facile judgment that does not suit every case, and it would be especially misleading applied to Hector. His stories had always presented a home as, at its best, a small but unexclusive club with a mediocre staff and a level of conversation necessarily constricted by the fact that half the membership was women. At its worst, a home was indifference, suffocation and strife. So it was not the want of a home that weighed on Hector.

He had chummed with young men, and if his need for

companionship had outweighed the irritations and inevitable compromises of living with another person, by the age of forty he could have secured a mate. Nor would it seem that his lack of fortune made him downhearted. His tastes were simple, his straitened circumstances he treated as something of a game. Nights when he did not play bridge at the Cocoa Tree he stayed at home plying a hobby called "tapestry painting." Its object was to make the background of a painting, "A Boar-Hunt in the Middle Ages," for example, look as though it were actually faded needlework. Ethel was surely no impartial critic but she pronounced his work remarkably good and regretted that he gave the best of it so freely to his friends.

He may have resented in his restrained way his lack of a wider fame. Later, critics would rejoice in his limited appeal, as though by being wine from a select vineyard, he conferred an unqualified distinction wherever he was uncorked. "There is no greater compliment to be paid the right kind of friend," said Christopher Morley, "than to hand him Saki, without comment." But the vintner in his lifetime may prefer to intoxicate a banquet hall, and when Hector parodies Shaw as "Sherard Blaw," one has the feeling that Shaw's offense lay not in being a Socialist but in being successful. Still, the small worm of envy could not alone explain the changes that were coming over Hector. He was tiring of his world, of himself, with the vehemence that sometimes overtakes an actor who has lost respect for his craft. Hector had come from a proud tradition of military imperialism. For as long as he remained a youth, he was exempt from following that tradition and he had managed to feel youthful for a remarkably long time. Whenever he felt his spirit flagging, there was always another impudent gesture to make. One gray summer at Ethel's cottage, he planned to tempt out the sun with a Greek ritual. "We will invoke Apollo's aid tonight," he said, "round a bonfire." He draped himself, Ethel and a guest in bed sheets and led them in prayer around the fire, asking for the boon of sunshine. The next day the sun appeared and shone for three weeks, which did not surprise Ethel.

New Year's Eve, a melancholy holiday on most calendars, drove Hector to particular despair. Since it fell only two weeks after his birthday, time's passage was borne doubly upon him each year. One New Year's he met a party of strangers in Oxford Circus and insisted that they all join hands with him and skip around a circle singing, "Here We Go Round the Mulberry Bush." Ethel observed his intensity at such moments, the way he could block out the world and yield to his abandon, and gave the credit to their mother's family, the Mercers, for a vitality and youthfulness that let him do it; she did not acknowledge the repression and hostility of the Munros that made him do it. On another New Year's Eve, Hector brought to a dinner party at a restaurant a new toy that made the sound of a dog's growling, and while it was causing hilarity at his table, he said with satisfaction, "Foreigners must be puzzled by all this. I'm sure they never make as much noise themselves." Again Ethel recalled the scene fondly, and she would have been astonished to learn that some readers found it as jarring as if Whistler had brought a whoopee cushion to the Café Royal. The episodes do bear out, however, Willie Mercer's observations about the people with whom Hector surrounded himself; and they confirm that Hector's was a Trappist wit that did not speak aloud.

But now, past forty, Hector no longer had the excuses of youth or illness for having denied his destiny as a soldier. At a time when men took stock, Hector would not be less rigorous on himself than on his Lester Slaggby or Wilfred Pigeoncote. He had indulged the merry, feckless side of himself, but he wasn't feeling merry or feckless any longer. He had become that familiar anomaly, the entertainer with contempt for entertaining. Edward Lear had come to loathe the limericks that diverted attention from his paintings, and Conan Doyle hurled from a cliff the creation that had seized control of his life. It was with something of that intention that Hector wrote *The Unbearable Bassington*.

To his chagrin, Hector had passed through his phase as Comus Bassington and wound up more like Comus' mother, Francesca. Like her, Hector stayed huddled in a London flat beneath a painting. Francesca's had been part of her wedding dower; it was a scene by a great Dutch painter whom Hector named Van der Meulen. "There was a pleasing serenity about the great pompous battle scene with its solemn courtly warriors bestriding their heavily prancing steeds, grey or skewbald or dun, all gravely in earnest, and yet somehow conveying the impression that their campaigns were but vast serious picnics arranged in the grand manner."

Hector, too, had hung a battle scene in his drawing room. It was not by a great painter, only an old Flemish picture he had somewhere acquired of horsemen in doublets and plumed hats fighting beneath the walls of a city. But he prized it as much as Francesca valued the Van der Meulen; it was his only painting. The difference came when Francesca looked at her treasure and reveled in it and Hector looked at his painting and was reproached by a scene of men doing what men were meant to do.

The novel opens with Francesca drinking tea with her brother and eating small cress sandwiches, as though Hector has put them on the stage of the Criterion Theatre and they were only pretending to be in her drawing room. The prose, too, shows signs of a strain unusual in Hector's writing. He seems to have felt that so ambitious an enterprise must be immediately more compelling than his stories for the newspapers. But the wit is there—"Francesca herself, if pressed in an unguarded moment to describe her soul, would probably have described her drawing room" —even though it shines less boldly among the more ornate language than among the fine precision of his stories. Nor does the plot compensate, since Francesca's dilemma has been so evidently contrived. She has been willed the use of this charming house on Blue Street, Westminster, only until a young woman named Emmeline Chertoff marries. At that time Francesca must vacate. Her son is not quite eighteen. Should he be the man Emmeline takes for her husband, Francesca may go on living in her adorable retreat. If this were a story by Wodehouse, we would suspect that after pages of sunny facetiousness Francesca would be allowed to stay. If it were a story by Maugham, we might guess that, because the author wanted to deprive some other character of the house even more than he wished to punish Francesca, she might not be evicted. But this is Saki, and Hector detests any sign of greed or materialism. From the very luxuriating eye with which Francesca surveys her domain, we know that she will pay for her complacency.

Throughout the novel, Francesca is never much more than her desire for possessions and ease. When, at the end, Hector tries to wring a tear about her belated maternal love, he seems more cynical in that paragraph than in the whole of *Reginald* and *Clovis*. Her son is to Francesca only what Hector had been to his aunts—a care, a burden, never a source of pleasure—and Comus Bassington is an amalgam of Hector as he was, Hector as he wished he had been, and those young men Hector had loved at the moment of their perfection. To Roy Reynolds, Hector had said, "There is one thing I care for and that is youth." Now, over and over, he makes the point that for certain untamable young lords, life after eighteen always represents a pathetic and inevitable decline. Other writers have said that, too; that the physical grace that allows a young man to win at sport or love is the great gift in most lives; that when it goes there is nothing that can replace it. But few other writers have identified so wholeheartedly with the young as Hector still could. The others found at least a consolation in their own ability to survive to tell the story. For Hector there were no consolations.

"Sometimes they sober down in after-life and become uninteresting, forgetting that they were ever lords of anything; sometimes Fate plays royally into their hands, and they do great things in a spacious manner, and are thanked by Parliaments and the Press and acclaimed by gala-day crowds. But in most cases their tragedy begins when they leave school and turn themselves loose in a world that has grown too civilized and too crowded and too empty to have any place for them. And they are very many."

Hector is speaking as himself in that passage. By the next chapter, he has decided that such boys may be only a precious remnant. The change comes as one form master at Comus' school upbraids another for not being able to tame the boys. The other man replies that it would be too great a responsibility to interfere with Nature in the case of the obviously untamable.

" 'Nonsense; boys are Nature's raw material.'

" 'Millions of boys are. There are just a few, and Bassington is one of them, who are Nature's highly finished product when they are in the schoolboy stage, and we, who are supposed to be moulding raw material, are quite helpless when we come in contact with them.'

" 'But what happens to them when they grow up?'

" 'They never do grow up,' said the housemaster; 'that is their tragedy. Bassington will certainly never grow out of his present stage.'

" 'Now you are talking in the language of Peter Pan,' said the form-master.

" 'I am not thinking in the manner of Peter Pan,' said the other. 'With all reverence for the author of that masterpiece I should say he had a wonderful and tender insight into the child mind and knew nothing whatever about boys.' "

By telling us early in his novel that Comus will not develop or change, Hector seriously underbids for our interest. Then he goes himself one better and, in our first view of Comus, trumps his own suit by making his hero less unbearable than simply unpleasant. Francesca has written to tell Comus to be especially kind to Emmeline Chertoff's young brother, Lancelot, when he arrives at Comus' school. This will be our introduction to young Bassington, and Hector lists the characteristics likely to win his own heart and assumes they will also win ours.

"In appearance he exactly fitted his fanciful Pagan name. His large green-grey eyes seemed for ever asparkle with goblin mischief and the joy of revelry, and the curved lips might have been those of some wickedly-laughing faun; one almost expected to see embryo horns fretting the smoothness of his sleek dark hair. The chin was firm, but one looked in vain for a redeeming touch of ill-temper in the handsome, half-mocking, half-petulant face. With a strain of sourness in him Comus might have been leavened into something creative and masterful; fate had fashioned him with a certain whimsical charm, and left him all unequipped for the greater purposes of life. Perhaps no one would have called him a lovable character, but in many respects he was adorable; in all respects he was certainly damned."

At that point, Hector commits either a blunder or an act of daring. He shows Comus whipping the Chertoff boy. The point of the scene is clear enough. Hector wants to establish that Comus will always understand where his self-interest lies and then betray it, and had Hector closed the door while Comus got on with the caning, he might have achieved his effect. The reader does accept that beatings are a cherished part of public school life, that they can create such an appetite that in later life an alumnus will pay prostitutes by the stroke for chastisements he once got free of charge. To know that, however, is different from watching the discipline being exultantly laid on. Comus starts by drawing a chalk line across the boy's buttocks so that every cut may be aimed at exactly the same spot. It is supposed to hurt much more that way.

"Comus drew the desired line with an anxious exactitude which he would have scorned to apply to a diagram of Euclid or a map of the Russo-Persian frontier.

" 'Bend a little more forward,' he said to the victim, 'and much tighter. Don't trouble to look pleasant, because I can't see your face anyway. It may sound unorthodox to say so, but this is going to hurt you much more than it will me.'

"There was a carefully measured pause, and then Lancelot was made vividly aware of what a good cane can be made to do in really efficient hands. At the second cut he projected himself hurriedly off the chair.

" 'Now I've lost count,' said Comus; 'we shall have to begin all over again. Kindly get back into the same position. If you get down again before I've finished Rutley will hold you over and you'll get a dozen.'

"Lancelot got back on to the chair, and was re-arranged to the taste of his executioner. He stayed there somehow or other while Comus made eight accurate and agonizingly effective shots at the chalk line.' "

It is only the end of Chapter Two, and Comus has lost both his heiress and the reader's sympathy. If he wins back the reader, it is less because of any positive virtue—Comus gambles, loses and cadges money for his debts from another wealthy young woman, one he may even fancy—than because Hector so obviously finds him winsome, and it is hard not to be guided in these matters by the narrator. Hector never tips the scales unfairly. Except for one or two lapses, he deprives Comus of any of Reginald's saving wit. We must take Comus to our hearts, if we will, entirely because he is unusually good-looking and because he refuses to play by society's rules. And each time Hector has almost convinced us that Comus may have a right after all to the lovely and rich Elaine de Frey, he breaks the spell with another example of Comus' utter selfishness. At John Lane, Ben Travers had criticized the title, *The Unbearable Bassington*. It was Hector's invention after he decided against calling the novel after the painting in Francesca's drawing room, and Travers thought they should find something more appealing. But Hector was as adamant about his title as about his theme.

The only other character of any dimension is a rising young politician who becomes Comus' rival for Elaine. Courtenay Youghal is calculating in the ways Comus is not, and while it would be overstating the case to call him sympathetic, the chill that surrounds him is offset by his considerable intelligence and practiced charm. As the story ends, we are left to believe that he will make Elaine only passively and intermittently unhappy; that in the world's judgment, if not in Hector's, her life with Youghal will be preferable to the active and steady misery that Comus would have caused her.

In the course of the book, Hector includes two irrelevant chapters, each of them touching in a conventional way, that suggest that if he could have cast off his obsessions and extended to his other characters the affection he felt for Comus, he might have written a less idiosyncratic, more popular novel. Not a better one, probably a worse. Merely more popular. In the first of these interludes, Courtenay Youghal goes to the Zoological Society's gardens to inform his mistress of long standing that he is giving her up for Elaine de Frey. There are touches of Hector to most characters in this novel, but he comes closest to making a personal statement about love and sex in the person of Molly McQuade, "a good sort." Her love affairs, Hector says, were the all-absorbing element in her life. "She possessed the happily constituted temperament which enables a man or woman to be a 'pluralist,' and to observe the sage precaution of not putting all one's eggs into one basket. Her demands were not exacting; she required of her affinity that he should be young, good-looking, and at least moderately amusing; she would have preferred him to be invariably faithful, but with her own example before her, she was prepared for the probability, bordering on certainty, that he would be nothing of the sort."

When Youghal imparts his news to her, Molly takes it splendidly. "She watched his retreating figure with eyes that grew slowly misty; he had been such a jolly comely boy-friend, and they had had such good times together. The mist deepened on her lashes as she looked round at the familiar rendezvous where they had so often kept tryst since the day when they had first come there together, he a school-boy and she but lately out of her teens. For the moment she felt herself in the thrall of a very real sorrow.

"Then, with the admirable energy of one who is only in town for a fleeting fortnight, she raced away to have tea with a world-faring naval admirer at his club. Pluralism is a merciful narcotic."

The second episode has even less relation to the core of the novel, and it affronted Evelyn Waugh's tidy artistic sense, especially since he saw a logical place later in the book to tuck this loose end back into the tapestry. But no. The scene is important to Hector because it speaks for the side of his character that wants to be rough-hewn and manly, as healthy as the Devon soil. This side was not yet strong enough to take command of his writing or his life, but it had to be expressed, even when there was no natural place for it in the book. To make a place, Hector contrives to have Elaine meet again a childhood idol, Tom Keriway. Keriway had done many of the things from Hector's own life, but Hector describes them at a heroic pitch he would have scorned for his autobiography. As with Molly's brave self-control, Keriway represents an idealized version of Hector, not so much in a way he cared to impress upon others but in the way, increasingly, he wished to look to himself.

"He had wandered through Hungarian horse-fairs, hunted shy crafty beasts on lonely Balkan hillsides, dropped himself pebble-wise into the stagnant human pool of some Bulgarian monastery, threaded his way through the strange racial mosaic of Salonika, listened with amused politeness to the shallow ultra-modern opinions of a voluble editor or lawyer in some wayside Russian town, or learned wisdom from a chance tavern companion, one of the atoms of the busy ant-streams of men and merchandise that moves untiringly round the shores of the Black Sea. And far and wide as he might roam, he always managed to turn up at frequent intervals, at ball and supper and theatre, in the gay Hauptstadt of the Habsburgs, haunting his favourite cafés and wine-vaults, skimming through his favourite news-sheets, greeting old acquaintances and friends, from ambassadors down to cobblers in the social scale. He seldom talked of his travels, but it might be said that his travels talked of him; there was an air about him that a German diplomat once summed up in a phrase: 'a man that wolves have sniffed at.' "

Severe illness has laid Keriway low, and he has retired to a farm that may appear charming and peaceful to others but, to his experienced eye, is seething with blood-driven stoats and crafty foxes. For Elaine he weaves a spell from that lore that borders on witchcraft—of prowlers and hunters and farmers stranger than their animals—and Elaine is enrapt. " 'You are a person to be envied,' she said to Keriway; 'you have created a fairyland, and you are living in it yourself.'

" 'Envied?'

"He shot the question out with sudden bitterness. She looked down and saw the wistful misery that had come into his face.

" 'Once,' he said to her, 'in a German paper I read a short story about a tamed crippled crane that lived in the park of some small town. I forget what happened in the story, but there was one line that I shall always remember: 'it was lame, that is why it was tame.'

"He had created a fairyland, but assuredly he was not living in it."

They are all prisoners except perhaps for the character least like Hector's own. Courtenay Youghal's selfishness and ambitions seem sure to bring him success and, with it, freedom. All the rest are trapped and, because there is no escape for them, doomed.

Yet *The Unbearable Bassington* is a comedy. The novel's sheen is what one remembers about it afterward, and as a comedy of manners it is never better than in the two scenes in which Comus loses the respect of Elaine de Frey and with it his chance to marry her. First he wheedles from her a silver basket dish that he carried off to feed her swans.

" 'Swans were very pleased,' he cried gaily, 'and said they hoped I would keep the bread-and-butter dish as a souvenir of a happy tea-party. I may really have it, mayn't I?' he continued in an anxious voice; 'it will do to keep studs and things in. You don't want it.'

" 'It's got the family crest on it,' said Elaine. Some of the happiness had died out of her eyes.

" 'I'll have that scratched off and my own put on,' said Comus.

" 'It's been in the family for generations,' protested Elaine, who did not share Comus's view that because you were rich your lesser possessions could have no value in your eyes . . .

" 'I know you don't really want it, so I'm going to keep it,' persisted Comus.

" 'It's too hot to argue,' said Elaine."

Next come loans of money, until there is one too many. Hector knew that love was not blasted away by grand debates over philosophy or religion but slipped off noiselessly, pennies lost in the carpet until the next accounting. How often had Hector listened, cold as Elaine, to requests —demands—for a pound or two on account?

" 'Four shillings and fivepence and a halfpenny,' said Comus reflectively. 'It's a ridiculous sum to last me for the next three days, and I owe a card debt of over two pounds.'

" 'Yes?' commented Elaine dryly, and with an apparent

lack of interest in his exchequer statement. Surely, she was thinking hurriedly to herself, he could not be foolish enough to broach the matter of another loan.

" 'The card debt is rather a nuisance,' pursued Comus, with fatalistic persistency . . .

"The conversation strayed away from the fateful topic for a few moments; and then Comus brought it deliberately back to the danger zone.

" 'It would be awfully nice if you would let me have a fiver for a few days, Elaine,' he said quickly; 'if you don't I really don't know what I shall do.'

" 'If you are really bothered about your card debt I will send you the two pounds by messenger boy early this afternoon.' She spoke quietly and with great decision. 'And I shall not be at the Connors' dance tonight,' she continued; 'it's too hot for dancing. I'm going home now; please don't bother to accompany me, I particularly wish to go alone.' "

Because the author of the novel is a miniaturist, he achieves his finest effects in the supporting characters, each drawn with so sure a stroke that they would only be smudged by more detail. Henry Greech, Francesca's brother, is one of Hector's finest bores: "His talents lay so thoroughly in the direction of being uninteresting, that even as an eye-witness of the massacre of St. Bartholomew he would probably have infused a flavour of boredom into his description of the event." Merla Blathington earns her name by being "one of those human flies that buzz; in crowded streets, at bazaars and in warm weather, she attained to the proportions of a human bluebottle."

The young artist Mervyn Quentock is "just receiving due recognition from the critics; that the recognition was not overdue he owed largely to his perception of the fact that if one hides one's talent under a bushel one must be careful to point out to every one the exact bushel under which it is hidden."

Stephen Thorle does good among the London poor; once he encountered two slum families eating from one damaged soup plate, and by regaling a dinner party with the story, he provokes Comus to one of his few bright remarks. " 'The gratitude of those poor creatures when I presented them with a set of table crockery apiece, the tears in their eyes and in their voices when they thanked me, would be impossible to describe.'

" 'Thank you all the same for describing it,' said Comus."

Thorle's female counterpart is Ada Spelvexit, "one of those naturally stagnant souls who take infinite pleasure in what are called 'movements.' 'Most of the really great lessons I have learned have been taught by the Poor,' was one of her favourite statements. The one great lesson that the Poor in general would have liked to have taught her, that their kitchens and sickrooms were not unreservedly at her disposal as private lecture halls, she had never been able to assimilate . . . Hostesses regarded her philosophically as a form of social measles which every one had to have once."

The author is less charitable. He brings Ada back repeatedly, once to tell of a rapturous weekend at the home of Canon Besomley. " 'Such an exquisite rural retreat, and so restful and healing to the nerves. Real country scenery: apple blossoms everywhere.'

" 'Surely only on the apple trees!' said Lady Caroline."

Ada's Nemesis is Lady Caroline Benaresque, "a professed Socialist in politics, chiefly, it was believed, because she was thus enabled to disagree with most of the Liberals and Conservatives, and all of the Socialists of the day."

After Lady Caroline's rebuff, Ada "gave up the attempt to reproduce the decorative setting of the Canon's home-life, and fell back on the small but practical consolation of scoring the odd trick in her opponent's declaration of hearts.

" 'If you had led your highest club to start with, instead of the nine, we should have saved the trick,' remarked Lady Caroline to her partner in a tone of coldly gentle reproof; 'it's no use, my dear,' she continued, as Serena flustered out a halting apology, 'no earthly use to attempt to play bridge at one table and try to see and hear what's going on at two or three other tables.'

" 'I can generally manage to attend to more than one thing at a time,' said Serena rashly; 'I think I must have a sort of double brain.'

" 'Much better to economize and have one really good one,' observed Lady Caroline."

Serena Golackly is not alone in her eavesdropping. The novel echoes with overheard conversation, a testimony to Hector's years as a solitary man, dining alone in Sofia, walking alone through the streets of St. Petersburg, going alone to the theatre in London. Francesca overhears a woman at a dinner party point out Elaine de Frey for the first time to Courtenay Youghal: "Tons of money and really very presentable. Just the wife for a rising young politician. Go in and win her before she's snapped up by some fortune hunter." Francesca also overhears news about the marital plans of Emmeline Chetroff, the heiress whose wedding, when it comes, will displace her from Blue Street. Most of the time, however, the speakers who are caught in mid-fatuity do not advance the plot; many do not have names. It is enough for Hector to bring pests and nuisances to a public place and let them rend the air:

" 'Whenever I hear his music I feel that I want to go up into a mountain and pray. Can you understand that feeling?'

"The girl to whom she was unburdening herself shook her head.

" 'You see, I've heard his music chiefly in Switzerland, and we were up among the mountains all the time, so it wouldn't have made any difference.'

" 'In that case,' said the woman, who seemed to have emergency emotions to suit all geographical conditions, 'I should have wanted to be in a great silent plain by the side of a rushing river.'

" 'What I think is so splendid about his music—' commenced another starling-voice on the farther side of the girl. Like sheep that feed greedily before the coming of a storm, the starling-voices seemed impelled to extra effort by the knowledge of four imminent intervals of acting during which they would be hushed into constrained silence."

" 'We all said, 'It can't be Captain Parminter, because he's always been sweet on Joan,' and then Emily said—'

"The curtain went up, and Emily's contribution to the discussion had to be held over till the entr'acte."

Sometimes the author provides only a final line to taunt the reader with the engrossing story he has missed: " 'And there, dear lady,' concluded the Colonel, 'were the eleven dead pigeons. What had become of the bandicoot no one ever knew.' "

Some of these snippets no doubt came from memory. In Paris, Hector had copied out for Ethel a conversation he overheard among a group of American tourists. "I seem fated," he complained, "to learn the inmost yearnings of American stomachs; was dining at Constan's one night when an elderly American lady was leaving the restaurant after her dinner, and informing the busy manager in a high scream which grew higher and higher as she neared the door: 'I like *roast lamb*. My sister likes *roast lamb*. At the Grand hô-tel Godknowswhere we had some roast lamb that was *real good*. Yes, we both like *roast lamb*.' Then the Roumanian orchestra struck up, so I never knew what her little son's feelings were toward roast lamb."

By the time Hector turned that episode into a rather drab turn for Elaine and Youghal to overhear on their honeymoon, he had mastered his initial repugnance and was trying to understand the nature of the obsession. " 'So these people think of nothing but their food?' asked Elaine, as the virtues of roasted mutton suddenly came to the fore and received emphatic recognition, even the absent and youthful Jerome being quoted in its favour.

" 'On the contrary,' said Courtenay, 'they are a widely-traveled set, and the man has had a notably interesting career. It is a form of homesickness with them to discuss and lament the cookery and foods that they've never had the leisure to stay at home and digest. The Wandering Jew probably babbled unremittingly about some breakfast dish that took so long to prepare that he had never time to eat it.' "

Lady Veula Croot might be taken as Hector's Greek chorus for *The Unbearable Bassington* except that all her lamentations are silent. A woman who sees everything and suffers pangs of helpless sympathy, Lady Veula in turn is pitied by her creator. "She had a devoted husband, some blond teachable children, and a look of unutterable weariness in her eyes. To see her standing at the top of an expensively horticultured staircase receiving her husband's guests was rather like watching an animal performing on a music-hall stage. One always tells oneself that the animal likes it, and one always knows that it doesn't."

It is Lady Veula who sees with Comus the black dog foretelling his death. And Comus must surely die; the book was written toward his death. In his final reflections among the West African villagers, Comus speaks of the loneliness of a man who must live outside the natural human connections, and his thoughts could apply to three different sorts of melancholy. We can understand most readily that any man far from home might be visited by feelings of abandonment; Hector had experienced them in Burma during his months with the police. But what Comus feels could also be the isolating pain when a loved one—Cyril?—goes off and when even a good sort, a pluralist, wishes there were someone to tell about the separation. And, last, it could be the cry of an outsider whose thin lips ache from forty years of smiling.

Comus has watched the native boys frolicking like fighting kittens. "Presently two girls of their own age, who had returned from the water-fetching, sprang out on them from ambush, and the four joined in one joyous gambol that lit up the hillside with shrill echoes and glimpses of flying limbs. Comus sat and watched, at first with an amused interest, then with a returning flood of depression and heartache. Those wild young human kittens represented the joy of life, he was the outsider, the lonely alien, watching something in which he could not join, a happiness in which he had no part or lot. He would pass presently out of the village and his bearers' feet would leave their indentations in the dust: that would be his most permanent memorial in this little oasis of teeming life . . . He had loved himself very well and never troubled greatly whether anyone else really loved him, and now he realized what he had made of his life. And at the same time he knew that if his chance were to come again he would throw it away just as surely, just as perversely. Fate played with him with loaded dice; he would lose always."

At home, notified that Comus has been taken ill, Francesca Bassington awaits the telegram that will pronounce his death and realizes that her son was the only thing in life she had truly loved. As long as readers can be reached through self-pity, death will have a poignance for them, and some may grant to Francesca at that moment a trivial dignity. But Hector will not stop there. By any rule, the cherished painting, which she had refused to sell to establish Comus in business and keep him safe at home, must be genuine, if only for a practical reason: Should it prove to be a copy, it would not have raised the money needed to save Comus and Francesca's self-reproach would be in vain. There are better reasons, too, that the novel should end with the painting, now worthless to Francesca, still valuable to the world.

But her brother comes with the news: He has brought an expert to appraise it, and the Van der Meulen is a fake. It would have done—had done, many times—as the ending for a story. But novels rarely can rest upon twists. The reader has made a different sort of compact with a novel, and although its conclusion may surprise or astonish him, it cannot trick him with a minor turn of the plot. The British have always been alert to the sort of cleverness that undoes itself; Hector knew it and wrote about it often. But it is a cleverness that can help itself no more than Comus could, and to conclude his novel Hector succumbed to it.

The Unbearable Bassington, finally, represents a success only for the skills that Hector was trying to surmount, for vignettes as sharply edged as any in his stories, for the flawless sentences on almost every page that could have been the work of no other English writer. Yet even as a failure the novel suited the true purpose that Hector had demanded from it, and that was not simply to widen his renown. His author's note at the beginning read, "This story has no moral. If it points out an evil at any rate it suggests no remedy."

The evil was in his own way of living, and Hector did in fact find a remedy. He had set out to bury his youth, and in *The Unbearable Bassington* he provided an elegant coffin for it.

12

Shock Tactics
(1912-1913)

olidays had become as routine for Hector as the rest of his life. The family of Charlie's wife, Muriel, had a cottage on the sea in the north of Ireland at a village called Carrig Cnoc. From 1908, Hector and Ethel became accustomed to spending August there. Charlie had been promoted and was governor of Mountjoy Prison, in Dublin, a post he held until Ireland was partitioned in 1922.

Getting to Carrig Cnoc—Welsh for "the rock on the hill"—was a two-day enterprise; first a train up from London to Liverpool and an overnight boat train to Derry, then a pilot boat that would let them off at their end of the bay, twelve miles across the water from Portstewart. The house was small and painted pink. Downstairs were drawing room, dining room, a minuscule room for guests, and a bathroom created from a former pantry. Upstairs were two good-sized bedrooms, one facing the hill, the other the sea, along with a maid's room, a small nook where Muriel's father developed photographs, and a room that

Charlie called "the mosquito cabin" because it was the tiniest room of all and the one to which he was relegated when Hector and Ethel came to stay.

Summer days meant unceasing activity under the harsh light of the North Irish coast. Charlie dove from rocks into the sea. Hector and Ethel ran out in their bathing costumes from the small house directly into the water. A rugged golf course had been practicable, and Charlie enjoyed it, but the terrain was too rough for a tennis court. None of the grown Munros cared much for fishing. At night the costume box was raided for any games that required dressing up, and there was a lot of commotion but not much laughing. The three Munros had grown up hearing little and they considered their own humor a bit above mere laughter.

When Hector did laugh aloud, it was likely to be at a nonsense rhyme. Even then there was the suggestion that he was making the effort only to gratify a friend. One colleague later boasted that he had roused a laugh by repeating for Hector a rhyme written on the death of the Arcoon of Swat, which described the sorrow of his subjects and their question, "What's got Swat?"

Meals at Carrig Cnoc were simple. Muriel kept a recipe book with instructions for the cook on how to make sponge cake, flakemeal biscuits, lemon curd and "French meat for eight." (Two pounds thinly sliced steak, two or three rashers of bacon, one well-boiled cabbage; very little salt; bay leaf if liked; pepper or paprika; dripping.)

Charlie and Muriel's daughter, Felicia, was eight years old in 1913, a small, frail child, and although girls were not a favored sex with either of them, Hector and Ethel included her in their games. Hector was Otter, Ethel was Big Wolf and Felicia was Little Wolf, and Otter and Big Wolf spun stories about creeping through the woods looking for farmers' wives to devour. At last Muriel put a stop to the game. She told Felicia that she was getting too old for such fancies, but it is more likely that, a mild-natured woman herself, she had misgivings about the blood-thirstiness.

Aunt Ethel, it had to be admitted, was scarcely a fit model for a little girl, although the worst of her oddities were still in the future. After Hector's death, she began to travel with three dolls: a hand-puppet bear named Teddy, a rabbit named Wilfy, and a Master Owl. By that time Charlie and Muriel had another daughter, Juniper, but the dolls were not brought to amuse her. They were Ethel's entourage and given places of honor on her dressing table. As Juniper grew up, Ethel encouraged her to write separate notes to each of the dolls as though they were living things. Ethel also took to wearing a huge pad to make her hair bouffant, and she cleaned the pad with mentholated spirits. Her family was afraid that anytime she got near a match she would burst into flame.

Ethel's diet, on the other hand, was only a nuisance. She became a vegetarian during those unhappy years without Hector, and she subsisted on black-strap molasses, dandelion tea, honey and the health food called Bemax. But she would hang about the kitchen while Ida, Muriel's cook, made cakes, begging for a taste of the batter. Ethel would have eaten the whole cake raw if Ida had let her, and when she was cut off Ethel would cry, "Oh, you mean creature!"

All of that came after the World War. In the cloudless years before, Ethel was still a representative maiden lady, if considerably more headstrong than most. Her bullying of her sister-in-law was due entirely to temperament, not to any presumption of a superior background. At seventeen, Muriel had been presented to Victoria in London and then, as a married woman, again to Edward VII at the Vice Regal Lodge in Dublin, on the latter occasion wearing a black dress with ostrich feathers and the obligatory six yards of train. At the end of her life, strangers found Muriel a formidable woman with an air of strong resolve. But as a bride she had hit upon the one way of dealing with her sister-in-law and never did otherwise: she gave way to Ethel on everything.

Charlie and Hector got along well for two men whose lives had taken such different paths. Although he had become a prison governor, a career not entirely unpredictable from his upbringing, Charlie had retained a love of the theatre and a dry humor that kept him attuned to Hector, and he was generously and happily proud of his brother's success. Charlie wrote a little himself, a nonsense rhyme about "the elderly tablecloth / Went to the laundry / Had a wrangle / With the mangle / And came back as six young napkins." And there was a verse about a local figure named Mr. Love, who courted late in life and took his intended, also not young, to the promenade.

> *"And when she bent to fix her stocking*
> *Her swain cried out, This is too shocking.*
> *No wonder people thought me daft,*
> *Now that I've seen you fore and aft,*
> *Begone, begone, o ponderous one,*
> *Your goose is cooked and overdone."*

A cheerless visitor from the north of England once said to Charlie, "Now I am going to tell you a funny story," and launched upon a tedious description of his motor car breaking down. Charlie heard him out and, when he finished, waited a moment, fixed him with his monocle, and said, "Tell the funny part over, slowly."

Since little about the habits and predilections of mankind goes unknown to a prison governor, it is safe to assume that Charlie had a good idea about the nature of Hector's life in London. It is equally likely, given their reserve, that neither would have found a reason to discuss it. After Hector's death, Charlie often let his daughters know how much he missed his brother, and he told them about a night that he and Muriel had taken Hector to a pantomime. When they arrived at the theatre, the manager asked whether they would mind if the fiend of the piece sang a number from their box. They had no objection at all and welcomed the player to their midst. Later, Hector wrote from London that he was feeling quite gloomy these days without the company of the fiend.

Once or twice every month throughout 1912, always on a Tuesday morning, Hector published a new story in the *Morning Post*. Other weeks he sent pieces to the *Westminster Gazette* or to a new outlet for him, a glossy weekly called the *Bystander*. When three dozen stories had accumulated, John Lane brought out a collection entitled *Beasts and Super-Beasts,* one of Hector's japes against GBS, whose *Man and Superman* had appeared in 1905. To promote the volume in his monthly circular, the *Bodleian,* Lane called upon Ben Travers, by now its editor, to select one of Hector's stories to run in full. Travers chose his favorite, "Dusk," but when it appeared, Lane let him know that he was unhappy with the choice. The story was out of Saki's usual method, Lane explained, and that made it an inappropriate selection.

And by 1914, when "Dusk" appeared in the book, Lane was right. During the intervening years since he first wrote it, Hector had drawn back from plots that depended on their final paragraphs. "Dusk," which involves the loss of a cake of soap, has little to recommend it but its ingenuity, and even its one joke is shopworn. " 'To lose an hotel and a cake of soap on one afternoon suggests willful carelessness,' said Gortsby," suggesting that Hector hoped his memory of Lady Bracknell was better than his readers'.

It could not have occurred to Travers at the time, but the story does have a telling passage in which the central character, Norman Gortsby, reflects upon his life. His despondency is so pervasive, so inexplicable, and yet so deeply felt, that it seems to speak for Hector's mood at the time he was working on his first novel. "Dusk, to his mind, was the hour of the defeated. Men and women, who had fought and lost, who hid their fallen fortunes and dead hopes as far as possible from the scrutiny of the curious, came forth in this hour of gloaming, when their shabby clothes and bowed shoulders and unhappy eyes might pass unnoticed, or, at any rate, unrecognized . . .

"So Gortsby's imagination pictured things as he sat on his bench in the almost deserted walk. He was in the mood to count himself among the defeated. Money troubles did not press on him; had he so wished he could have strolled into the thoroughfares of light and noise, and taken his place among the jostling ranks of those who enjoyed prosperity or struggled for it. He had failed in a more subtle ambition, and for the moment he was heart sore and disillusioned, and not disinclined to take a certain cynical pleasure in observing and labelling his fellow wanderers as they went their ways in the dark stretches between the lamp-lights."

Travers' selection was the more eccentric because *Beasts and Super-Beasts* included "The Open Window," one of the five or six of Hector's stories that were to prove irresistible to editors compiling an anthology. Even if one prefers another of his pieces, the appeal to that tart romance is undeniable, and it is, in itself, an anthology of Hector's later methods. This time the central character is presented as a girl of fifteen, but she is obviously only a younger and even more delicate Clovis. Although Hector's tone was near the surface whenever Reginald or Clovis spoke, there had never been any discernible trace of Ethel in Hector's young women. His sister was too hearty for his purposes and she was not inventive. In life, Ethel was ever the audience, and in the stories that role is taken by the reader.

We find the girl entertaining a new visitor to her aunt's house, a man named Framton Nuttel. Mr. Nuttel has come to the country to rest his nerves; this notion is a chimera that tempts several of Hector's characters. J. P. Huddle in "The Unrest-Cure," for example, thinks he is safely entombed in the country, and then a religious war breaks out on his doorstep.

In "The Open Window," after assuring herself that Nuttel knows no one in the neighborhood, the girl, whom Hector calls Vera for reasons he will make clear, regales him with the story of her aunt's tragic loss. " 'You may wonder why we keep that window wide open on an October afternoon,' said the niece, indicating a large French window that opened on to a lawn.

" 'It is quite warm for the time of the year,' said Framton; 'but has that window got anything to do with the tragedy?'

" 'Out through that window, three years ago to a day, her husband and her two young brothers went off for their day's shooting. They never came back. In crossing the moor to their favorite snipe-shooting ground they were all three engulfed in a treacherous piece of bog. It had been that dreadful wet summer, you know, and places that were safe in other years gave way suddenly without warning. Their bodies were never recovered. That was the dreadful part of it.' Here the child's voice lost its self-possessed note and became falteringly human. 'Poor aunt always thinks that they will come back some day, they and the little brown spaniel that was lost with them, and walk in at that window just as they used to do. That is why the window is kept open every evening till it is quite dusk. Poor dear aunt, she has often told me how they went out, her husband with his white waterproof coat over his arm, and Ronnie, her youngest brother, singing, Bertie, why do you bound? as he always did to tease her, because she said it got on her nerves. Do you know, some-times on still, quiet evenings like this, I almost get a creepy feeling that they will all walk in through that window—'

"She broke off with a little shudder. It was a relief for Framton when the aunt bustled into the room with a whirl of apologies for being late in making her appearance.

" 'I hope Vera has been amusing you?' she said.

" 'She has been very interesting,' said Framton.

" 'I hope you don't mind the open window,' said Mrs. Sappleton briskly; 'my husband and brothers will be home directly from shooting, and they always come in this way. They've been out for snipe in the marshes today, so they'll make a fine mess over my poor carpets. So like you men-folk, isn't it?' "

Nuttel sits edgily and wonders how he can escape from this madwoman. Then Mrs. Sappleton brightens.

" 'Here they are at last!' she cried. 'Just in time for tea, and don't they look as if they were muddy up to the eyes!'

"Framton shivered slightly and turned towards the niece with a look intended to convey sympathetic compre-hension. The child was staring out through the open win-dow with dazed horror in her eyes. In a chill shock of nameless fear Framton swung round in his seat and looked in the same direction.

"In the deepening twilight three figures were walking across the lawn towards the window; they all carried guns under their arms, and one of them was additionally bur-dened with a white coat hung over his shoulders. A tired brown spaniel kept close at their heels. Noiselessly they neared the house, and then a hoarse young voice chanted out of the dusk: 'I say, Bertie, why do you bound?' ''

Nuttel grabs up his stick and hat as Mrs. Sappleton is welcoming her family from the hunt. When he is gone, she tells them about Nuttel's strange behavior. '' 'I expect it was the spaniel,' said the niece calmly; 'he told me he had a horror of dogs. He was once hunted into a cemetery somewhere on the banks of the Ganges by a pack of pariah dogs, and had to spend the night in a newly dug grave with the creatures snarling and grinning and foaming just above him. Enough to make any one lose their nerve.' ''

That is the story's end but for one line. Hector was killed in such a way that there could be no gravestone or marker. Otherwise, the sentence, with adjustment for gender, might have served for his epitaph:

"Romance at short notice was her specialty."

Ten months later, Hector tried the same formula in "The Lull." This time it is Latimer Springfield, a politician exhausted from electioneering, who must be coddled and kept from brooding about the coming vote. His hosts are a Mr. and Mrs. Durmot but their niece once again is Vera, now sixteen and no less inventive. She persuades the exhausted Springfield that the local reservoir has burst and he must give refuge in his bedroom to a gamecock and a pig. The night passes as hectically as Vera had wished, but by morning Springfield has penetrated the hoax. He confronts Vera on the way to breakfast.

'' 'I should not like to think of you as a deliberate liar,' he observed coldly, 'but one occasionally has to do things one does not like.' '' To which Vera responds that at least she has kept his mind off politics.

One difference between the two stories explains why the first is a classic of its kind and the second a diverting farce. In "The Lull," the reader is privy to the hoax; in "The Open Window," he is not. In Hector's hands, we are all Nuttels, and by giving us an entirely satisfactory ghost story he doubles the effectiveness of his trick.

Making the taleteller a young girl rather than a boy also improves the joke. Girls were thought to be the more truthful sex, even if, as they grew up, a peculiar reversal could be expected. Since Hector shared the view that girls were less creative, Vera was less suspect for his purposes. Indeed, in Hector's mind it was a compliment to be considered an accomplished liar. Even as an adult he defended the glories of a fanciful concoction against stale reality, and he recognized that children have no power worth the name except their lies and their retreats into fantasy. Surely they couldn't pray; the adults in their lives had made it clear that God was a grown-up. They could try to call down the wrath of dark gods even mightier than their guardians, and once in a millennium a spirit would respond. But, in the main, their best recourse was to lie.

In the year after "The Lull," when he had published one novel and was finishing a second, Hector returned to the subject of children and truth. "The Story-Teller" is a pure distillation of Hector's freshest ingredients, and it offers the best introduction to his work. If that story does not please a new reader, Hector has no more potent charms to win him over. A reviewer for the *Spectator* located the reason. Tracing the several currents and undertows to Saki's work, the critic concluded that despite, or because of, his peculiar gifts, he was too acid ever to become a popular writer: "The plain person cannot subsist on a diet of perpetual olives." The reviewer appreciated both the freakishness and the flippancy in Saki, but he added, "We like him best when he is least malicious." "The Story-Teller" gives us Saki at his least malicious.

This is the tale of an aunt traveling by train with her three wards—two girls and a boy, so that it will not be exactly himself and Ethel and Charlie—and another passenger, a bachelor. The four are trapped together in a railway carriage on a hot afternoon with the next stop an hour away. First comes a long and inconclusive dialogue between aunt and boy, whose name is Cyril, over why the sheep that he spies from the window are being driven to another field when there was ample grass for them where they were.

"The smaller girl created a diversion by beginning to recite 'On the Road to Mandalay.' She only knew the first line, but she put her limited knowledge to the fullest possible use. She repeated the line over and over again in a dreamy but resolute and very audible voice; it seemed to the bachelor as though someone had had a bet with her that she could not repeat the line aloud two thousand times without stopping. Whoever it was who had made the wager was likely to lose his bet.''

To distract them, the aunt begins a story about a little girl of such high moral character that everyone loves her, and when she is threatened by a mad bull, her admirers rush to save her. Since the children are not impressed, the bachelor volunteers to tell a story of his own. At first it sounds unpromising; it is also about an exemplary girl. But the bachelor wins them over by adding that the girl, named Bertha, was "horribly good," and for her goodness, Bertha not only received three medals but also an invitation to walk in the park of the ruling prince. The outing is a glorious experience until an enormous wolf comes prowling into the park looking for a fat little pig for its supper. By now the bachelor has the children enthralled.

"The first thing that it saw in the park was Bertha; her pinafore was so spotlessly white and clean and it could be seen from a great distance. Bertha saw the wolf and saw that it was stealing towards her, and she began to wish that she had never been allowed to come into the park. She ran as hard as she could, and the wolf came after her with huge leaps and bounds. She managed to reach a shrubbery of myrtle bushes and she hid herself in one of the thickest of the bushes. The wolf came sniffing among the branches, its black tongue lolling out of its mouth and its pale grey eyes glaring with rage. Bertha was terribly frightened, and thought to herself: 'If I had not been so extraordinarily good I should have been safe in the town at this moment.' ''

The wolf cannot sniff out the girl, however, because the scent of myrtle is too strong, and the bushes are so thick that he can catch no sight of her. The wolf resolves to leave and catch a little pig instead.

" 'Bertha was trembling very much at having the wolf prowling and sniffing so near her, and as she trembled the medal for obedience clinked against the medals for good conduct and punctuality. The wolf was just moving away when he heard the sound of the medals clinking and stopped to listen; they clinked again in a bush quite near him. He dashed into the bush, his pale grey eyes gleaming with ferocity and triumph, and dragged Bertha out and devoured her to the last morsel. All that was left of her were her shoes, bits of clothing, and the three medals for goodness.'

" 'Were any of the little pigs killed?'

" 'No, they all escaped.'

" 'The story began badly,' said the smaller of the small girls, 'but it had a beautiful ending.'

" 'It is the most beautiful story that I ever heard,' said the bigger of the small girls, with immense decision.

" 'It is the *only* beautiful story I have ever heard,' said Cyril."

When the aunt complains that it had been an improper story for children, the bachelor reflects as he leaves the carriage that for the next six months the children will assail her in public with demands for an improper story.

Aunt Tom was still alive when the story appeared. Had she ever remarked on the abundance of aunts in Hector's work? She seems not to have been a woman alert to coincidence. More curiously, did the fate of Hector's mother occur to him when the aunt told of a good little girl saved from a bull? His own mother had not been saved; had she not been good?

But Hector's strength was that he never let the restraints of the adult mind filter out the primitive streak that quickens his beautifully crafted stories. He was adept, for example, at the wounding game of insults that both children and adults would love to play but are rarely equipped to win. One critic said that only a man with a touch of the child to him could revel in a joke like this one:

" 'She's leaving her present house and going to Lower Seymour Street.'

" 'I daresay she will, if she stays there long enough.' "

There are scores of others:

" 'You're looking nicer than usual,' I said, 'but that's so easy for you.' "

" 'What an odious young cub Bertie Dykson has become!' pronounced Mrs. Dole, remembering suddenly that Bertie was rather a favourite with Mrs. Hatch-Mallard. 'The young men of today are not what they used to be twenty years ago.'

" 'Of course not,' said Mrs. Hatch-Mallard; 'twenty years ago Bertie Dykson was just two years old, and you must expect some difference in appearance and manner and conversation between those two periods.'

" 'Do you know,' said Mrs. Dole confidentially, 'I shouldn't be surprised if that was intended to be clever.' "

" 'I don't know why I shouldn't talk cleverly,' she would complain; 'my mother was considered a brilliant conversationalist.'

" 'These things have a way of skipping one generation,' said the Gräfin.

" 'That seems so unjust,' said Sophie; 'one doesn't object to one's mother having outshone one as a clever talker, but I must admit that I should be rather annoyed if my daughters talked brilliantly.'

" 'Well, none of them do,' said the Gräfin consolingly."

Sometimes the parry is better than the thrust:

" 'Is your maid called Florence?'

" 'Her name is Florinda.'

" 'What an extraordinary name to give a maid!'

" 'I did not give it to her; she arrived in my service already christened.'

" 'What I mean is,' said Mrs. Riversedge, 'that when I get maids with unsuitable names I call them Jane; they soon get used to it.'

" 'An excellent plan,' said the aunt of Clovis coldly; 'unfortunately I have got used to being called Jane myself. It happens to be my name.' "

Nothing in the spite and malice of these remarks need trouble a reader unless they remind him of occasions when he has been comparably discomposed. But Saki's aggression does not stop with words, and the uneasiness that his stories have provoked in some readers has led certain of his admirers to respond that he is never cruel, that his only victims are snobs and bullies who deserve their discomfiture. Or they are middle-aged and powerful enough to survive a momentary indignity. Much of the time the apologists are persuasive. Even when Hector is not settling scores deservedly, he is so playful in the way he discharges his victims that one would have to be a pacifist, and a remarkably dour one, to object:

"Dobrinton was bitten by a dog which was assumed to be mad, although it may only have been indiscriminating. The victim did not wait for symptoms of rabies to declare themselves but died forthwith of fright."

"At that moment a youngish man came up behind him, drew the blade from a swordstick, and stabbed him half a dozen times through and through. 'Scoundrel,' he cried to his victim, 'you do not know me. My name is Henri Leturc.' The elder man wiped away some of the blood that was spattering his clothes, turned to his assailant, and said: 'And since when has an attempted assassination been considered an introduction?' "

" 'Waldo is one of those people who would be enormously improved by death,' said Clovis."

All these passages provoke laughter. But into the reckoning must also go what we know of Hector himself, his hoaxes, his refined but very real blood lust. In Burma, he had watched with fascination as two men staged a ritual fight, scratching like cats with hands and feet to be the first to draw blood. Hector wrote, with the candor that Ethel stimulated in him, "I was quite disappointed to see them stop as soon as one was scratched. I had hoped (such is our fallen nature) that they would fight to the death and was trying hurriedly to remember whether you turned your thumbs up or down for mercy."

Later, in St. Petersburg, his cleaning woman developed a craving for mince pies and would filch a piece or two whenever there was pie to be had. Hector living by himself might have blinked an eye; it was part of the charm to his jokes that they have an audience. But he was chumming just then, and neither man spoke to the woman directly. Instead, they coated the underside of the top crust with mustard and chortled when the pilfering stopped. Hearing of the tactic back in England, Ethel enjoyed its indirection. If there was a nastiness to the joke, Ethel did not see it.

Even when he was past forty and living in London, the jokes went on. Invited to a dinner party with a journalist friend, E. B. Osborn, Hector on the way sketched out a quarrel for them to stage. Once arrived, Osborn followed the scenario and what began as a mild insult escalated during the meal to rasher invective, until, by the port, Hector and Osborn were threatening each other with violence. The other diners were now atwitter, and one gentle Scot laid his hand on Osborn's shoulder and begged him to pay no mind to Hector, he couldn't mean what he had been saying. When they were sure they had gulled everybody at the table, the hoaxers owned up.

At another dinner Hector sat gloating while he watched an heiress with a bad stomach eating her ration of milk puddings. "I had a hearty supper," he told friends afterward, "and for all her millions she couldn't eat anything."

Minor incidents, certainly, and any cruelty in them too trivial to deserve the name. But what of passages in the stories that we are inclined to glide over in the prevailing gaiety? What of Sylvia Seltoun, who makes the fatal error of affronting a woodland deity in the tranquil English countryside? It takes no overingenious reading to know that her true crime has been marrying a contented bachelor. But whether she has offended Pan or her husband, Sylvia pays.

"The huge antler spikes were within a few yards of her, and in a flash of numbing fear she remembered Mortimer's warning, to beware of horned beasts on the farm. And then with a quick throb of joy she saw that she was not alone; a human figure stood a few paces aside, knee-deep in the whortle bushes.

" 'Drive it off!' she shrieked. But the figure made no answering movement.

"The antlers drove straight at her breast, the acrid smell of the hunted animal was in her nostrils, but her eyes were filled with the horror of something she saw other than her oncoming death. And in her ears rang the echo of a boy's laughter, golden and equivocal."

What of the Baroness's tale of seeing a "small half-naked gipsy brat" seized by a hyena? " 'The gipsy child was firmly, and I expect painfully, held in his jaws.' " When the hyena lopes away to finish off its morsel, the Baroness's companion shudders. " 'Do you think the poor little thing suffered much?' came another of her futile questions.

" 'The indications were all that way,' I said; 'on the other hand, of course, it may have been crying from sheer temper. Children sometimes do.' "

What, finally, of his masterpiece, "Sredni Vashtar"? As a child Hector had made a particular pet of a Houdan cock in the backyard at Barnstaple. From Ethel's description, it was a clever bird that followed Hector everywhere, ate from his hand and thrived under his caresses. Then one leg of Hector's pet went bad. Ethel was sure that a veterinarian could have saved it but at Broadgate Villa such an extravagance for a mere bird would have been considered sinful. When the cock was destroyed, only Ethel knew the depths of Hector's misery.

More than thirty years later, Hector recalled his emotions from those days when the cock died and the local doctor pronounced its owner so frail that he would go soon afterward. In his story, Hector becomes Conradin, and the cock becomes a Houdan hen "on which the boy lavished an affection that scarcely had another outlet." Aunt Augusta becomes the boy's guardian, Mrs. De Ropp, who "would never, in her honestest moments, have confessed to herself that she disliked Conradin, though she might have been dimly aware that thwarting him 'for his own good' was a duty which she did not find particularly irksome. Conradin hated her with a desperate sincerity which he was perfectly able to mask."

But now Hector could make the fight a little fairer. He gives Conradin a second, secret pet in a cage. It is a large polecat-ferret that the boy calls Sredni Vashtar and worships as a god. One day Mrs. De Ropp—who figures in Conradin's thoughts simply as the Woman—sets out to pry among his hidden treasures in a locked shed. Watching her through the door, Conradin breathes an urgent prayer; by this point in the story, Hector did not need to say what he was praying. "But he knew as he prayed that he did not believe. He knew that the Woman would come out presently with that pursed smile he loathed so well on her face, and that in an hour or two the gardener would carry away his wonderful god, a god no longer, but a simple brown ferret in a hutch. And he knew that the Woman would triumph always as she triumphed now, and that he would grow ever more sickly under her pestering and domineering and superior wisdom, till one day nothing would matter much more with him, and the doctor would be proved right."

His despair causes Conradin to break forth defiantly into a hymn:

> "Sredni Vashtar went forth,
> His thoughts were red thoughts and his teeth were white.
> His enemies called for peace, but he brought them death.
> Sredni Vashtar the Beautiful."

And after waiting and watching and not daring to hope: "Out through that doorway came a long, low yellow-and-brown beast, with eyes a-blink at the waning daylight, and dark wet stains around the fur of jaws and throat."

Saki could be cruel. It was his second great gift.

ABOVE LEFT: George Munro, a son of Col. Charles Adolphus Munro, Hector's grandfather, upheld the family's military tradition by joining the Army and serving in India, where he was killed in the bloody Indian Mutiny of 1857. Sixty-five years earlier, another of Hector's military relatives had also perished in India when a tiger ate him.

ABOVE RIGHT: Hector's father, Charles Augustus Munro, upon the death of his wife, entrusted his three small children to his mother and his spinster sisters while he returned to the military police in Burma. (W. H. Hayles, London)

Hector, at the age of ten, was called "Chickie" by his aunts because of his frail constitution and his pale blond hair. "Conradin," Hector wrote of the young hero of "Sredni Vashtar," "was ten years old, and the doctor had pronounced his professional opinion that the boy would not live another five years." (J. D. Vickery)

Broadgate Villa. "In the dull, cheerless garden," Hector wrote in "Sredni Vashtar," "overlooked by so many windows that were ready to open with a message not to do this or that, or a reminder that medicines were due, he found little attraction." *(William K. Tuohy)*

RIGHT: Charles Arthur Munro, Hector's brother, whose weak eyes had kept him from the Army, compensated by joining the military police in Burma and sporting a fashionable monocle.

BELOW: On leaving the police in Burma, Charlie Munro took up a career as a prison administrator in Ireland until the establishment of the Irish Free State in 1922. With him are his young daughter, Felicia, and his wife, Muriel.

After Hector's death, Ethel Munro kept this picture framed along with his telegram to her announcing his enlistment. Every Memorial Day, the picture was festooned with fresh poppies. *(E. O. Hoppé)*

Francis Carruthers Gould, born in Barnstaple some twenty years before Hector was reared there, became his patron at the *Westminster Gazette* by introducing him to its editor, J. A. Spender. *(The Mansell Collection)*

In Francis Carruthers Gould's sketch for Hector's "Alice in a Fog," Alice and the Cheshire Cat ponder the meaning of a verse by the Poet Laureate, Alfred Austin. "'I'd give sixpence to any one who can explain it,' said Alice." *(Westminster Gazette)*

H. W. Nevinson, already an experienced journalist when Hector set out in 1902 as a correspondent for the *Morning Post,* recalled later the peculiar allure of those days, when the prevailing misery and war were tempered by the exhilarating beauty of the Balkans. *(The Mansell Collection)*

A. Rothay Reynolds, a fellow journalist whom Hector met in St. Petersburg, became a lifelong friend. Of Hector, Reynolds wrote, "He cared nothing for money . . . When a friend once suggested a profitable field for his writings, he dismissed the idea by saying he was not interested in the public for which it was proposed that he should write."

In St. Petersburg in 1905, Hector left the sanctuary of the nearby Hôtel de France to press against a doorway for a better view of the Tsar's Cossacks firing into the crowd of reformers as they marched on the Winter Palace. *(Granger Collection)*

Georgy Apollonovich Gapon, who instigated the march on the Winter Palace, was a Russian Orthodox priest of about Hector's age. A prominent leader in the growing movement against the Tsar's intransigence, he fled Russia after the march became the bloodbath that so enthralled Ethel Munro. *(BBC Hulton Picture Library)*

Carrig Cnoc, the vacation retreat in Northern Ireland of Muriel Chambers Munro's family and the spot where Hector and Ethel joined their brother for their August holidays. Both Hector and Ethel reveled in running in their bathing costumes directly from the house into the sea.

Hector, at left, in 1908, with Ethel, who hated having her picture taken and watched her brother rather than the camera. Muriel steadies her three-year-old daughter, Felicia, and her husband, Charlie, stands at her side.

John Lane, after World War I, published two posthumous volumes of Saki's stories and essays. The publisher of Oscar Wilde, Lane had been mortified by the Wilde scandal, and he put his hands over his ears when his editors taunted him that in Saki he had signed another homosexual author. *(BBC Hulton Picture Library)*

Lady St. Helier, in her youth. As the widow of Sir Francis Jeune, she became a hostess whose "at homes" and formal parties Hector frequented. A collector of literary men, she recalled fondly his bad temper on the morning that Tennyson had burned his mouth on hot bread and milk at her breakfast table. *(BBC Hulton Picture Library)*

On transferring to the 22nd Battalion of the Royal Fusiliers, Munro had a picture taken in his enlisted man's uniform. The Army had pulled his decaying upper teeth, and he had raised a mustache to offset the loss.

Gᵥ R I

HE whom this scroll commemorates was numbered among those who, at the call of King and Country, left all that was dear to them, endured hardness, faced danger, and finally passed out of the sight of men by the path of duty and self-sacrifice, giving up their own lives that others might live in freedom. Let those who come after see to it that his name be not forgotten.

L/Serjt. Hector Hugh Munro
Royal Fusiliers

Munro had put on his enlisted man's uniform, wrote Rothay Reynolds, "with the exaltation of a novice assuming the religious habit."

The scroll from the King to Munro's family commemorates Munro's death from a sniper's bullet on November 14, 1916. "He was absolutely splendid," wrote an officer in command of Munro's unit. "What courage! The men simply loved him."

13

The Penance
(1913)

In London, life was changing in ways disturbing to a man whose conservative side now exerted a greater control over his temperament. Two dozen men and women named Munro had installed telephones, but Hector was not among them, and in his stories people went on communicating by note and wire. By 1911, ten of the music halls in London had begun showing pictures on the Cinematograph; Hector's characters never went to see them. Nor did they ride the electric carriages down Bond Street.

New literary voices were being heard. Katherine Mansfield published "Old Tar" in the *Westminster Gazette* in 1913, and early the next year Rupert Brooke appeared there with "The Indians." But Hector chose to remain in the age of Kipling and Lewis Carroll, his concession to modernity an occasional swipe at Shaw, who, for that matter, was his elder by fourteen years. The *Bystander* was running full-page displays of such nudes as *September*

Morn, with a caption to reassure readers that the picture had been selected only to represent the beautiful art currently gracing Paris salons. But Hector's men still hesitated to disrobe, even with a mouse in their clothes, unless it was at the Turkish bath. His females paid no heed to fashion, though all around him women were demanding that their dressmakers free them from the Edwardian lace and frills. They were not all sure what they wanted instead, and they settled on confining hobbleskirts and hats with brims wider than their shoulders.

An increasing sexual tolerance was reflected in the less guarded language. Lytton Strachey used the word "semen" in a mixed company that included Virginia Woolf. Rupert Brooke wrote to a young woman that he knew all about "people in love with people of the same sex as themselves" and promised one day to enlighten her. And in *Pygmalion,* Shaw used for the first time on the British stage the epithet "bloody"; the *Bystander* critic, present for the premiere, recorded the response: "For a single instant we all had to look as if we had never heard such an expression before and had certainly never used it; and then the human element in the audience prevailed, and a healthy show of laughter went up to high heaven."

Historians would stretch the Edwardian Age in each direction, until it took in the end of the nineteenth century and the four years after Edward's death but before the Great War. Literary critics then made use of that license to treat Saki as a representative—some said an embodiment —of the Edwardian era, even though he had written almost entirely during the reign of George V. Allowing for a certain elasticity, it is still hard to accept Hector, untuned as he was to his time, as speaking for a generation. Nor had that ever been his aim. As early as the Reginald stories, Hector had been writing historical romances; his imagination had preferred to dwell in the orderly time of his boyhood, a time when women traveled in graceful barouches; when family prayers and bicycles were going out of style in tandem; when a young man of fashion was embarrassed to be seen in a horse bus or carrying a bulky parcel through the streets. That age was ending just as Hector started to write about it, and he could take it as a finished subject and paint its nuances, knowing that they might vanish but would not change.

John Gore, the journalist and biographer, had first heard Hector's stories at Oxford from Willie Mercer, who learned them by heart and recited them to his friends. Gore's circle found Reginald rather unwholesome but they questioned only his morals, never his wit, and to Gore the name of Saki ever afterward conjured up a vision of spires, paneled rooms and shaven lawns sloping down to a silver river. Even as Hector was publishing in the *Morning Post,* each story with the day's date clearly printed at the top, he was offering to his readers that same respite, that retreat into nostalgia.

Like other observant people of his time, Hector Munro knew that a change was coming and that it did not involve Marconi or Wilbur Wright. Munro's powers as a prophet were selective. He did not foresee why the Russian Revolution would succeed or why the British Empire would one day dissolve. But he watched the growth of Germany and predicted an inevitable clash with the Kaiser. In 1913, he published a novel aimed at alerting his countrymen to the threat.

Munro believed he understood the timeliness of his book better than his publisher did, and when he had finished a first draft he wrote to John Lane to urge haste. "Since our informal conversation yesterday about deferring publication of the novel till July or thereabouts I have consulted several literary friends (including Robert Ross) and they unanimously advise immediate publication, that is to say some time in March. Apart from the political setting of the book it has a strong society undercurrent and I cannot help thinking that it would stand a better chance of being read and talked about during the Season than it would just at the fag-end."

Lane was not moved by Munro's appeal or by its support from Robert Ross, a literary columnist for the *Bystander* and Oscar Wilde's editor and steadfast friend. The publisher seems to have called for revisions; as late as August 1913, Munro was tinkering with the last chapter. When the book was published at last, it was six months later than Munro had hoped and less than a year before the war it posited.

The novel is set nominally in the near future, but like the rest of Munro's writing it owed its texture to the age just passed. *When William Came*—William stands for Kaiser Wilhelm and his troops—is bitter, despairing and, less often, clever. Munro does not show the struggle between the German and British forces. Instead he moves directly to the consequences of an English defeat, and the first scene is one of light comedy. Cicely Yeovil, at home with her young admirer, Ronnie Storre, is awaiting with mild apprehension the return of her husband, Murrey. She is not concerned about his reaction to Ronnie; so tepid is their flirtation that we, too, expect Murrey to be indulgent. What concerns her is that Murrey Yeovil has been hunting and collecting birds in Eastern Siberia and has missed the brief war and the subsequent German occupation. Effortlessly, Cicely has adapted to the *fait accompli*. Will Yeovil spoil her life by being difficult?

On his arrival, Yeovil is as stunned as his wife anticipated, and he turns to a doctor friend for an explanation of what caused the war. Apparently the fuse had been an unimportant frontier clash in East Africa. " 'War between two such civilized and enlightened nations is an impossibility,' one of our leaders of public opinion had declared on Saturday; by the following Friday the war had indeed become an impossibility, because we could no longer carry it on. It burst on us with calculated suddenness, and we were just not enough." The British seamen had been better than the Germans, but the Germans had the superiority in aircraft. British soldiers were as good as the German soldiers but Germany had many more of them under arms. The British reserves did their best but they could not master the science of war at a moment's notice. In sum, the doctor says, "There was courage enough running loose in the land, but it was like unharnessed electricity, it controlled no forces, it struck no blows. There was no time for the heroism and the devotion which a drawn-out struggle, however hopeless, can produce; the war was over almost as soon as it had begun.' "

Yeovil demands to know whether Englishmen are to

remain a subject people, like the Poles, and the doctor argues that the most they can hope for is that Germany—"the Master Power," as he calls it—gets involved in an unsuccessful war somewhere else. Many thousands of working people have emigrated from England, along with some of the upper and middle classes. Those who have stayed are trying, like Cicely, to make the best of it.

The doctor gives an odd disquisition on the role of the Jews, especially odd from Munro, who had traveled through Europe enjoying the pleasures of boulevard life. But now Munro is back in London and what he had learned for himself about the Jews in Russia is blurred once more by the prevailing English attitudes. "I am to a great extent a disliker of Jews myself, but I will be fair to them, and admit that those of them who were in any genuine sense British have remained British, and have stuck by us loyally in our misfortune; all honour to them. But of the others, the men who by temperament and everything else were far more Teuton or Polish or Latin than they were British, it was not to be expected that they would be heartbroken because London had suddenly lost its place among the political capitals of the world, and became a cosmopolitan city. They had appreciated the free and easy liberty of the old days, under British rule, but there was a stiff insularity in the ruling race that they chafed against. Now, putting aside some petty Government restrictions that Teutonic bureaucracy has brought in, there is really, in their eyes, more license and social adaptability in London than before. It has taken on some of the aspects of a No-Man's-Land, and the Jew, if he likes, may almost consider himself as of the dominant race; at any rate he is ubiquitous. Pleasure, of the café and cabaret and boulevard kind, the sort of thing that gave Berlin the aspect of the gayest capital in Europe within the last decade, that is the insidious leaven that will help to denationalize London."

Yeovil's shudder gives the doctor the opportunity to extol a life that Munro had admired, never lived, but which he embraces now as passionately as though he had never succumbed to "A Lady of No Importance," or asparagus, or the Jermyn Street Baths.

" 'I know, I know,' " said the doctor, sympathetically; 'life and enjoyment mean to you the howl of a wolf in the forest, the call of a wild swan on the frozen tundras, the smell of a wood fire in some little inn among the mountains. There is more music to you in the quick thud, thud of hoofs on desert mud as a free-stepping horse is led up to your tent door than in all the dronings and flourishes that a highly-paid orchestra can reel out to an expensively fed audience.' "

Four years earlier, a retired colonel in one of Hector's stories would have offered that panegyric at a dinner table only because Clovis was armed with the perfect deflating non sequitur. Now Munro is serious, and he has written an unsettling book that is not always unsettling in the ways he intended. *The Unbearable Bassington* had killed the self that had sustained Hector's best work, and that suicide had been sad to witness. The self-betrayal of this second novel is worse: Munro exhumes the corpse to defile it.

The chief victim is called Percival Plarsey, but he is only Reginald who has sinned by getting old. "Plarsey had never been able to relinquish the idea that a youthful charm and comeliness still centred in his person, and laboured daily at his toilet with the devotion that a hopelessly lost cause is so often able to inspire." Without the virtues of being nineteen and faunlike, Plarsey cannot expect his conversation to bubble and intoxicate. Munro has gone off champagne, particularly when the bottle's label is faded and torn.

" 'One gets tired of everything,' said Plarsey, with a fat little sigh of resignation. 'I can't tell you how tired I am of Rubinstein, and one day I suppose I shall be tired of Mozart, and *violette de Parme* and rosewood. I never thought it possible that I could ever tire of jonquils, and now I simply won't have one in the house. Oh, the scene the other day because someone brought some jonquils into the house! I'm afraid I was dreadfully rude, but I really couldn't help it.'

"He could talk like this through a long summer day or a long winter evening.

"Yeovil belonged to a race forbidden to bear arms. At the moment he would gladly have contented himself with the weapons which nature had endowed him, if he might have kicked and pommelled the abhorrent specimen of male humanity whom he saw before him."

Plarsey is scarcely the only offender. Ronnie Storre, although still young and a talented pianist, is no more than a social parasite, and to Munro, living off others, nicking those who can afford it, has become detestable. Only in the sketch of Tony Luton, a secretary-valet-companion, are there reminders of the Hector of the stories. Luton "was a young man who had sprung from the people and had taken care that there be no recoil." Possibly because Luton has usually paid his own way and because there are to him hints of a buried virility, Munro as he calls the roll squints and lets Tony pass muster. "Tony Luton was just a merry-eyed dancing faun, whom Fate had surrounded with streets instead of woods, and it would have been in the highest degree inartistic to have sounded him for a heart or a heartache."

If the men about town are now to be despised, who are Munro's new heroes? In grace, intelligence, patience and will, many turn out to be the German conquerors. At first we may wonder whether it is not merely a shrewd artistic device to give us urbane and farsighted men when we expect villainous blockheads, and no doubt there is some of that calculation in their portrayal. But after a few passages it becomes clear that these are men whom Munro sincerely admires. And why not? His quarrel is not truly with Germany but with England, with the society he had once adored for the opportunities it gave him to be clever at its expense. Now, with the genius of his youth spent, he looks around him as though waking from a dream. One cannot go on being Reginald into middle age; that way lies the shame of Percival Plarsey. Better, at forty-two, to be a distinguished politician, a baron like Charnwood or a triumphant soldier. Since he had made the Germans victorious, how could he help but admire them? Some critics even saw in his treatment of a German political adviser, a Herr von Kwarl, an identification so thorough that they read Munro's explanation of von Kwarl's unmarried state as an apologia for his own. It may be that Munro, embarrassed now by a way of life that no longer pleased him, had dropped in a set piece so that new friends like Charnwood could cite it should the need arise.

"He was a bachelor of the type that is called confirmed, and which might better be labelled consecrated; from his early youth onward to his present age he had never had the faintest flickering intention of marriage. Children and animals he adored, women and plants he accounted somewhat of a nuisance. A world without women and roses and asparagus would, he admitted, be robbed of much of its charm, but with all their charm these things were tiresome and thorny and capricious, always wanting to climb or creep in places where they were not wanted, and resolutely drooping and fading away when they were desired to flourish. Animals, on the other hand, accepted the world as it was and made the best of it, and children, at least nice children, uncontaminated by grown-up influences, lived in worlds of their own making."

However much he might have wished it, the passage had little to do with Munro. Assuredly there are such asexual men, and many of them marry. But Munro, if he could only remember it, had been luckier in his life than that.

The question of social class arises more persistently and overtly in this ostensibly political novel than in most of the short stories with their pasteboard duchesses and working people who turn up only so that a beast can carry off their children. The reason for this new consciousness is that *When William Came* is something of a mystery story. Munro is trying to establish who has betrayed England, and the villains are not solely pleasure-seeking fops and cosmopolitan Jews. A young clergyman identifies another culprit. This young man is one of Munro's new breed: "He had a keen, clever, hard-lined face, the face of a man who, in an earlier stage of European history, might have been a warlike prior, awkward to tackle at the council-board, greatly to be avoided where blows were being exchanged."

The clergyman explains to Yeovil that the poor have been left helpless and bitter by the German conquest and are looking for scapegoats: "One thing you may be sure of, they do not blame themselves. No true Londoner ever admits that fault lies at his door. 'No, I never!' is an exclamation that is on his lips from earliest childhood, whenever he is charged with anything blameworthy or punishable. That is why school discipline was ever a thing repugnant to the schoolboard child and his parents . . . Public schoolboys and private schoolboys of the upper and middle class had their fling and took their thrashings, when they were found out, as a piece of bad luck, but 'our Bert' and 'our Sid' were of those for whom there is no condemnation; if *they* were punished it was for faults that 'no, they never' committed. Naturally the grown-up generation of Berts and Sids, the voters and householders, do not realize, still less admit, that it was they who called the tune to which the politicians danced. They had to choose between the vote-mongers and the so-called 'scare-mongers,' and their verdict was for the vote-mongers all the time."

Munro makes another final reversal in *When William Came* as thorough as his disavowal of his younger self. An elderly and titled woman is no longer something to defy and mock as a surrogate of Aunt Tom. She has now become, in the person of Eleanor, Dowager Lady Greymarten, the very spine of the Empire. "The affairs of the county had not sufficed for her untiring activities of mind and body; in the wider field of national and Imperial service she had worked and schemed and fought with an energy and a far-sightedness that came probably from the blend of caution and bold restlessness in her Scottish blood . . . Spadework when necessary and leadership when called for, came alike within the scope of her activities, and not least of her achievements, though perhaps she hardly realized it, was the force of her example, a lone, indomitable fighter calling to the half-caring and the half-discouraged, to the laggard and the slow-moving."

Gentlemen write a bread-and-butter note to their hostess. Munro wrote a bread-and-butter chapter.

Though old and lacking strength, Lady Graymarten has the spirit to urge that Yeovil never accept the German occupation as a *fait accompli*. Whom can they enlist in the cause? There is only the future generation, and Munro, however many ties to his younger self he has severed, still puts his faith in England's youth. Not in their untrammeled individualism or the romance of their separate worlds, not in Clovis or Bertie van Tahn. Munro counts upon those young men who wear uniforms and march in lock step. In his vision, England is to be saved by her Boy Scouts.

The Scouts have been scheduled to march through Hyde Park, a ceremony that will crown England's acceptance of the new regime. To guarantee their allegiance, they have been flattered and cosseted and deluged with examples of Teutonic favor. Waiting for them to appear, one British collaborator assures another that these khaki-clad boys will be the Janissaries of the Empire. A throng has turned out to watch the march through Hyde Park gate, and the Emperor and his suite have come to inspect the young troops. Behind the police lines, the crowd starts to stretch and crane expectantly. A clock clangs three, the hour for the march to begin. Yeovil has come, ashamed that so far he has made no resistance.

Now a restlessness sweeps the crowd, a murmur. Something has gone wrong. The novel ends:

"And in the pleasant May sunshine the Eagle standard floated and flapped, the black and yellow pennons shifted restlessly, Emperor and Princess, Generals and guards, sat stiffly in their saddles, and waited.

"And waited. . . ."

Ethel watched her brother writing a part of the novel while they were together on holiday at Rye, in Sussex, and she asked herself where his gift had come from. Their paternal grandfather had once been told by a marquis that he wrote "purely classical language," and Aunt Tom believed that Hector had inherited his talent from him, even though Grandfather Munro had written exclusively about the politics of India. Ethel was inclined to share the credit with their maternal grandmother, Lucy—a clever woman, a Celt and a McNab. All Ethel knew for certain was that Hector's talents were entirely native. Writing her memoir, she assured the reader disarmingly that her brother never "went through a literary correspondence course."

At Rye, Munro had sometimes gone off alone in the woods to write; for absolute quiet, he explained to Ethel. But he could write anywhere, on anything. During a stay in Barnstaple in August 1913, he had jotted down a paragraph of the last chapter of *When William Came* on the back of his bill from the Golden Lion Hotel. His rapid flow did not pause for full names. Cicely was "Cic," Ronnie "Ron." Nor did he render simple words in full. Going back to make a fair copy, Munro would know that "t" stood for "the" and "wi" for "with." The passage dealt with Cicely's trading Ronnie Storre for a new admirer, and it went into his novel almost exactly as he drafted it. The most extensive addition was a summation that had come to him later: "To feminine acquaintances with fewer advantages of purse and brains and looks she might figure as 'that Yeovil woman,' but never had she given them justification to allude to her as 'poor Cicely Yeovil.'"

A writer can hardly be more serious than to predict the fall of his civilization, and the reviewers rewarded Munro accordingly. The *Times Literary Supplement* found *When William Came,* at six shillings, a "remarkable *tour de force* worked out with great cleverness," and the review praised the ending for introducing a note of hope without falling into sensationalism. The *Spectator's* long and admiring review a month later praised the book as a clever and bitter fantasia. The reviewer's one concern was whether the author might have neutralized the scathing nature of his satire with so much wit.

The notice that pleased Munro most was not a public one. He had sent a copy of his novel to Lord Roberts, a hero of the Boer War and an advocate of national service for home defense. Roberts was past eighty when he responded to the gift; ten months later, called back to duty as head of the India Expeditionary Force, he caught a chill and died in France.

"Dear Sir," Roberts wrote, "I have now read your book 'When William Came' and must tell you how much interested I have been by it and how thoroughly I approve the moral it teaches. I hope the book will be widely read and generally appreciated as it deserves to be."

Munro treasured the note and parted with it only long enough to send it to Charlie that he might make a copy. Their father, dead for seven years, was not available to appreciate the man Hector Munro had become. But Roberts, graduate of Eton and Sandhurst, field marshal and earl, came near to making an acceptable substitute.

14

The Mappined Life (1914)

If short-story writers produce novels to satisfy a public expectation, novelists write plays from the more private prompting of avarice. No doubt it looked as easy to Munro as it had once looked to Henry James: six weeks' work for a lifetime annuity. It was time to hear the audience cheering his imperishable lines. Twice before, Munro had set a foot toward the stage in melodramatic playlets, "Karl-Ludwig's Window" and "The Death Trap." They had been mere exercises. When Munro turned serious about a stage success, he wrote a drawing-room comedy called *The Watched Pot* and took it to Frederick Harrison, manager of the Haymarket Theatre. Harrison returned the manuscript with the remark that it was interesting but unplayable, and suggested that Munro join talents with Charles Maude, whose brother, Cyril, was one of Harrison's leading actors, in the hope that Maude's craftsmanship could salvage the play. That initial rejection left Munro wary. As early as the *Bodleian* interview in 1912, he had been making gentlemanly apologies on behalf of any producer who might decline his play.

"You have written for the theatre?" the interviewer asked.

" 'Yes,' was the grim reply. 'But I have not yet had anything produced.'

" 'That is surprising, for you have great gifts for writing dialogue.'

" 'Well, I have been very near making my public appearance as a dramatist, but it has not come off yet. Personally I don't believe it ever will. But you know how difficult it is to get a drama by a new man accepted. One can't blame the managers. Most of them have their plans arranged for some years ahead—two or three years ahead, anyway—and after all, there are only a very limited number of theatres.' "

Hector worked with Charles Maude over an extended period, Maude urging the cutting of any line that impeded the action, Munro standing firm for his jokes. Many of those jokes, while undeniably luscious, were no longer fresh. As Munro's mind became increasingly occupied with political matters, he went back to his stories and plucked out their best lines like raisins from a pudding. By the time Maude gave way and the play was finished, the war was upon them and, as Munro had predicted, *The Watched Pot* went unproduced in his lifetime.

Ben Travers, who had the playwright's knack, speculated later on why a writer so gifted as Saki should translate badly to the stage. He decided that the very triumph of wit was its artificiality. One could visualize Saki's world but one could not represent it literally, and, for all its tricks and artifices, the stage is very literal.

Munro and Maude had also disagreed over plot, and it is hard to see that either of them won. Several women are scheming to marry Trevor Bavvel and thus become the mistress of his estate, Briony. Trevor's mother is called Hortensia Bavvel, but she is Aunt Tom once again, a village tyrant who decides every dispute in the neighborhood. Like Francesca Bassington, Hortensia will lose her dominion when a marriage occurs, and she has frightened away all candidates for her son's hand. Now, however, she will be absent briefly from Briony, and the women gathered there plan to stage a revel of the sort Hortensia specifically proscribes in the hope that, in the excitement, Trevor will propose to one of them. The play's other characters are also familiar Saki people traveling under new names. René St. Gall is Reginald. ("This suit I've got on was paid for last month, so you may judge how old it is.") Ludovic Bavvel, Trevor's uncle, plays René's Other. ("Things that are lent to you, René, are like a hopeless passion, they're never returned.") Agatha is clearly another Agnes. ("Agatha is one of those unaccountable people who are impelled to keep up an inconsequential flow of conversation if they detect you trying to read a book or write a letter, and if you should be suffering from an acknowledged headache she invariably bangs out something particularly triumphant on the nearest piano by way of showing that she at least is not downhearted.") Sybil Bomont has the requisite sharp tongue, although her lines have occasionally been honed elsewhere. Sybil says, "A husband with asthma has all the advantages of a captive golf ball; you always know pretty well where to put your hand on him when you want him," exactly as though the same thing hadn't been said one afternoon at Cicely Yeovil's house. For that matter, René St. Gall has no idea that his best stroke—"Sparrowsby is one of those people who would be enormously improved by death"—is a quotation from Clovis Sangrail.

Trevor is another of those lackadaisical young men who must be treed into matrimony. Trevor never says, with the resignation and greater candor of a similar young man in "Karl Ludwig's Window," that since he would never marry anyone he loved, it doesn't matter whom his mother marries him to. Truths like that are left to René: "I dislike the idea of women about a house; they accumulate dust." Trevor will marry all right, but when he does he wants a chum.

Over the course of three acts, the calculating women have many chances to insult and backbite. Their dialogue is not always consistent with their characters, but well-bred misogyny seemed to gratify a matinee audience.

"Sybil: Why is it that plain women are always so venomous?

"Agatha: Oh, if you're going to be introspective, my dear."

Then it is Sybil's turn. "Agatha: But if I had a really nice man for a husband I should want him to be able to come with me wherever I went."

"Sybil: A woman who takes her husband about with her everywhere is like a cat that goes on playing with a mouse long after she's killed it."

Sybil is described as having "a fatal gift for detecting the weak spots in her fellow humans and sticking her spikes into them. Matrimony is not reputed to be an invariable bed of roses, but there is no reason why it should be a cactus-hedge." For Mrs. Vulpy, who is waiting impatiently for news of her ailing husband's death so that she may enter the Bavvel sweepstakes, Munro dusts off another line from Clovis: "Brevity is the soul of widowhood." Near the final curtain, the banter runs down and a few moments of stilted exposition reveal that Trevor and Clare, a good sort, have been married all along but were forced to maintain the secret because Clare's aunt forbade the marriage.

The Watched Pot had to wait for another war to have its London premiere. In 1943, the play was chosen to represent the Edwardian Age in a festival of English comedy. When it went to New York four years later, Brooks Atkinson expressed surprise that it had languished for more than thirty years; worse plays had made it to the stage regularly. Another critic found in the dialogue evidence that had Munro survived the war he could have written comedies throughout the twenties to match those of Maugham, Coward and Frederick Lonsdale. But in fact there is little evidence in *The Watched Pot* of a theatrical sense, still less evidence that Munro would have been flattered by the comparison, and none at all after 1914 that he had any intention of writing another comedy.

Munro's invention might be flagging but his facility was not. He was now writing two stories a month for the *Morning Post,* topical verse for the *Daily Express,* imaginary dialogues between famous men for the *Bystander,* and, for the *Outlook,* a weekly review of actions in the House of Commons under the title "Potted Parliament." Munro had written of the greedy feeding of sheep before a storm, and there was something of that same frantic air in his outpouring of work throughout 1913 and the first half of the next year.

The verse was the most negligible of his production. In place of Carruthers Gould, Munro had teamed himself with a cruder cartoonist who signed his work "Pat." Their collaboration exploited such predictable themes as British military unreadiness, the Irish nationalist movement and the suffragettes. One of Hector's verses speaks amply for the others: "A suffragette Lobelia was / She early left this life because / (She had the rottenest of luck) / She too sincerely hunger-struck."

Hector was speaking to different readers from those he had first delighted in the *Westminster Gazette.* He had moved to a more commercial, less literary venue when he began selling stories to the *Bystander,* and its editors had showed their appreciation by inviting him to a dinner for contributors at the Trocadero restaurant. Then, with the publication of *When William Came,* Hector became a figure worthy of being included when John Lane gave a tea party in his office for Stephen Leacock.

The *Bystander* published three of what Munro labeled "Heart-to-Heart Talks." They ran with a mock disclaimer: "We have no other authority than that of our contributor that the conversations between the persons in question have actually taken place." The first was a dialogue between Nijinsky and the House of Commons' Liberal whip, the joke being that the dancer wants to be a politician and the politician wants to talk about the ballet. Another promised conversation between Bernard Shaw and the Baron Marschall von Bieberstein, the German Ambassador, but there was no dialogue, only a torrent from Shaw. "I am not a happy man," Munro had him complaining. "In recent years my life has been overshadowed with a great dread. *What has happened to Shakespeare may happen to me.* My works will live for all time, but I, physically speaking, am mortal; fifty or sixty years after my death who knows but that a school of critics may arise, in America and in your country, and perhaps here in England, who will attribute all my plays to Arthur Balfour? There is a horrible plausibility about the idea which never ceases to haunt me. Shall I be depicted to future generations as a chattering, posing, after-dinner-talkative individual who screened with his noisy personality the identity of the cynical, retiring, world-indifferent man of affairs and man of letters?"

Shaw speculated that the way he had treated marriage in his plays might only feed the controversy. "Will not the theorists of a future generation fasten on my handling of the subject and declare it to be the work of a man who stood outside the marriage-tie as a philosophic and satirical onlooker, the attitude of a Manx cat towards a cat that has got its tail jammed in a door, and will they not triumphantly point out that Arthur Balfour was a persistent bachelor?"

The last heart-to-heart talk was between Oscar Hammerstein, the American impresario, and Dom Manoel, lately deposed as king of Portugal. " 'You and I have this much in common,' said the purveyor of grand opera, 'we are both kings. You are the sometime king of a sometime kingdom, with a seating capacity for about six million souls and emergency exits all along the frontier.'

" 'Don't,' said the ex-king, 'omit to mention its unseating capacity, which is considerable.' "

Hammerstein hit upon an idea that, in the seventy years since Munro wrote the piece, has come to look more like prophecy than satire. Grand opera, churchgoing and county cricket matches were not drawing crowds because they did not involve their audiences. Hammerstein would revivify opera, at least, by making it obligatory for everyone to come in the costume of the opera being given.

" 'Just imagine what the house would be like on a *Carmen* night, the mantillas and combs and roses in the hair, the toreador costumes and Spanish uniforms. How the audience would love themselves, and what crowds would gather outside to see them come in. What *éclat,* what advertisement, what receipts! Not of course that I care about the money. And there would be lots of other operas that would be equally popular. For instance, how the young bucks would fancy themselves in the costumes of the "Eugene Onégin" period. It is one of the rules of grand opera that the singers are never good-looking, so the bloods in the stalls and boxes could compare themselves favourably with their counterparts on the stage . . . Can't you imagine some titled dowager saying to another, 'Yes, she sings quite well, and her technique is faultless, as far as I'm any judge, but this lace that I'm wearing really belonged to the Queen of Bohemia.' "

" 'By the way,' said the ex-king, 'what about the operas placed in classical times, in which the characters are supposed to wear next to nothing—just a panther-skin and a garland of ivy? Wouldn't they present rather a problem?'

" 'A problem that I am quite ready to grapple with,' said Mr. Hammerstein. 'I should merely have to build a larger opera house.' "

His new affiliation with the *Outlook* reflected the gradual hardening of Munro's views. Owned by a Conservative member of Parliament, Walter Guinness, it was literate, informed and fiercely biased. Munro signed his weekly dispatches Saki, but there was little of Saki's amused tolerance to his reporting.

His friend from St. Petersburg days, Roy Reynolds, published a book on his experiences, *My Russian Year,* and Munro arranged to review it for the *Morning Post.* Reynolds' text was enlivened with the author's photographs, many of young men; Munro did not comment on them. He praised his friend's natural passion for investigation, which he claimed was a national trait of British journalists, and his sympathetic temperament, which was not. British correspondents more often hid their feelings "under an impenetrable crust of reserve and shyness." As a fellow journalist, Munro could assure readers that Reynolds' many anecdotes were true. "And every now and then he breaks off into an apposite piece of gossip concerning the life-story of Dmitri Pavlovitch or Anna Mikhailovna or some other unit in his crowd of acquaintances—and they have the merit of being real people with disguised names, and not names journalistically disguised as real people."

But when Munro himself returned to weekly reporting, he did not find that literalness worth emulating. To make a point, he often fell back on his storyteller's imagination, and he peopled the Commons with characters of his own invention. Valerian, who sits for North Subbage, is a dapper Liberal. ("Doubtless there are many men in the House who know how to dress; Valerian is one of the comparatively few who put that knowledge into practice.") Clode was Munro's Conservative voice, willing to debate any issue the author thought needed illuminating. "Rather annoying," says Clode at one juncture, "for a man to boast that he's 'got the Tories on the run,' and then to find that he's left their candidate in a comfortable sitting position." These are the years of Munro recycling his wit, and he had already given the same construction to Mrs. Vulpy in his play. ("Nothing is more discouraging than to have a man say that you've ruined his life, and then find out that you haven't even given him after-dinner insomnia.")

When he dealt with genuine Members of Parliament, Munro's descriptions were deftly partisan; he could always find more delectable frailties in men of the opposition. There was Sir David Brynmor Jones, "with his voice of honey, suggestive of a July afternoon in an apiary." Mr. John Ward was "a samovar, bubbling over with self-esteem." After Herbert Samuel elucidated the Liberal budget, Munro decided that he "would really be invaluable as menu-writer in a cheap restaurant. A better attempt at disguising a hash under a wealth of consoling language has seldom been witnessed."

Indignation could overcome urbanity. Munro truly detested Lloyd George, "armed with his meanness and his inaccuracy, the one as glaring as the other." When some members of the House considered taxing Lloyd George with his inaccuracies, Munro warned that "one might as well lecture to a mole on colour-blindness." "One understands of course that Mr. Lloyd George feels that these attacks on him are a little unreasonable; a Cabinet Minister who talks about Tory dungheaps may naturally claim to have infused a certain dignity and pleasantness into party politics, and to expect in return a generous measure of courtesy and consideration from his opponents. However, public life is full of these disappointments."

Munro could depend on Ramsay MacDonald, the ranking Labour Minister, to provide magnificent denunciations "delivered with the gusto of an orator who can seldom command a hearing from a public meeting of his own supporters." Winston Churchill "intervened in the guise of a peacemaker, and succeeded in making matters rather worse." When appropriate, Munro could reach back ten years and insult a member with an exotic image from his travels. "Russell sat on the Treasury Bench, incessantly muttering and chattering to himself, reminding one of a Pomak deputy in the Bulgarian Sobranye industriously telling his beads and reciting verses of the Koran."

Much of the debate during that session was over Home Rule for Ireland. Even if Munro had not had a brother whose livelihood depended on English sovereignty, his opinion would have been predictable, and he had no patience with attempts to be politic. He complained, for example, that to try to pin down Asquith on the subject was to set a trap to catch a moonbeam. Meantime, Munro saw the uncertainty breeding great danger. "The country had been brought to the brink of civil war and left there, as one leaves a parcel at left-luggage office."

For the author of *When William Came,* the debate over defense measures took on special significance. He was irritated when the War Minister called for the mustering of a few well-to-do reserve outfits rather than mobilizing the mass of the population for home defense. "In making a charge of neglect of public duty it is always well to single out the few for condemnation and absolve the many—the many will be certain to applaud the justice of your discrimination. If you do not go down to posterity as a statesman who looked ahead, you will at least be remembered as a politician who looked carefully around."

Munro was alert to his opponents' hedging in parliamentary debate, their judicious interpositions of "as far as I know" or "technically speaking." He generously gave Clode the stanza that came out of his frustration and contempt: "As Clode has aptly improvised on Omar: 'The moving finger writes, and having writ / Not all their irony nor all their wit / Can pin you down to anything you *said.*' "

Debate in the House over the Irish question had become so heated that the *Westminster Gazette* took to pleading for decorum. Munro noted that the greatest offenders were the Liberals and then indulged in a bit of reminiscence to show why no Liberal yapping would deter a stout heart like Andrew Bonar Law's. "It used to be required of me once that I should ride about the highways and byways of Mandalay at dead of night, visiting sleepy police patrols, and I almost invariably had a pack of native dogs yelping and demonstrating at my pony's heels; they doubtless thought that they were a source of extreme embarrassment, but I missed them dreadfully if private feuds or other business drew them off in some other direction."

The Commons put aside the Irish question briefly for a flurry over how to exploit the oil reserves recently found in Persia. Otherwise, it was Ireland night and noon. Munro quoted the observation of "a youthful Liberal peer," who may have been as genuine as Clode: "If George III. had only had the sagacity to lose us Ireland as well as the American colonies what a world of trouble we should have been saved!"

What is striking about the sessions is how little notice the House was taking of any threat from Germany. Thomas Guthrie recalled seeing in the New Year 1914 at a supper party at the Carlton, and as the couples waltzed and tangoed he had the feeling that the year would be happy and lucky. Guthrie had run into Munro at a party a few weeks earlier, but the author of *When William Came* was giving his fellow guests no cause for alarm. Instead, Munro treated them to an imitation of Sarah Bernhardt reciting "The Walrus and the Carpenter" in French.

His prolific output was slightly cramping Munro's social rounds, and if Lady Charnwood had been as inclined as Lady St. Helier to cherish literary detritus, she could have added this note to her collection: "Dear Lady Charnwood, I hoped to have been able to call this afternoon, but it is one of my involved Sundays—that is to say I have work on hand that must be finished. Will Thursday or

Friday of this week suit you for dinner?" So little of Munro's handwriting has survived that it is impossible to say whether the misspellings in the next paragraph speak of haste or the slapdash nature of his early schooling: "The prescious parcel arrived safely. Sincerely your's H.H. Munro."

The first Saturday night in August 1914 Munro spent in his customary fashion. He went with a friend for a swim at the baths; then tea and a walk in the Green Park, and dinner and a look-in at the Cocoa Tree. Coming out, he passed the Geographical Society's club, where a dinner was being given for Sir Ernest Shackleton, the explorer, who was about to set off for the South Pole. That prospect brought back to Munro the leavetakings in his own life, and for a moment he felt sorry for Shackleton, leaving England and losing touch with all that was happening. By now the impending crisis was impossible to ignore. On July 29, the German Imperial Council at Potsdam had decided on war with Russia and France but hoped for England's neutrality. At noon on this Saturday, August 1, a state of war between Germany and Russia was officially declared, and German troops were reported to be massing along the French border. One could hear the exhilaration in the newsboy's cry and in the nervous speculation on the street. Munro found it hard to concentrate on anything. It was Saturday night and early, but he went home to wait.

On Monday, August 3, Munro pushed through the crowds at the House of Commons to hear Sir Edward Grey, the Secretary of State for Foreign Affairs, respond to the weekend's developments. Would Grey proclaim that Belgium was vital to Britain's interests? The German force had moved across the French frontier on Sunday, and there was little doubt that they would cross into Belgium today. Grey could choose war or peace, and Munro was in a fever of excitement, not sure which path the nation would take.

"For one memorable and uncomfortable hour the House of Commons had the attention of the nation and most of the world concentrated on it. Grey's speech, when one looked back at it, was a statesman-like utterance, delivered in an excellent manner, dignified and convincing. To sit listening to it, in uncertainty for a long time as to what line of policy it was going to announce, with all the accumulated doubts and suspicions of the previous forty-eight hours heavy on one's mind, was an experience that one would not care to repeat often in a lifetime. Men who read it as it was spelled out jerkily on the tape-machines, letter by letter, told me that the strain of uncertainty was even more cruel; and I can well believe it. When the actual tenor of the speech became clear, and one knew beyond a doubt where we stood, there was only room for one feeling; the miserable tension of the past two days had been removed, and one discovered that one was slowly recapturing the lost sensation of being in a good temper."

We know that in psychology, as in economics, war can sometimes alleviate depression. But not everyone in the House that day found the impending conflict a tonic. For the pacifists, especially those from the Labour Party, Munro felt a depth of hatred that it was now his duty to proclaim. "Many of them are men who have gloatingly threatened us with class warfare in this country—warfare in which rifles and machine-guns should be used to settle industrial disputes; they have seemed to take a ghoulish pleasure in predicting a not-far-distant moment when Britons shall range themselves in organized combat, not against an aggressive foreign enemy, but against their own kith and kin. Never have they been more fluent with these hints and incitements than during the present Session; if a crop of violent armed outbreaks does not spring up one of these days in this country it will not be for lack of sowing of seed. Now these men read us moral lectures on the wickedness of war . . . There are other men in the anti-war party who seem to be obsessed with the idea of snatching commercial advantages out of the situation, regardless of other considerations which usually influence men of honour.

"There seems to be some confusion of mind in these circles of political thought between a nation of shopkeepers and a nation of shoplifters.

"If these men are on the side of the angels, may I always have a smell of brimstone about me."

Here stood revealed the moralist hidden within the satirist. Once freed, this scourge and scold could never be cajoled into taking up again with raillery and innuendo. Critics who lamented the loss of the bright social comment that Saki might have made throughout the twenties had not read attentively Munro's writings from the day England went to war.

15

The Quest
(1914-1916)

Leaving the House after Grey's speech, Munro went with Roy Reynolds and two friends to a chophouse in the Strand. On the way, pushing the others along at a tremendous pace, already in training for the exertions to come, he told them about Grey's delivery, how he had put on his eyeglasses to read a memorandum and then carefully taken them off before continuing, building an intolerable suspense, until Munro had found himself sweating from the strain.

At their table, a hapless waiter was the butt of Munro's new fervor. "Butter?" he asked.

"Cheese, no butter," Munro answered peremptorily. "There's a war on."

Within a day or two, Munro was hiring a horse to take exercise, something he had not done in recent years, and he was reviling himself for the slackness of his years in London. With approval, he watched the youths who were marching and shouting in the streets and waving the flags of France and Britain. Here were his Boy Scouts come to life. Perhaps sheer high spirits rather than true patriotism lay behind those outbursts, but Munro was relieved to see them all the same. How else could the young show their feelings? How could he?

Reynolds realized that Munro was determined to fight, but for the first week or two it looked impossible. However much his health had revived after Paris, Munro was still not strong and he was forty-three years old. To Reynolds he said, "And I have always looked forward to the romance of a European war." Then, on August 25, Munro was accepted as an enlisted man in the 2nd King Edward's Horse. He rushed from the military headquarters to the telegraph office to send his sister the one word she had been awaiting. Ethel considered it the most exciting and delightful message she had ever received, even though the operator had erred in the transcription. "Enroled," Munro's wire read, and perhaps it was a mistake but not an error. He was entering upon the last impersonation of his life.

We do not know how many men have gone off to war hoping not to come back because it is one of those wishes that, when fervent enough, is always granted. Certainly most men past the age of forty, because they have accepted the decline in their bodies, or because they have families to support, or because they are less brave than they may have been at twenty, either wait on the sidelines of a war or accept commissions that will make use of their talents and experience. When a man like Munro demands to enter the ranks, the questions arise that followed T. E. Lawrence into the service when he tried to pass as Airman Shaw or Ross. Saki's view of human nature would have prepared him for the fact that the popular response was apt to be a snigger. At John Lane, the editors gossiped that Munro had chosen to enter the ranks because his inverted tastes would find the pickings easier there. Leaving aside the dubious premise that young men of the lower economic classes were riper for seduction than those from public schools, we can see that the speculation missed the reverse metamorphosis that Saki had been willing upon himself, the transformation from a butterfly to one more earthbound slug.

Munro's writing had reflected the change and so had his reading. He sent away to the publisher for a life of Jesus, a purchase that would have been unlikely ten years ago from a man so mockingly anticlerical. But Munro was not the first doubter to be attracted in middle years to that holy rage against the times or to the idea of release through martyrdom from an intolerable world. Munro was also drawn to *The Golden Journey to Samarkand* by James Elroy Flecker, friend of Rupert Brooke and victim of consumption, who would soon go to Davos to die. Very likely Flecker's posturing recalled to Munro the youthful Hector. "Humour," Flecker had written at college, "is an abortive attempt at wit." And with their perfumed despair, his verses could take Munro back to the *Rubaiyat:* "When even lovers find their peace at last / And Earth is but a star, that once had shone."

A year after he read these thoughts, consoling in their finality, the war gave Munro a way to make his own peace. Marching resolutely, he set out for his Golgotha, a man tired of his earlier incarnations—of Hector and Saki and H. H. Munro. For such a man, accepting a commission would be to sustain those identities; certainly wearing an officer's uniform in Burma had given him little pleasure. Charlie chuckled proudly over his brother's enlistment and told his friends that Munro had "forgot a few years" to persuade the army to take him. But Munro had not forgot those years and they were not a few. He wanted to expunge half his life. He would start over. This time he would live his life the right way or he would end it.

King Edward's Horse was a natural choice for Munro. It dated, like his own political coming of age, from the Boer War and it drew largely on the overseas dominions, appropriate for a man whose family had served the crown in India and Burma. In 1914, the regiment was mobilized on the ninth of August, and some five hundred splendid horses were brought to the grounds of the Alexandra Palace. About the time Munro was enrolling, three hundred of those horses, most of them hunters, stampeded in their strange surroundings, and six had to be shot. A few days later, during a parade, the whistles of a river barge set off a second stampede. But by the time Munro joined the regiment, the skittishness had passed and training was proceeding again, although slowly and slackly. The grumble among officers and men alike was that the war would be over before they got to fight in it.

When it came, Munro's enlistment had been sudden, and on his second week in the regimental camp at Slough, near Windsor, he picked up some cheap purple-lined paper to notify his associates in London. "Dear Lane," he scrawled in a big round hand to his publisher, who had always been "Mr. Lane" before, "I am a trooper in the above force, and I've asked A. R. Reynolds (permanent address: National Liberal Club, Whitehall) to look after my literary affairs while I am on service. If anything 'conclusive' happens to me, my brother, C. A. Munro, governor, H. M. Prison, Mountjoy, Dublin, is my executor.

"I hope to get out" (here, lest he be misunderstood, Munro added a caret and "to the front") "in the course of a couple of months. It is only fitting that the author of 'When William Came' should go to meet William half way. I hope that things are going well with you. Very sincerely yours, (Trooper) H. H. Munro."

When Lord Kitchener came in late September to inspect Munro's division in Gornhambury Park, the men were sure they were on their way to the front. But another month passed and they were still in England. Lord Roberts, who had admired *When William Came,* had established a fund to help equip the hastily mobilized troops. From it King Edward's Horse received fifty excellent binoculars, but for the time being there was no enemy upon which to train them. Impatient privates and NCOs began seeking discharge from the regiment to take up commissions and get to France with the infantry. One second lieutenant went as reinforcement to the 9th Lancers; within a week he had reached the front, been wounded, and was back visiting his former comrades in King Edward's Horse.

Munro also left the regiment during the autumn, but

not to take up a commission. The demands of the cavalry had proved too strenuous, after all, for a man of his age and condition. He arranged a transfer to the 22nd Battalion of the Royal Fusiliers.

Three months before war was declared, Sir William Davison, the mayor of Kensington, had begun raising the 22nd Battalion as a service unit. Late in the fall of 1914, an artist designed a recruiting poster for the battalion that showed a wounded British soldier who had just dispatched three Uhlans. The caption read, "It's 4 to 1—come and help us lads, quick." Lord Kitchener saw the sketch and admired its spirit but he complained that the dead German cavalrymen looked too smart. "No Uhlan," he said, "ever had decently-cut breeches." The artist put in deep creases and Kitchener gave his approval.

Munro's own khaki uniform, like those of his comrades in the battalion, was a source of pride, since khaki was scarce and most government-raised regiments were still drilling in what was disparagingly called "work-house blue." But the 22nd's new commander, Major Randle Barnett Barker, a relative by marriage of Sir William's wife, had sent around to Harrod's and bought some of the last khaki to be had in London. Messrs. Lillywhites, the cricket outfitters, had a limited supply of leather, and they were induced to use it on equipment for Sir William's unit. The mayor also bought and distributed eleven hundred of the best quality Kropp razors.

An exemplary soldier in all other regards, Munro had not joined the army to maintain a smart appearance. The one snapshot that has survived shows him toting a pail, shirt unbuttoned, sleeves carelessly rolled and no evidence that he had used his Kropp razor. He had grown a raffish mustache as consolation for having his upper teeth pulled sometime during training; Charlie's family regretted the loss and blamed the bad army diet. Whatever the cause, with its new dental plate Munro's mouth looked incapable of smiling. Ethel loathed the picture and refused to use it in her memoir. But his own scowling visage pleased Munro enough for him to send it to the *Bystander* for use with a reprint of one of his battalion articles.

Munro's fluency in German was a nuisance to him in his

role as trooper. The high command put continuing pressure on those who spoke the language to take jobs as interpreters, and during the time the 22nd was based at Horsham, Munro was conscripted to teach German to his mates. Beginning in December 1914, he was to teach for four hours each week, overseen by the Board of Education, which quickly confirmed his worst view of bureaucracy by ordering the teachers to start with principles of German grammar. Munro and the other instructors refused. A class of tired men, they said, simply would not listen to a lot of dry rules about an unknown language. But Lady Charnwood sent him two dictionaries for the classes, and her mother dispatched a box of chocolates and lemon drops, which Munro shared with the other men, especially the poorer ones who could not afford many treats on pay of one shilling a day.

His unit was doing a good deal of marching—twenty-three miles one day, much of it quick time—and Munro was gratified to find that the next day he was neither stiff nor tired. He had no reason to regret refusing a commission although the offers continued to come in. Besides his mastery of German, Munro was demonstrably a gentleman and that could make his service as a trooper awkward. Only one approach seems to have tempted him: an officer's rank in the Argyll and Sutherland Highlanders. After a short deliberation, Munro rejected it. He told Roy Reynolds that he distrusted his ability to be a good officer; he may have meant that he was not sure he could send his men to their death. More likely his reluctance was for his own sake, not theirs. He had joined the army to be at one with other men; pinning bars to his shoulders would only separate him from them.

After Munro's death, Lord Charnwood took offense at the idea that his friend might have questioned his own fitness, and he questioned Reynolds' accuracy. Munro, he said, would never have funked a challenge; his motive in refusing a commission must have been entirely lofty. To Ethel, Munro had offered what he considered a practical reason for staying in the ranks: to become an officer would require so much additional training that he would be starting all over again and might never get to the war at all. He also repeated the misgivings about his temperament that had ruffled Charnwood. "The 3½ months' training that I have had will fit me to be a useful infantry soldier and I should be a very indifferent officer. Still it is nice to have had the offer."

In February 1915, Aunt Tom died in Barnstaple. She had been the goad to much of his best work, a compelling incentive for remaining detached and amused throughout his prolonged youth; a model during his middle age, when he turned intolerant and martial. On February 13, Munro wrote to Charlie from the Golden Lion to tell him about the funeral. Munro was now forty-four years old, but his letter tried to reach across the years and extend to Charlie the puny consolations of the nursery.

"The funeral went off all right yesterday; Mrs. H. Munro and Effie came with me, and we had Manning and Colman, Aunt Tom's old gardeners, among the bearers and there was a good deal of genuine sorrow shown by the old men and others whom she had befriended. Also, considering that she had outlived so many of her friends, the display of flowers was a fine one. As I have to go back early tomorrow, Sunday, I am having power of attorney granted to Ethel to act for me, as executor, and we are employing Toller and Co. as lawyers to wind up the estate. Among the stacks of letters I have gone thro (only a fraction of the whole) is one from Uncle W. which I enclose, written in 1889, the year after we were in Dresden. Besides some plain and salutary speaking to Aunt Tom about the aunts' indebtedness to the Gov. he alludes in scathing terms to a campaign of abuse which Aunt Augusta seems to have directed against us 3. All of that generation are dead now, so the letter may as well be destroyed when you have read it. I think Ethel and you and I may feel some pride in reflecting that the old folks at the end of their lives came to see that we were likable and loveable and they obviously greatly preferred us to our cousins."

To be back with his unit meant more marching and waiting. Late in February 1915, the 22nd moved from

Horsham to new barracks at Roffey, a couple of miles away. After eight days, Munro wrote that most of his company found life very jolly although the move had meant a lot of extra chores. He himself had spent three days digging in water-logged trenches, and while he knew that Ethel would regard that as a formidable job, he had found that he was a good digger and could take satisfaction in watching the water drain off. The previous day, Munro had been orderly for the thirty men in his hut and discovered that drawing their rations, cleaning the hut and washing up their plates and cups had kept him busy from 5:45 A.M. until 5:30 P.M., with only a hasty interval for his own meals.

Despite what his family believed, camp food was substantial and nourishing, with a large breakfast of porridge and milk, plus steak and tomatoes or eggs and bacon. Dinner at midday included meat carefully measured to weigh twelve ounces with the bone; in a typical week that meant roast beef with Yorkshire pudding on Monday and Wednesday, and on the other days meat pie, boiled beef, mutton or curry. The evening meal was light—tea with bread and butter, plus salmon, herring, sardines or bloaters. For a man who had been content with lunch at a corner house, army fare was no deprivation.

It might be exaggerating to say that these were the happiest days in Munro's life. Most writers are happy, if at all, only on the days that they write. But since other men were now free to leave their wives and children behind, perhaps Munro experienced that same parole from writing. At least his letters to Ethel smack of physical joy. "We have a good deal of fun, with skirmishing raids at night with neighbouring huts, and friendly games of footer; it is like being boy and man at the same time. All the same I wish we could count on going away soon; it is a poor game to be waiting when others are bearing the brunt and tasting the excitement of real war-fare."

Excitement. Romance. Those were Munro's usual words for war. In "The Toys of Peace," a story published in the spring of 1914, he had argued that his fascination was normal for the human race, taking as his text a newspaper clipping about an organization that was proposing to do away with toy soldiers and guns and substitute "peace toys"—plows and the tools of industry. Munro's story follows two brothers, both under twelve, who receive those worthy playthings with indifference until they find that they can use them to fight the wars of Louis the Fourteenth. It is a clever piece, a plea for the primacy of the Hannibals and Bonapartes of history. Young Bertie's enthusiasm for gore makes us smile. He is only a child and he has never seen a war. But Munro was no child, and his enthusiasm was even greater. He boasted of it now in the *Morning Post* under the heading "An Old Love."

" 'I know nothing about war,' a boy of nineteen said to me two days ago, 'except, of course, that I've heard of its horrors; yet, somehow, in spite of the horrors, there seems to be something in it different to anything else in the world, something a little bit finer.'

"He spoke wistfully, as one who feared that to him war would always be an unreal, distant, secondhand thing, to be read about in special editions, and peeped at through the medium of cinematograph shows. He felt that the thing that was a little bit finer than anything else in the world would never come into his life.

"Nearly every red-blooded human boy has had war, in some shape or form, for his first love; if his blood has remained red and he has kept some of his boyishness in after life, that first love will never have been forgotten. No one could really forget those wonderful leaden cavalry soldiers; the horses were as sleek and prancing as though they had never left the parade-ground, and the uniforms were correspondingly spick and span, but the amount of campaigning and fighting they got through was prodigious. There are other unforgettable memories for those who had brothers to play with and fight with, of sieges and ambushes and pitched encounters, of the slaying of an entire garrison without quarter, or of chivalrous, punctilious courtesy to a defeated enemy. Then there was the slow unfolding of the long romance of actual war, particularly of European war, ghastly, devastating, heartrending in its effect, and yet somehow captivating to the imagination. The Thirty Years' War was one of the most hideously cruel wars ever waged, but, in conjunction with the subsequent campaigns of the Great Louis, it throws a glamour over the scene of the present struggle. The thrill that those far-off things call forth in us may be ethically indefensible, but it comes in the first place from something too deep to be driven out; the magic region of the Low Countries is beckoning to us again, as it beckoned to our forefathers, who went campaigning there almost from force of habit."

Munro had written recently to Ethel about the temerity of a young man at home who asked whether Munro would use his influence to get him an engagement on the London stage. Munro lacked that sort of connection. But that was not the point. Here was a healthy youth of twenty-two thinking that it was more important to study voice than to join the battle as Munro, twice his age, had done. "You may imagine the perfectly horrible reply he got," Munro assured his sister.

He returned to that sort of young man in his article for the *Morning Post:*

"One must admit that we have in these Islands a variant from the red-blooded type. One or two young men have assured me that they are not in the least interested in the war—'I'm not at all patriotic, you know,' they announced, as one might announce that one was not a vegetable or did not use a safety-razor. There are others whom I have met within the recent harrowing days who had no place for the war crisis in their thoughts and conversations; they would talk by the hour about chamber-music, Greek folk-dances, Florentine art, and the difficulty of getting genuine old oak furniture, but the national honour and the national danger were topics that bored them. One felt that the war would affect them chiefly as involving a possible shortage in the supply of eau-de-Cologne or by debarring them from visiting some favourite art treasure at a Munich gallery. It is inconceivable that these persons were ever boys, they have certainly not grown up into men; one cannot call them womanish—the women of our race are made of different stuff. They belong to no sex, and it seems a pity that they should belong

to any nation; other nations probably have similar en-
cumbrances, but we seem to have more of them than we
either desire or deserve."

With that, Munro abated, having confirmed the maxim
that no one is more intolerant than a convert. He turned
next to a more familiar object of contempt, the merchants
and traders who had urged neutrality because it would be
good for their commerce. Since Clovis had long scorned
such men, it was less jarring now to hear Munro denounc-
ing them than to hear him disavowing in the name of
national honor his most splendid creations.

At about the same time he was composing this screed,
Munro furnished Ethel with more details about the fun in
his hut—the men "never seem too tired to indulge in sport
or ragging"—and the equal pleasure he took in the work.
It was hard some days but not incessant, as it had been in
King Edward's Horse. "I was O.C.'s orderly on a field-
day on Wednesday and was jumping brooks and scrambling up slippery banks and through thickets with a pack
on my back that I should scarcely have thought myself
capable of carrying at all a few months ago, and I came
home quite fit."

For the 22nd Battalion's *Fortnightly Gazette,* Munro
compiled a "Diary of the War," as it was being chronicled
in the newspapers. His first entry, dated August 11, 1914,
ran, "The war a week old. Germany feeling the intolerable
strain of the campaign," and his last, on April 16, 1915,
was "Financial strain beginning to be felt in Germany.
Famine in Dresden. Positively the last available Austrians
being hurried into the fight."

Munro whiled away the remainder of the spring of 1915
by writing more articles for the *Gazette.* They were always signed "By Saki, 'A' Company," and the soldiers in
the other companies did not always know that they were
reading the work of a noted London writer. Some of them
remembered years later that there had been a "Sarky" in
their battalion who had got his name from being always a
little, don't y'know, acid, a little sarcastic.

Any young actor in London, if he had seen the Fusiliers'
journal, would have agreed about the sarcasm. Once

safely in uniform, Munro was showing no mercy toward the civilian life he had put behind him. His years of listening impassively to jokes about nancy boys might have deepened his contempt for society but instead that contempt had turned inward. If it were not for the evident pain in it, Munro's constant effort to ally himself finally with the majority might be distasteful rather than simply sad.

"Many of their comrades of the stage have gone to the war or to train for the war," one of his short pieces concludes, "but the 'Boys of the Lap-dog breed' remain trilling their songs, capering their dances, speaking their lines as complacently as though no war was in progress . . . They have set themselves as something apart, and after the War let them be treated as something apart; something human and decorative and amusing; but something not altogether British, not exactly masculine, something that one does not treat as an equal."

Other articles were mere entertainment. In "The Soldier's Guide to Cinema," Munro anticipated for his less urbane mates some of the plot devices that were already trite barely twenty years after the invention of motion pictures. "If a man goes to work in a lonely waste, leaving his wife alone in the log hut, it is a moral certainty that he will hear her scream for help before the morning is very far advanced. He stands and listens; she is probably the only wife he possesses, at any rate within a radius of a couple of hundred of miles, but he listens to make sure that the screams really concern him. When he has convinced himself that it is certainly his wife that is screaming, he puts down his axe and shades his eyes to find out what she is screaming about; in those remote solitudes so many women scream out of sheer boredom. It dawns on him at last that the two strangers who are dragging her about by the hair and hacking at her with knives have something to do with the noise that she is making. Even then he does nothing violent and immediate in the way of sprinting till he has turned round to express astonishment, annoyance and manly resolve in his features. But then he probably knows, as everyone in the audience knows, that these log-hut wives are practically indestructible."

His diligence as a trooper got Munro promoted to corporal, an advance that thrilled Felicia, his ten-year-old niece back in Ireland, who remembered him fondly as a man who always took time for children. To explain his new rank Munro wrote "On Being Company Orderly Corporal," and he thought enough of the piece to send it for reprinting in the *Bystander,* along with his stern new photograph. His inventory of the job gave a good picture of the way Munro had spent the past spring.

"When one has drawn the milk and doled out the margarine, and distributed the letters and parcels, and seen to the whereabouts of migratory tea-pails and flat-pans—and paraded defaulters and off-duty men under the cold scrutiny of the canteen sergeant—and disentangled recruits from messes to which they do not belong—and induced unwilling hut-orderlies to saddle themselves with buckets-full of unpeeled potatoes which they neither desire nor deserve—and has begun to think that the moment has arrived in which one may indulge in a cigarette and read a letter—then some detestably thoughtful friend will sidle up to one and say, 'I suppose you know there's the watercress waiting at the cookhouse?' "

Imparting advice to future orderlies, Munro included one of his best lines: "Develop your imagination; if the officer of the day remarks on the paleness of a joint of meat hazard the probable explanation that the beast it was cut from was fed on Sicilian clover, which fattens quickly, but gives a pale appearance; there may be no such thing as Sicilian clover, but one-half of the world believes what the other half invents."

One of his duties was distributing mail, and Munro claimed to have pulled off a hoax, although perhaps we are not meant to believe him. "There was one young man in Hut 3 whose reproachful looks got on my nerves to such an extent that at last I wrote him a letter from his Aunt Agatha, a letter full of womanly counsel and patient reproof, such as any aunt might have been proud to write. Possibly he hasn't got an Aunt Agatha; anyhow the reproachful look has been replaced by a puzzled frown."

They marched and waited. One trooper wrote a song with the line, "Are we downhearted?" to which the marching men shouted back, "No, no, no!" For diversion there were cross-country runs and concerts given by the YMCA. And drink. Munro and a friend from civilian days, W. R. Spikesman, were the only two of the thirty troopers in their hut who could go out for a night in town and return sober. It was a distinction Munro wanted to shed, and one night he and Spikesman went to Roffey to visit a friend, Captain Cyril Winterscale, who had lately returned wounded from the front. After a good dinner and talk, they headed back to the camp at 11:30 P.M., entirely clear-headed. Once home in Number 2 Hut, however, they began to stagger and play drunk. Munro had always been good at fooling people, and when he tried to explain the next day that it had been only a rag, the others remained unconvinced.

They moved camp again. The villagers turned out early to cheer and then weep as the men were moved to Clipstone, which was near enough to Nottingham for weekend leave. Barely a month later they were off once more, and the civilians at the stations their train passed made the men of the 22nd feel that they were truly off to serve their country. But the destination was only Tidworth, and they would tarry there most of the autumn, going out occasionally for long maneuvers in nearby turnip fields or camping in trenches they had dug along Salisbury Plain. Once—the fall's highlight—they were reviewed by Queen Mary.

Rumors of their next destination abounded. One fanciful report had them headed to the Balkans, and that prospect revived in Hector's mind the image of his favorite beast. "My dear little Wolf," he wrote to Charlie's daughter, disregarding Muriel's ruling against the game. "Many thanks for your letter. I am sorry the mousie died" (a bee had stung Felicia's pet mouse to death) "but I expect you gave it a fine funeral and all the other mice will talk a lot about it. We went out on the march for three days this week and slept out in the open fields behind haystacks and hedges. A little black and white goat strayed away from some other regiment and marched at the head of our columns, but it did not know that we are the fastest marching regiment in this Division, and before the three days were over it was too tired to walk and had to be carried in one of our transport carts; it is resting now and will be quite fit again. Perhaps I may be going out to Serbia and may meet some wolves in the forests there, which will be fun. With much love, your affectionate uncle Hector."

The next day he wrote in the same contented vein to Ethel, praising the beauty of the villages they moved through on their field operations, particularly Amport and Abbots Ann, and the generosity of villagers who ran out to them with baskets of apples. He said that he had warned one timorous youth—obviously a boy made of softer stuff than his niece—that the forests of Serbia swarmed with wolves, which pounced upon men standing sentry duty. Munro added that he would like to go back there; he only hoped they wouldn't be sent to Gallipoli.

By early November, it looked as though their waiting was done. The men received overseas kits and they found, to their disgust, that for anything extra they wanted to buy, they were badly overcharged by the same townsmen who had welcomed them with such gratitude. Worse yet, their neighbors from the cavalry walked off with anything from the camp that they could carry. Souvenirs, they explained. By the time the orders came to ship out, most of Hector's battalion was in debt.

The farewell dinner in the sergeants' mess gave some clue to the sort of barracks humor Munro had been enjoying for the past year. The tomato-bean soup was described on the menu as the "bean soup that made Jack and the beans-talk." That night, Major Barnett Barker consolidated his hold over the men's hearts by ending his speech, "Incidentally, anyone who cleans his buttons out there will be shot at dawn."

On November 7, 1915, Munro wrote to Ethel, "After the long months of preparation and waiting we are at last on the eve of departure and there is a good prospect of our getting away this week. It seems almost too good to be true that I am going to take an active part in a big European war. I fear it will be France, not the Balkans, but there is no knowing where one may find oneself before the war is over; anyway, I shall keep up my study of the Serbian language. I expect at first we shall be billeted in some French town."

Nine days later, snow was falling as the men marched from their barracks behind a cavalry band. To the fluttering of handkerchiefs in the crowd at the train station, they shouted that eerie call of the First War, "Good-by-ee!" ("Wipe a tear, baby dear, / From your eye-ee.") The band played "Auld Lang Syne" and they were off. At Ashford, they paused for a long while at a station that the men agreed could not enjoy much repute in railway circles. It was after sunset by the time they reached Folkestone. Their crossing was calm, with only the mildest of swells beneath a bath of moonlight. They were forbidden to smoke or talk, but they sailed happily, unconscious of any danger. A few hours later, word came that the hospital ship behind them had struck a mine.

Boulogne was not a sight to lift the hearts of men seeing France for the first time. After a rain, the town was a morass of deep puddles, muddy cobblestones, and gangs of men who had been waiting for days for a leave boat to take them back to England. And another dampening of their spirits: Their popular commanding officer had been called away to the infantry. "My parting words to you all are," shouted "B. B." to his battalion, "to keep happy and endeavor to make each other merry and bright."

The first few nights, the men loved hearing the sounds of the guns. They had not even left Boulogne before their war stories began, and the censor held back one letter that started, "I am writing this on the back of a dead German." The men traveled by train to St. Omer on November 18 and then marched throughout the night; the battalion now consisted of thirty officers and just less than a thousand men.

After Béthune and Beuvry, they began to meet morose and exhausted soldiers coming the other way, and the sight assured them that they were truly in a war zone. Taking up billets in the ruined houses of Annequin South, the 22nd Battalion sent working parties every day to the trenches to learn what shell and rifle fire was like away from Salisbury Plain. Munro ignored the wisdom of every veteran by volunteering to be part of the first "wiring party"—stretching out barbed wire during A Company's first visit to the trenches at Vermelles. He was selected; the foray went smoothly and all its members returned alive.

The battalion's first casualty came on December 5. A shell, what the men called a "whizz bang," fell on the road in the midst of B Company, killing one private and wounding ten others. Two weeks later, Munro was sent temporarily away from further danger. He was ordered to a nearby town for two weeks' instruction with a few officers and other NCOs. The training looked interesting enough, and it could lead in time to his being promoted to lance sergeant. His one concern was whether he might miss any lively fighting.

He was being the model soldier. On marches, Munro never bent the rules, as others did, by throwing his pack onto the back of a truck that was headed in the same direction. Once, when he thought his friend Spikesman had been derelict in a minor duty, he gave him a severe dressing down. But his anger always passed immediately, and he took to heart his former commander's injunction to keep his fellow troopers merry. Every reminiscence by the men of his unit mentions his determined good cheer, although the few examples given suffer from the usual inability to recapture the moment that made a quip seem funny. One instance came when the men finally got to the war and then were relieved periodically from the trenches; it turned out that their "rests" meant even harder work at digging and fortifying. Munro raised a laugh by claiming that some of the men, hearing that heaven was a place of eternal rest, had renounced their religion. Other jokes that the battalion claimed for its own were variations on standards that date back to Troy: After a long pack drill, a voice in the ranks sighs plaintively, "O death, where is thy sting?" The sergeant calls the men to attention and shouts, " 'Ere now, 'oo said that?" The same weary voice responds, "Actually, Sarge, I think it was Shelley."

To Ethel, Munro could let down a bit when his age told on him. "I had a longish way to march" to the training center, "with all my possessions on my back, my overcoat in addition to being twice its normal weight through soaked-in mud, so I was glad enough to get to my billet, especially as I had had very little sleep for the previous 3 or 4 nights." Just as in his letters to Felicia, Munro never overlooked the chance to tell Ethel of an animal he had encountered or boast gently of his concern for it. "At a village where we were quartered for a few days' rest there was a dog in a farmyard chained always to a kennel without any floor, and only sharp cobblestones to lie on. I gave it a lot of straw from my own bed allowance, much to the astonishment of the farm-folk."

Christmas Eve 1915 found much of Munro's battalion on the front line. It rained throughout the night, and the men huddled under their waterproof sheets. The next day the sun appeared, and they broke into song, trying to forget that one of their sentries had been blinded during the night and another private killed in the early hours. On the whole, the men agreed, they had done pretty well during these first tours in the trenches. On Boxing Day, the battalion went back to Annequin for a belated Christmas celebration with festoons of lanterns and paper flowers. Still at the training center, Munro missed sharing Christmas with his company, but he sent Ethel his adaptation of a carol for the holiday:

> "While Shepherds watched their flocks by night
> All seated on the ground
> A high-explosive shell came down
> And mutton rained around."

By mid-January 1916, the battalion was installed at Festubert in solid breastworks while the front line was held by a series of islands, called "grouse-butts," where the men went for shifts of twenty-four hours. There were a few more casualties, but the days turned sunny and time passed indolently. Then the battalion moved to Givenchy and more action. On February 8, Munro took a moment to write to his niece. "My dear Felicia, I have been meaning to write to you for a long time but we are kept fairly busy. It is nice being out·here, except the marching which is tiring because we carry so much, but that cannot be helped. I think you would enjoy going out at night to mine the wire entanglements in front of our lines: You have to creep, creep like a prowling cat, and when the enemy sends up a flare light every few minutes, you have to press yourself flat on the ground and pretend to be a lump of earth. It reminded me of the times when you and I were wolves and used to go prowling after fat farmers' wives. At night lots of owls come to the trenches to catch the mice that swarm all over the place and they must have plenty of sport. Our kitchens are drawn by horses and mules and follow us wherever we go, and the cooks of our company have a jolly little tabby kitten that goes everywhere with them and is quite used to a travelling circus as it wont understand living in one place. Please tell Daddy that I got the parcel he sent me, with the candles and cooker refills and that they come in very useful, and I was able to make tea early in the morning without causing smoke for the enemy to see. With much love to your Mother and Father and yourself. Your loving uncle Hector."

On the same day, Hector wrote to Ethel about the owls, too, but he also gave her a less whimsical account of life in the trenches. "We are holding a rather hot part of the line and I must say I have enjoyed it better than any we have been in. There is not much dug-out accommodation so I made my bed (consisting of overcoat and waterproof sheet) on the fire-step of the parapet; on Sunday night, while I was on my round looking up the sentries, a bomb came into the trench, riddled the overcoat and sheet and slightly wounded a man sleeping on the other side of the trench. I assumed that no 2 bombs would fall exactly in the same spot, so remade the bed and had a good sleep."

A fellow trooper later filled in the details of that near-miss. Other men who were due for a four-hour patrol were often hard to rouse; it took a rough hand or the toe of a boot to get them up, and the result was that men coming off patrol sometimes lost ten to fifteen minutes of their rest time before the guard could be changed. But Munro was always up and ready to meet his shift, and it was because he had been off his ground sheet fifteen minutes early that the shell missed him. As his friend concluded, "One knows of many narrow escapes, but few happening because of that fixed idea of being just."

Their sandbagged trenches brought the British troops close enough to the Germans that they could talk together through the "sap end," the part of the trench that jutted out from the front line toward the enemy. A British soldier might throw out cigarettes and a German soldier throw back a packet of pipe tobacco. Once a German called to Munro to say that the war would soon be over, and Munro answered, "In about three years' time," which provoked a groan from the German and his comrades.

Back in London, Roy Reynolds had just published a new book, *My Slav Friends,* which he dedicated to Munro. He sent a copy by way of the trenches, along with some chocolate, and when the parcel arrived, Munro told Ethel that he had found the dedication to him very charming: "To Corporal H. H. Munro (22nd Royal Fusiliers) My dear 'Saki,' I beg you to accept this book in gratitude for your friendship, in admiration for your writings, and in reverence for the patriotism that has made you exchange a tender and witty pen for the bayonet. R. R."

There were other reminders of civilization. Munro found an excellent Burgundy in one village, but his stay there was brief. He described prices in France as "semi-famine," writing to Ethel, "The French have been saying all their lives, 'La Vie Coûte Chére' and now it really does."

Offers to take Munro away from the mud and bursting shells persisted. One day he was scrubbing potatoes when a general came to inspect the troops, a man at whose house Munro had played bridge. "What on earth are you doing here, Munro?" the general asked, and he tried, with no success, to persuade him to accept a transfer away from the line. The general could not be expected to understand that for Munro the rigors were the reward. In the March snow, he stood his night watch without bundling up, and when he didn't feel the cold he concluded that his blood must be in very good condition.

Such robust health for a man of frail constitution was one of war's unexpected bonuses, and Munro mentioned it often to Ethel. "I am in very good health and spirits; the fun and adventure of the whole thing and the good comradeship of some of one's companions make it jolly, and one attaches an enormous importance to little comforts such as a cup of hot tea at the right moment." In the trenches, there were happenings grotesque enough to slake even Saki's taste. Robert Wright of the 22nd, for example, found what he described as "a perfectly good ear" on Vimy Ridge. It was "no use to me so I threw it over the parapet to the rats, remembering that rats were traditionally very fond of ears."

As a man who had enjoyed his London club, Munro on occasion tried to institutionalize the battalion's camaraderie. In England during training, he had launched a "Creeper's Club"; to qualify for membership, a man had to be seen talking confidentially to someone of higher rank. In those days of agitated rumor, it did not matter what one was saying. The surreptitious contact alone qualified a man as a Creeper. In April 1916, at Ham-en-Artois, Munro tried for more lasting bonds. He and three mates had found some pork in the village, and Munro persuaded an old French woman to cook it for them. She told them to return to her back kitchen promptly at 7:30 P.M. When they did, they found the pork ready for them, along with dressing, roast potatoes and peas. *"Messieurs,"* said the old woman, *"bon appétit."* When they were finished, she told them that her back kitchen was available to them any time they could come back. Munro's friend Spikesman took down a card advertising Chocolate Ménier and on the reverse wrote "The Back Kitchen Club." The four signed their names, Munro first since he was the acknowledged founder.

Munro then laid down the rules. The membership was not to exceed nine; a replacement for a member who "passed on" required unanimous approval—making Munro's club more exclusive than some in London, where one blackball was no longer enough to bar an applicant. Club members were to eat together every day; being company orderly was the only excuse for an absence. They were to pool their packages from home and to pay expenses for any member who was broke. The last rule was inviolate: "The conduct of all members to be beyond reproach."

In June 1916, Munro went back to England on a short leave. He registered at the Richelieu Hotel, and Charlie and Ethel hastened to London to join him there. Munro wanted to see everything—friends and family, paintings at the Academy, the latest plays at the theatre. Both Ethel and Roy Reynolds thought he showed signs of what he had been through; he was thin, and Reynolds found his face haggard. But he was in splendid high spirits and he had a project in mind that excited Ethel perhaps even more than it did him.

From France, Munro had written to Reynolds that he had become aware that after the war he could never return to his old life in London. Would Reynolds check with a friend of theirs in Russia to find out whether it was possible to buy acreage in Siberia? Munro wanted to go there to live, to farm and hunt. Reynolds saw the plan as evidence of the spiritual change that had come over his friend in uniform. Munro was returning to that love of the woodland and its wild inhabitants that he had felt as a child. "The dross," Reynolds wrote, meaning the life of a writer in London, "had been burnt up in the flames of war."

Ethel embraced the scheme with her customary vigor. She pictured herself trailing after her brother to Siberia, indispensable because she had remembered to carry with her all he forgot to bring. "It would have been a remarkable life," she imagined, "wild animals beyond the dreams of avarice, at our very doors, and, before long, inside them." Possibly she did not know that Munro had told Reynolds that he intended to set up housekeeping with a couple of Yakutsk lads as servants.

The leave was all too brief, and the time came to see Munro off. Charlie, Ethel and a friend went down to Victoria Station in high spirits. Corporal Munro had survived in the trenches for eight months. It was unthinkable that anything could happen to him now.

Because civilians were not allowed near the troop train, Ethel's parting message to her brother had to be shouted over a barrier at the platform's edge. Afterward, she took satisfaction in her last words to him. She knew of his ambition to take part in a bayonet charge, and even if that had never been realized, she assumed that he had found other ways to dispatch the German enemy. In any case, she was attuned exactly to his mood when she leaned across the barricade to cry, "Kill a good few for me!"

Such was the spirit of 1916, and some of that intoxication with bloodletting lingered even after the war ended. When Munro's last two volumes of stories were brought out posthumously, he was reviewed less as a writer than as a killer of Germans. By then King George had sent to Ethel the obligatory message from Buckingham Palace and she had framed it. "I join with my grateful people in sending you this memorial of a brave life given for others in the Great War." Ethel nailed the accompanying scroll to her wall, along with the wistful portrait by Hoppé and her brother's enlistment telegram, creating a satisfactory shrine that she maintained until her own death.

After the war, Charlie bought a blank album and collected the admiring reviews that *The Toys of Peace* was getting. This latest volume, said the *Guardian,* was "to be the more treasured since, as his commanding officer testified, its author 'was one of the heroes of the war.' " "Peace to you, brave soul, bright spirit," wrote another reviewer. "There will be none in our time to write like you; none to leave a finer example." "We doubt," said the *Observer,* after paying tribute to Saki's "imperishable work," "if anyone who died in the war quite so definitely represented an idealism and a patriotism which no German could ever begin to understand."

Only the critic for the *Daily News* took exception to the florid praise for Munro as soldier. Quoting from Munro's hymn to "An Old Love," the reviewer commented that even when preached by a writer like Saki, glorification of war "is still a lie more dangerous and more destructive than any of the great emotional untruths which capture a man's heart in childhood and bolt the door against reason." It was a dissent so singular that it sounded subversive.

Several reviewers quoted the expectation of a comrade from the 22nd that when peace finally came, "Saki will give us the most wonderful of all the books about the war," and they regretted that the prophecy must now go unfulfilled. The *Westminster Gazette,* in a proprietary tone, claimed that once Saki came home from Russia as a correspondent he had never seemed quite at home in London. It was a theme picked up by other critics, who preferred the translucent fancies of Reginald to anything Saki wrote afterward.

J. C. Squire, the influential critic, noted in the *Westminster* that now that he was gone Munro would be far more appreciated than he had been in his lifetime. Yet Squire could not quite understand why Saki had never reached a wider public, especially since he had discovered for himself how well Saki's crystalline sentences rang when they were read aloud. That discovery was confirmed later when, grudgingly, Ethel allowed a few of the stories to be read on the British Broadcasting Corporation; it was proved still again in the late 1970s, when the Welsh actor Emlyn Williams presented an evening of readings from Saki that he called *The Playboy of the Weekend World.*

Squire concluded that the problem for Saki was that he never got "publicity" and that he wrote for only a few journals. "He employed a pseudonym of the recondite sort that makes people shy," Squire added, "and he kept his personal habits and private life, contrary to the modern practice, in the background." John Lane had promised that a collected edition would appear shortly, and Squire saluted the idea as a way to have Saki recognized as one of the wittiest writers of his time. But the *Spectator,* while agreeing that it was their loss when readers overlooked Saki, doubted that it would ever be different. "He had great gifts—wit, mordant irony and a remarkable command of ludicrous metaphor—but an intermittent vein of freakish inhumanity belied his best nature, and disconcerted the plain person."

16

"Down Pens"
(1916)

At the front, Munro's euphoria over the war was slowly leaking away. He got news from London of one friend who was dying, and then in a single day three men from his section were hit by a shell. Munro wrote to Ethel, "One, a dear, faithful, illiterate old sort, who used to make tea for me and do other little services, was killed outright, so I am not feeling at my gayest, but luckily there is a good deal to take the mind off unhappy things." To lighten his mood, he wrote an essay for the *Westminster Gazette* on his enthusiasm of a lifetime. "Birds on the Western Front" was the title, and sixty years later, when Emlyn Williams read from it as the conclusion to his performance, many people in his audience took it for a poem. It was the last piece Munro wrote.

"The skylark in this region has stuck tenaciously to the meadows and crop-lands that have been seamed and bisected with trenches and honeycombed with shell-holes. In the chill, misty hour of gloom that precedes a rainy

dawn, when nothing seemed alive except a few wary wa-
terlogged sentries and many scuttling rats, the lark would
suddenly dash skyward and pour forth a song of ecstatic
jubilation that sounded horribly forced and insincere. It
seemed scarcely possible that the bird could carry its in-
souciance to the length of attempting to rear a brood in
that desolate wreckage of shattered clods and gaping shell-
holes, but once, having occasion to throw myself down
with some abruptness on my face, I found myself nearly
on the top of a brood of young larks . . .

"At the corner of a stricken wood (which has had a
name made for it in history, but shall be nameless here), at
a moment when lyddite and shrapnel and machine-gun
fire swept and raked and bespattered that devoted spot as
though the artillery of an entire Division had suddenly
concentrated on it, a wee hen-chaffinch flitted wistfully to
and fro, amid splintered and falling branches that had
never a green bough left on them. The wounded lying
there, if any of them noticed the small bird, may well have
wondered why anything having wings and no pressing
reason for remaining should have chosen to stay in such a
place . . .

"The only other bird I ever saw there was a magpie,
flying low over the wreckage of fallen tree-limbs; 'one for
sorrow,' says the old superstition. There was sorrow
enough in that wood."

Whenever Hector had been wretched, as he had been in
Burma and in Paris when he was becoming bored with
reporting, his body obliged him by providing excuses that
his mind was too dutiful to invent. Now, in the autumn
of 1916, Munro came down with malaria. His fever ran so
high that when the commanding officer saw him, he immediately sent Munro back to headquarters. Without him,
Spikesman was desolate and his other friends told him to
stop "being such a misery." A few weeks before Munro
was stricken, he had been promoted to lance sergeant.
Now more battles were looming, and he was apart from
his troops. From the infirmary he wrote to Charlie, "I
keep thinking of the boys all the time; when one is sharing
dangers they don't seem so big, but when one is in safety

and the others in the front line all sorts of catastrophes seem possible and probable."

Another consideration was much worse. Throughout October, the men of the 22nd believed that within the month they would be facing a major battle, and sometimes men without Munro's rectitude would sham an ailment to miss the fighting. To Munro it was intolerable that there might be even the slightest hint that he was such a shirker, and as reports of an attack on Beaumont-Hamel became more persistent, he got up from bed on November 11 and reported to the trenches. Spikesman was glad to welcome him back and aware of why he had made the effort. But he knew, too, that Munro should still be in the hospital.

The British had tried to take Beaumont-Hamel early in July, but the German encampment had proved impregnable. Since that time the Germans had strengthened their forces, and the weather went against the British. An autumn of constant rain and mud made the trenches all but unendurable. Tours of duty were cut to two days, but all the same many troopers had joined Munro in the infirmary. Even when the battalion rested at Acheux Wood, their huts were submerged in a sea of mud and the only connecting walkways were tracks of duckboard. The day of the attack was set and then postponed. That happened once, twice, again. So many briefings were held, so many special badges passed out, that the men had become sick of the battle before it began.

At last a zero hour was set and not called off. On November 12, the 22nd assembled in battle order at Betrancourt, and the next morning, at 1:30 A.M., the men marched in darkness to the trenches. They went by way of Mailly Maillet with A Company at the head. Just before 6 A.M., the Fifth Infantry Brigade moved out of the trenches to attack, and every British gun from Ancre at the far north opened its bombardment. The noise was ferocious. and it was amplified at once by the Germans' return fire. Munro's battalion edged forward, peeling off to right and left to fill what had been the front lines. It was afternoon before C and B companies were sent across No

Man's Land to face north and form a defensive guard for the exposed flank of the Fifth Infantry.

Twelve hours later, at 4 A.M. on the morning of November 14, they were joined by A and D companies. In the cold of the early morning, the men felt the chill begin with their toes and fingers and spread through their bodies. A thick mist made it impossible to see more than a few yards ahead.

The men of A Company were sent out of the trenches to flank at the left of the battalion's advancing line. Behind them, the ground was a deep marsh, and men were sinking to their bellies in the mud, not able to work themselves forward. There was a sudden roar of guns and then silence; one trooper thought it was as though the guns themselves felt the need of a rest. It was still very dark when all at once A Company was hailed by voices speaking English. A figure, possibly from the Fifth Infantry, rose to the top of the trenches and shouted greetings to the A Company commander. As the two officers began to talk, the men sank to the ground to rest. Munro found a shallow crater and leaned back against its lip. Through the darkness an air of serenity was spreading among the troops. One of the men lighted up. But Munro, ever the noncom, knew it was too dangerous to be smoking, and he shouted an order to stop.

Spikesman heard the shout and then a shot from a German sniper. But he did not connect the two sounds until an hour later, after the fighting had started up and died down again. A trooper said to him, "So they got your friend." Spikesman understood then that he had heard Munro's last words on earth and that they had been, "Put that bloody cigarette out."

Particularly because he had been the victim, the irony to the story might have made Saki laugh.

SIX
UNCOLLECTED
STORIES
BY SAKI

Tracing Saki's short stories through newspaper and magazine archives has brought to light a number of uncollected pieces. For their two posthumous collections, *The Toys of Peace* and *The Square Egg,* Ethel Munro and the publisher apparently relied on Munro's own files rather than the British Library, and as a result, the stories presented here have never been published in book form. If they do not represent Saki's best work, they are more typical of his style than most of what appears in *The Square Egg.*

"The Holy War" and "The Pond" show the way in which Saki could take similar situations and nudge them toward either comedy or, with a bit more obvious strain, tragedy. "A Shot in the Dark" reverses another of his regular themes and presents a case of unmistaken identity. "A Sacrifice to Necessity" resembles "The Stake," except that the wager involves a bride instead of a cook. "The Almanack" brings together Clovis Sangrail and Vera Durmot in a commercial venture suited to their peculiar talents, and "The Solution of an Insoluble Dilemma" offers one last crisis at a house party.

For Saki fanciers, the recovering of the stories represents six causes for celebration, and they will not object that none of them rivals "Sredni Vashtar" or "The Background." Other readers will want to consult at least two dozen of Saki's prime stories and not judge his achievement on the six stories presented here.

In his own time, critics were made uneasy by the lack of heart they detected in Saki's writing, and they despaired at his ever finding a larger public. But as the century has wound down, that public has absorbed so many artistic and political shocks that Saki's ruthlessness and lack of sentimentality have made him modern and kept him fresh. Wit has one prime virtue amid its limitations: it does not fade. Until human nature reforms itself, it will be true that "all decent people live beyond their income nowadays, and those who aren't respectable live beyond other people's." And until the triumph of genetic engineering, there will be men like Lucas Harrowcliff with "colouring that would have been accepted as a sign of extensive culture in an asparagus, but probably meant in this case mere abstention from exercise. His hair and forehead furnished a recessional note in a personality that was in all other respects obtrusive and assertive."

It is perhaps not to our credit that Saki's undeniable cruelty troubles us less than it did the critic who reviewed *The Toys of Peace* for the *Spectator,* or that what was taken sixty years ago as freakish inhumanity should now seem only the observable norm. Saki, aloof and condescending to his own times, turns out to be one of us.

But embracing him is easier than establishing his place in English letters. An unbeliever, he did not concern himself with the relationship of man to God, and critics have often used that theme to test an author's seriousness. Then, by shunning love in all of its disguises, he banished another of the four characters of Western literature's primal cast. God was gone, Eve was gone, and Hector had left himself with only Adam and the snake. Yet, rejoicing in that narrow range, he fashioned a comedy of manners that looks to be enduring.

Hector Munro was too proud to make claims for himself, and those made on his behalf should respect the unerring proportion of his work. If genius is doing a thing perfectly, he was a genius. If genius is doing all things perfectly, he was not. Does it matter? He makes us laugh.

The Pond

Mona had always regarded herself as cast for the tragic rôle; her name, her large dark eyes, and the style of hairdressing that best suited her, all contributed to support that outlook on life. She wore habitually the air of one who has seen trouble, or, at any rate, expects to do so very shortly; and she was accustomed to speak of the Angel of Death almost as other people would speak of their chauffeur waiting round the corner to fetch them at the appointed moment. Fortune-tellers, noting this tendency in her disposition, invariably hinted at something in her fate which they did not care to speak about too explicitly. "You will marry the man of your choice, but afterwards you will pass through strange fires," a Bond Street two-guinea palm-oilist had told her. "Thank you," said Mona, "for your plain-speaking. But I have known it always."

In marrying John Waddacombe, Mona had mated herself with a man who shared none of her intimacy with the shadowy tragedies of what she called the half-seen world. He had the substantial tragedies of his own world to bother about, without straining his mental eyesight for the elusive and dubious distractions belonging to a sphere that lay entirely beyond his range of vision; or, for the matter of that, his range of interests. Potato blight, swine fever, the Government's land legislation, and other pests of the farm absorbed his attention as well as his energies, and even if he had admitted the possibility of such a disease as soul-sickness, of which Mona recognised eleven distinct varieties, most of them incurable, he would probably have prescribed a fortnight at the seaside as the most hopeful and natural remedy. There was no disguising the fact, John Waddacombe was of the loam, loamy. If he had cared to go into politics he would have been known inevitably as honest John Waddacombe, and after that there is nothing more to be said.

Two days, or thereabouts, after her marriage, Mona had made the tragic discovery that she was yoked to a life-partner with whom she had little in common, and from whom she could expect nothing in the way of sympathetic understanding. Anyone else, knowing both her and John and their respective temperaments, could have advanced her that information the moment that the engagement was announced. John was fond of her in his own way, and she, in her quite different way, was more than a little fond of him; but they trafficked in ideas that had scarcely a common language.

Mona set out on her married life with the expectation of being misunderstood, and after a while John arrived at the rather obvious conclusion that he didn't understand her—and was content to "leave it at that." His wife was at first irritated and then disheartened by his attitude of stolid unconcern. "Least said, soonest mended," was his comfortable doctrine, which failed woefully when applied to Mona's share of the reticence. She was unhappy and perturbed about their lack of soul-fellowship; why couldn't he be decently distressed about it also? From being at first theatrically miserable she became more seriously affected. The morbid strain in her character found at last something tangible to feed on, and brought a good appetite to the feeding. While John was busy and moderately happy with his farm troubles, Mona was dull, unoccupied, and immoderately unhappy with her own trouble.

It was at this time, in the course of one of her moody, listless rambles, that she came across the pond. In the high chalky soil of the neighbourhood, standing water was a rarity; with the exception of the artificially made duck-pond at the farm and one or two cattle pools, Mona knew of no other for miles round. It stood in a clay "pocket" in the heart of a neglected beech plantation on the steep side of a hill, a dark, evil-looking patch of water, fenced round and overspread with gloomy yews and monstrous decaying beeches. It was not a cheerful spot, and such picturesqueness as it possessed was all on the side of melancholy; the only human suggestion that could arise in connection with the pool was the idea of a dead body floating on its surface. Mona took to the place with an instantaneous sense of fascination; it suited her temperament, and it mightily suited her mood. Nearly all her walks led her to the beechwood, and the Mecca of the wood was always the still dark pond, with its suggestion of illimitable depths, its silence, its air of an almost malignant despondency. If one could indulge in such a flight of fancy as to imagine a hill rejoicing, or a valley smiling, one could certainly picture the pond wearing a sullen, evil scowl.

Mona wove all sorts of histories about the pool, and in most of them there was some unhappy, fate-buffeted soul who hung wearily over its beckoning depths and finally floated in sombre spectacular repose among the weeds on its surface, and each time that she reshaped the story she identified the victim more and more with herself. She would stand or sit on the steeply inclined bank that overhung the pond on every side, peering down at the water and reflecting on the consequences that would follow a slip of her foot or an incautious venturing over-near the edge. How long would she struggle in those unfathomed weed-grown depths before she lay as picturesquely still as the drowned heroine of her tale-weavings, and how long would she float there in peace, with the daylight and moonlight reaching down to her through the over-arching catafalque of yew and beech, before searchers discovered her resting-place, and haled her body away to the sordid necessities of inquest and burial? The idea of ending her despondencies and soul troubles in that dark, repose-inviting pool took firmer and clearer shape; there seemed a spirit lurking in its depths and smiling on its surface that beckoned her to lean further and yet further over its edge, to stand more and more rashly on the steep slope that overhung it. She took a subtle pleasure in marking how the fascination grew on her with each visit; how the dread of the catastrophe that she was courting grew less and less. Every time that she reluctantly tore herself away from the spot there seemed a half-jeering, half-reproachful murmur in the air around her, "Why not to-day?"

And then, at a timely moment, John Waddacombe, hearty as an ox, and seemingly proof against weather exposure, fell suddenly and critically ill with a lung attack that nearly triumphed over doctors and nurses and his own powers of stubborn resistance. Mona did her fair share of the nursing while the case was critical, fighting with greater zeal against the death that threatened her husband than she had shown in combatting the suggestion of self-destruction that had gained so insidious a hold on her. And when the convalescent stage had been reached she found John, weak and rather fretful as he was after his long experience of the sick-room, far more lovable and sympathetic than he had been in the days of his vigour. The barriers of reserve and mutual impatience had been broken down, and husband and wife found that they had more in common than they had once thought possible. Mona forgot the pond, or thought of it only with a shudder; a healthy contempt for her morbid weakness and silliness had begun to assert itself. John was not the only one of them who was going through a period of convalescence.

The self-pity and the coquetry with self-destruction had passed away under the stress of new sympathies and interests; the morbid undercurrent was part of Mona's nature, and was not to be cast out at a moment's notice. It was the prompting of this undercurrent that led her, one day in the autumn, to pay a visit to the spot where she had toyed so weakly with stupid, evil ideas and temptations. It would be, she felt, a curious sensation to renew acquaintance with the place now that its fascination and potential tragedy had been destroyed. In outward setting it was more desolate and gloom-shrouded than ever; the trees had lost their early autumnal magnificence, and rain had soaked the fallen beech leaves into a paste of dark slush under foot. Amid the nakedness of their neighbours, the yews stood out thick, and black, and forbidding, and the sickly growth of fungoid things showed itself prominently amid the rotting vegetation. Mona peered down at the dark, ugly pool, and shuddered to think that she could ever have contemplated an end so horrible as choking and gasping to death in those foul, stagnant depths, with their floating surface of slime and creeping water insects and rank weed-growth. And then the thing that she recoiled from in disgust seemed to rise up towards her as though to drag her down in a long-deferred embrace. Her feet had slipped on the slithery surface of sodden leaves and greasy clay, and she was sliding helplessly down the steep bank to where it dropped sheer into the pool. She clutched and clawed frantically at yielding roots and wet, slippery earth, and felt the weight of her body pull her downward with an increasing momentum. The hideous pool, whose fascination she had courted and slighted, was gaping in readiness for her; even if she had been a swimmer there would have been little chance for her in those weed-tan-gled depths, and John would find her there, as once she had almost wished—John who had loved her and learned to love her better than ever; John whom she loved with all her heart. She raised her voice to call his name again and again, but she knew that he was a mile or two away, busy with the farm life that once more claimed his de-voted attention. She felt the bank slide away from her in a dark, ugly smear, and heard the small stones and twigs that she had dislodged fall with soft splashes into the water at her feet; above her, far above her it seemed, the yews spread their sombre branches like the roof-span of a crypt.

"Heavens alive, Mona, where did you get all that mud?" asked John in some pardonable astonishment. "Have you been playing catch-as-catch-can with the pigs? You're splashed up to the eyes in it."

"I slipped into a pond," said Mona.

"What, into the horse-pond?" asked John.

"No, a pond out in one of the woods," she explained.

"I didn't know there was such a thing for miles round," said John.

"Well, perhaps it would be an exaggeration to call it a pond," said Mona, with a faint trace of resentment in her voice; "it's only about an inch and a half deep."

The Morning Post, May 6, 1913

The Holy War

R evil Yealmton sat in the swaying dining-car of a
Nord Express train that raced westward through the
Prussian plain in the dusk of an early summer day. After
nearly two years of profitable business pilgrimage in the
border regions of Asiatic Russia he was returning to his
wife and home in the English West Country. It was a
house that, as a matter of fact, he had never inhabited, and
yet he was looking forward to reaching it as eagerly as
though it had been the hallowed dwelling place of his
childhood. Old memories endeared the place to his recollection, even though they were the memories of one who
had dreamed rather than of one who had experienced. In
his early days, when he had lived with his parents in a
prim and rather dreary cottage in a sleepy West Country
village, the old gabled house at the foot of the hill had
been occupied by a bachelor uncle, who had not encouraged his relatives to intrude too freely on his seclusion.
From the evergreen fastness of a conveniently placed holly
hedge the boy had been able to look, unobserved, on the
domain with which he seldom enjoyed closer acquaintance, and in his eyes it had been a wonderful and desirable
abode for mortal man. Every detail stood up in his mind
now with undimmed distinctness as he sat finishing his
dinner in the jolting train. There was the broad pond at
the entrance, whereupon a company of drakes and ducks,
mottled and ringstraked and burnished, went to and fro

like a flotilla of painted merchantmen on an inland sea; there were high white gates that led into a yew-begirt garden on one side and a wide straw-yard on the other, a yard in which radiant-plumaged gamecocks led their attendant trains of hen folk in endless busy forays, and sleek, damson-hued pigs grabbed and munched and dozed the day long. And on the hillside beyond the yard there was an orchard of unspeakable delight, where the gold-finches nested in the spring, and the apples and greengages and cherries made one's eyes ache with longing in fruit time. There were a hundred other heart-enslaving things that he remembered from his boyhood's days, and the wonder was that the clamour of them had stood the criti-cal test of maturing years. After his parents had passed into a pious memory he had revisited the neighbourhood with the assurance of a successful mercantile career to his credit, and had found the old uncle more human and friendly than of yore, and the old gabled house and all that stood with it as bewitching as ever. And then, a few months later, as he had been setting out on his important eastward journey, the uncle had died and left his nephew all that earthly paradise to have and to hold. Yealmton had sent his wife to take possession, and deferred the joy of entering into his desired land until he should have seen his Russian enterprise to a successful conclusion. And now he was returning, with a riot of expectant longing in his brain, to his home—and to Thirza. But a thought kept intruding itself with unwelcome cynicism: was his wife really included in the anticipations that piled themselves so pleasantly before him?

Thirza Yealmton was what is known as a managing woman. Of such there are many that are only to be spoken of with honour and incense-burning, but Thirza was of the regrettable kind that can never realise that nature, and particularly human nature, is sometimes devised and con-structed to be unmanageable, for its own happiness and its own good. Yealmton thought, with a suppressed psalm of thanksgiving at the back of his mind, of the comfortable discomfort of his last two years of travel, and of how Thirza's presence on the scene would assuredly have en-tailed a distressing accompaniment of arranging and supervising and general dislocation of the accepted way of things. He knew that he was impatiently counting the slow hours that separated him from the old homestead at the foot of the hill, but he could not assure himself that any of the impatience was honestly due to a desire to be once more in his wife's company and within the sphere of her organising genius.

Later, when Thirza met him with the pony-cart at the small country station, Yealmton knew that his cynical self-accusation had been well founded. The anticipation still ran high in his brain and heart, none of it had found realisation in the meeting with his wife. It was unfortunate, he admitted to himself, but he was too engrossed with other crowding sensations to give the matter more than a perfunctory vote of censure. He hardly heeded Thirza's unstemmed torrent of talk that kept pace with the rattle of the pony's hoofs, until suddenly a sentence detached itself with unpleasant distinctness.

"You will find a lot of improvements since you last saw the place."

"Improvements?"

He jerked out the question wonderingly. It had never crossed his mind that any improvement could be desirable in the wonderland that he remembered.

"For one thing," said Thirza, as the cart swung round a corner and brought them into view of the gates, "I've had that old pond at the entrance drained away; it made things damp and looked untidy."

Yealmton said nothing, and Thirza did not see the look that came into his eyes. He remained silent, too, when his wife introduced him to a monotonous colony of white Leghorns, in wired runs, that she had substituted for the lively poultry yard of strutting, gorgon-hued game fowl that had been his uncle's special pride.

"The miller bought most of the old stock," she informed him: "a quarrelsome straying lot those game fowl were. I was glad to get rid of them. These ones are record layers, and I make quite a lot by their eggs. This is where the orchard was."

She showed him a trim array of young fruit trees, planted in serried rows, in a carefully-wooded enclosure.

"When they are fully grown they will yield three times the profit that the old orchard did," she observed.

"We are not poor," said Yealmton.

Thirza was chilled and offended; how little her husband appreciated the trouble she had been to in the matter.

"Money is always worth having," she said sharply.

"Goldfinches used to build in the old orchard," said Yealmton, almost to himself.

"Birds are a mistake about a garden, I think," said Thirza: "we could have goldfinches in an aviary if you liked."

"I would not like," said Yealmton, shortly.

A yellow figure came down a garden path and made straight for the newcomer.

"Hullo, Peterkin!" cried Yealmton, gladly, and a golden-furred cat sprang purring into his arms.

"How funny!" said Thirza. "That cat hasn't been seen anywhere about the place since the first week I was here; I didn't know it was still in existence. Don't let it come into the house," she added; "I don't encourage cats about a house."

For answer Yealmton carried Peterkin into the morning-room and placed him on a broad shelf built into the ingle-nook.

"This was his throne in my uncle's time," he said: "It is his throne now."

Thirza promptly decided on a four days' headache, which was her invariable recipe whenever anyone thwarted or annoyed her. She had been known to postpone it during times of stress, such as Christmas week or a spring cleaning, but she would never forgo it altogether. For the moment she said nothing.

After dinner that evening Yealmton stood at an open window, with Peterkin purring rapturously at his side, and listened for some remembered sound that should have come to him through the dusk.

"Why aren't the wood owls hooting?" he asked. "They always used to call from the copse about this time. All the way across Europe I've been longing to hear those owls singing Vespers."

"Do you like their noise?" asked Thirza. "I couldn't

stand it. I got the local gameskeeper to shoot them. It was such a dismal noise, I think."

"Is there any other vile thing that you have done in this dear old place?" asked Yealmton. He spoke to himself, but he asked the question aloud. Then he added: "Something dreadful must surely happen to you!"

Thirza gasped and stared at him for half a minute.

"You are over-tired with your journey," she said at last, and went upstairs to inaugurate a headache, which, she felt, could scarcely last less than a week.

Judicious digging operations restored the pond to something like its old splendour, and a great company of ducks, mottled and ring-straked and speckled, went to and fro on its waters as though they had been doing it all their lives. A couple of young gamecocks, supplied by the sympathetic miller, made short work of the alien white cockerels that had reigned in their stead, and the local gameskeeper was warned of the dismal things that would befall him if any further owl slaughter was brought home to his account. Even the fruit paddock was induced to lose some of its nursery-garden air and to stray back toward the glory of a West Country orchard. The birds of heaven received no further discouragement, except such as was meted out to them by Peterkin in his capacity of warden of the currant bushes. And while these things were being done Yealmton and his wife waged a politely reticent warfare; it was a struggle which Thirza knew she must ultimately win, because she was fighting for existence—arranging and interfering and supervising were a necessary condition of her well-being. What she did not know, or did not understand, was that Yealmton was fighting a Holy War, and therefore could not be defeated.

As summer and autumn passed away into winter Thirza turned her managing energies in a greater degree upon the rural life of the village, where she encountered less formidable obstacles than Yealmton's overruling opposition presented in the narrower sphere. She was not popular with the cottagers, but she had thoroughly mastered the art of being penetrating.

"I am going down to the mill-ponds," she announced one afternoon, when a hard frost had held the land for a couple of days; "the children will be coming out of school about now. They've been warned not to go on the ice, and I mean to see that they don't."

"It can't possibly bear yet," said Yealmton.

"It bears at the shallow end," said Thirza.

"Then why not let them go on the shallow end?" asked Yealmton.

"They've been told not to," said Thirza; "I don't wish to argue the matter. I mean to see that none of them go on."

As a matter of fact the children were engrossed with a slide at the other end of the village, and Thirza had the lonely mill meadows to herself. From the orchard gate Yealmton could see her walking rapidly along the reed-fringed borders of the wide ponds, as though determined to see that no adventurous urchin was enjoying a furtive slide in some hidden nook among the bushes. As he watched the dark, solitary figure moving through the desolate wintry waste his involuntary prophecy shot across his mind: "Something dreadful must surely happen to you." And at that moment he saw something white rush out of the bushes and come flapping towards her, he saw Thirza start back, and fall on the slippery edge of the pond, and across the meadows a scream came on the frozen air. It was a long while before he could reach the spot, running at his highest speed, and when he arrived the woman was lying half under the scum of churned-up ice and slush at the pond's edge, and something white and ghostly was stealing away through the dusk. Yealmton knew it for a wild swan, wounded by some gunner on the coast, and harbouring among the reeds till it should die; savage and weak with hunger and death-fear, but with strength enough left to do—what it had done.

The Almanack

H as it ever struck you," said Vera Durmot to Clovis, "that one might make a comfortable income by compiling a local almanack, on prophetic lines, like those that the general public buy by the half million?"

"An income, perhaps," said Clovis, "but not a comfortable one. The prophet has proverbially a thin sort of time in his own country, and you would be too closely mixed up with the people you were prophesying about to be able to get much comfort out of the job. If the man who foretells tragic happenings for the Crowned Heads of Europe had to meet them at luncheon parties and tea-fights every other day of the week he would not find his business a comfortable one, especially towards the last days of the year, when the tragedies were getting over-due."

"I should sell it just before the New Year," said Vera, ignoring the suggestion of possible embarrassments, "at eighteenpence a copy, and get a friend to type it for me, so that every copy I sold would be clear profit. Everyone would buy it out of curiosity, just to see how many of the predictions would be falsified."

"Wouldn't it be rather a trying time for you later on," asked Clovis, "when the predictions began to 'lack confirmation'?"

"The thing would be," said Vera, "to arrange your forecast so that it couldn't go very far wrong. I should begin with the prediction that the vicar would preach a moving New Year sermon from a text in Colossians; he always has done so since I can remember, and at his time of life men dislike change. Then one could safely foretell for the month of January that 'more than one well-known family in this neighbourhood will be faced with a serious financial outlook which, however, will not develop into actual crisis.' Every other head of a family down here discovers about that time of year that his household is living far beyond its income, and that severe retrenchment will be necessary. For April or May or thereabouts I should hint that one of the Dibcuster girls would make the happiest choice of her life. There are eight of them, and it's really time that one of the family married or went on the stage or took to writing worldly novels."

"They never have done anything of the kind within human memory," objected Clovis.

"One must take some risks," said Vera. "I should be on safer ground," she added, "in predicting serious servant troubles from February to November. 'Some of the best mistresses and house managers in this locality will be faced with vexatious servant difficulties, which will be temporarily tided over.' "

"Another safe forecast," suggested Clovis, "could be fitted into the dates when there are medal competitions at the golf club. 'One or two of the most brilliant local players will encounter extraordinary and persistent bad luck, which will rob them of the deserved guerdon of good play.' At least a dozen men will think your prophecies positively inspired."

Vera made a note of the suggestion.

"I'll let you have an advance copy at half price," she said; "on the other hand, I expect you to see that your mother buys one at market rates."

"She shall buy two," said Clovis; "she can give one to Lady Adela, who never buys anything that she can borrow."

The almanack had a big sale, and most of its predictions came sufficiently near fulfillment to sustain the compiler's claim to prophetic powers of an eighteenpenny standard. One of the Dibcuster girls made up her mind to be a hospital nurse and another of them gave up piano playing, both of which might be considered happy decisions, while the forecast of servant troubles and unmerited bad luck on the golf links received ample confirmation in the annals of the home and the club.

"I don't see how she was to know that I was going to change my cook twice in seven months," said Mrs. Duff, who easily recognised an allusion to herself as one of the best mistresses of the neighbourhood.

"And it's come quite true about phenomenal vegetable products being recorded from a local garden," said Mrs. Openshaw; "it said 'a garden which has long been the admiration of the neighbourhood for its magnificent flowers will this year produce some marvels in the way of vegetables.' Our garden is the admiration of everybody, and yesterday Henry brought in some carrots, well, you wouldn't see anything to equal them at a show."

"Oh, but I think that refers to *our* garden," said Mrs. Duff, "it has always been admired for its flowers, and now we've got some Glory of the South parsnips that beat anything I've ever seen. We've taken their measurements, and I got Phyllis to photograph them. I shall certainly buy the almanack if it comes out another year."

"I've ordered it already," said Mrs. Openshaw; "after what it foretold about my garden I thought I ought to."

While the general verdict was in favour of the almanack as an inspired production, or, at any rate, a very fair compilation of successful prediction, there were critics who pointed out that most of the events foretold were of the nature of things that happened in one form or another in any given year.

"I couldn't risk being very definite about any particular event," said Vera to Clovis towards the end of the twelvemonth; "as it is I have rather tied myself up over Jocelyn Vanner. I hinted that the hunting field was not a safe place for her during November and December. It never is a safe place for her at any time, she is always coming off a jump or getting bolted with or something of that sort. And now she has taken alarm at my prediction, and only comes to the meets on foot. Nothing very serious can happen to her under those circumstances."

"It must be ruining her hunting season," said Clovis.

"It's ruining the reputation of my almanack," said Vera; "it's the one thing that has definitely miscarried. I felt so sure she would have a spill of some sort that could be magnified into a serious accident."

"I'm afraid I can't offer to ride over her, or incite hounds to tear her to pieces in mistake for a fox," said Clovis; "I should earn your undying devotion, but there would be a wearisome fuss about it, and I should have to hunt with another pack in the future, and that would be dreadfully inconvenient."

"As your mother says, you are a mass of selfishness," commented Vera.

An opportunity for being unselfish occurred to Clovis a day or two later, when he found himself at close quarters with Jocelyn near Bludberry Gate, where hounds were drawing a long woody hollow in search of an elusive fox.

"Scent is poor, and there's an interminable amount of cover," grumbled Clovis from his saddle; "we shall be here for hours before we get a fox away."

"All the more time for you to talk to me," said Jocelyn archly.

"The question is," said Clovis darkly, "whether I ought to be seen talking to you. I may be involving you."

"Heavens! Involving me in what?" gasped Jocelyn.

"Do you know anything about Bukowina?" Clovis asked with seeming inconsequence.

"Bukowina? It's somewhere in Asia Minor, isn't it—or Central Asia—or is it part of the Balkans?" hazarded Jocelyn; "I really forget for the moment. Where exactly is it?"

"On the brink of a revolution," said Clovis impressively; "that's what I want to warn you about. When I was staying with my aunt in Bucharest" (Clovis invented aunts as lavishly as other people invent golfing experiences) "I got mixed up in the affair without knowing what I was in for. There was a Princess—"

"Ah," said Jocelyn knowingly, "there is always a beautiful and alluring Princess in these affairs."

"As plain and boring a woman as one could find in

eastern Europe," said Clovis; "one of the sort that call just before lunch and stay till it's time to dress for dinner. Well, it seems that some Rumanian Jew is willing to finance the revolution if he could be assured of getting certain mineral concessions. The Jew is cruising in a yacht somewhere off the English coast, and the Princess had made up her mind that I was the safest person to convey the concession papers to him. My aunt whispered, 'For Heaven's sake agree to what she asks or she'll stay on to dinner.' At the moment any sacrifice seemed better than *that*, and so here I am, with my breast pocket bulging with compromising documents, and my life not worth a minute's purchase."

"But," said Jocelyn, "you are safe here in England, aren't you?"

"Do you see that man over there, on the roan?" asked Clovis, pointing to a man with a heavy black moustache, who was probably an auctioneer from a neighbouring town, and at any rate was a stranger to the hunt. "That man was outside my aunt's door when I escorted the Princess to her carriage. He was on the platform of the railway station when I left Bucharest. He was on the landing-stage when I arrived in England. I can go nowhere without finding him at my elbow. I was not surprised to see him at the meet this morning."

"But what can he do to you?" asked Jocelyn tremulously; "he can't kill you."

"Not before witnesses, if he can avoid it. The moment hounds find and the field scatters will be his opportunity. He means to have those papers to-day."

"But how can he be sure you've got them on you?"

"He can't; I might have slipped them over to you while we were talking. That is why he is trying to make up his mind which of us to go for at the critical moment."

"Us?" screamed Jocelyn; "do you mean to say—?"

"I warned you that it was dangerous to be seen talking to me."

"But this is awful! What am I to do?"

"Slip away into the undergrowth the moment that hounds get moving, and run like a rabbit. It is your only chance, and remember, if you escape, no talking. Many lives will be involved if you breathe a word of what I've told you. My aunt at Bucharest—"

At that moment there was a whimper from hounds down in the hollow, and a general ripple of movement passed through the scattered groups of waiting horsemen. A louder and more assured burst of noise came up from the valley.

"They've found!" cried Clovis and turned eagerly to join in the stampede. A crashing, scrunching noise as of a body rapidly and resolutely forcing its way through birch thicket and dead bracken was all that remained to him of his late companion.

Jocelyn's most intimate friends never knew the exact nature of the deadly peril she had incurred in the hunting field that day, but enough was made known to ensure the almanack a brisk sale at its new price of three shillings.

A Housing Problem

THE SOLUTION OF
AN INSOLUBLE DILEMMA

I'm in a frightful position," exclaimed Mrs. Duff-Chubleigh, sinking into an armchair and closing her eyes as though to shut out some distressing vision.

"Really? What has happened?" said Mrs. Pallitson, preparing herself to hear some kitchen tragedy.

"The more one tries to make one's house-parties a success, the more one seems to court failure," was the tragical reply.

"I'm sure it's been most enjoyable so far," said the guest politely; "weather, of course, one can't count on, but otherwise I can't see that anything has gone wrong. I was thinking you were to be congratulated."

Mrs. Duff-Chubleigh laughed harshly and bitterly.

"It was so nice having the Marchioness here," she said; "she's dull and she dresses badly, but people in these parts think no end of her, and, of course, it's rather a social score to get hold of her. It counts for a good deal to be in her good graces. And now she talks of leaving us at a moment's notice."

"Really? That is unfortunate, but I'm sure she'll be sorry to leave such a charming—"

"She's not leaving in sorrow," said the hostess; "no— in anger."

"Anger?"

"Bobbie Chermbacon called her, to her face, a moth-eaten old hen. That's not the sort of thing one says to a

Marchioness, and I told him so afterwards. He said she was only a Marchioness by marriage, which is absurd, because, of course, no one is born a Marchioness. Anyway, he didn't apologise, and she says she won't stay under the same roof with him."

"Under the circumstances," said Mrs. Pallitson, promptly, "I think you might help Mr. Chermbacon to choose a nice early train back to Town. There's one that goes before lunch, and I expect his valet could get the packing act done in something under twenty minutes."

Mrs. Duff-Chubleigh rose in silence, went to the door, and carefully closed it. Then she spoke slowly and impressively, with the air of a Minister who is asking an economically-minded Parliament for an increased Navy Vote.

"Bobbie Chermbacon is rich, quite rich, and one day he will be very much richer. His aunt can buy motor-cars as we might buy theatre-tickets, and he will be her chief heir. I am getting on in years, though I may not look it."

"You don't," Mrs. Pallitson assured her.

"Thank you; still, the fact remains. I'm getting on in years, and though I've a reasonable number of children of my own I've reached that time of life when a woman begins to feel a great longing for a son-in-law. Bobbie told Margaret last night that she had the eyes of a dreaming Madonna."

"Extravagance in language seems to be his besetting characteristic," said Mrs. Pallitson; "of course," she continued hastily, "I don't mean to say that dear Margaret hasn't the eyes of a dreaming Madonna. I think the simile excellent."

"There are many different types of Madonna," said Mrs. Duff-Chubleigh.

"Exactly, but it's rather outspoken language for such short acquaintance. As I say, he seems to be a rather outspoken young man."

"Ah, but he said more than that; he said she reminded him of Gaby What's-her-name, you know, the fascinating actress that the King of Spain admires so much."

"Portugal," murmured Mrs. Pallitson.

"And he didn't confine himself to saying pretty things," continued the mother eagerly; "actions speak stronger than words. He gave her some exquisite orchids to wear at dinner last night. They were from *our* orchid-house, but, still, he went to the trouble of picking them."

"That shows a certain amount of devotion," agreed Mrs. Pallitson.

"And he said he adored chestnut hair," continued Mrs. Duff-Chubleigh; "Margaret's hair is a very beautiful shade of chestnut."

"He's known her for a very short time," said Mrs. Pallitson.

"It's *always* been chestnut," exclaimed Mrs. Duff-Chubleigh.

"Oh, I didn't mean that; I meant that the conquest was sudden, not the colour of the hair. These sudden infatuations are often the most genuine, I believe. A man sees someone for the first time, and knows at once that it is the one person he's been looking for."

"Well, you see the frightful position I'm in. Either the Marchioness leaves in a fury, or I've got to turn Bobbie adrift just as he and Margaret are getting on so very well. It will nip the whole thing in the bud. I didn't sleep a wink last night. I ate nothing for breakfast. If I'm found floating in the carp-pond, you, at least, will know the reason why."

"It's certainly a dreadful situation," said Mrs. Pallitson; "how would it be," she added slowly and reflectively, "if I were to ask Margaret and Bobbie over to our place for the remainder of the Marchioness's stay? My husband has got a men's party, but we could easily expand it. Out of all your guests you could subtract three without unduly diminishing your number. We could pretend that it was an old arrangement."

"Do you mind if I kiss you?" asked Mrs. Duff-Chubleigh; "after this we must call each other by our Christian names. Mine is Elizabeth."

"There I must object," said Mrs. Pallitson, who had submitted to the kiss; "there is dignity and charm in the name Elizabeth, but my godparents christened me Celeste. When a woman weighs as much as I do—"

"I am sure you don't," exclaimed her hostess, in defiant disregard of logic.

"And inherits a very uncertain temper," resumed Mrs. Pallitson, "there is a distinct flavour of incongruity in answering to the name Celeste."

"You are doing a heavenly thing, and I think the name most appropriate; I shall always call you by it."

"I'm afraid we haven't an orchid-house," said Mrs. Pallitson, "but there are some rather choice tuberoses in the hothouse."

"Margaret's favourite flower!" exclaimed Mrs. Duff-Chubleigh.

Mrs. Pallitson repressed a sigh. She was fond of tuberoses herself.

The day after the transplanting of Bobbie and Margaret, Mrs. Duff-Chubleigh was called to the telephone.

"Is that you, Elizabeth?" came the voice of Mrs. Pallitson; "you must have Bobbie back. Don't say it's impossible, you must. The Bishop of Sokotra, my husband's uncle, is staying here. Sokotra, never mind how it's spelt. Bobbie told him last night at dinner what he thought of Christian missions; I've often said the same thing myself, but never to a Bishop. Nor have I expressed it in quite such offensive language. The Bishop refuses to stay another day under the same roof as Bobbie. He, the Bishop, is not merely an uncle, but a bachelor uncle, with private means. It's all very well to say he should show a tolerant and charitable spirit; charity begins at home, and this is a Colonial Bishop. Sokotra, I keep telling you; it doesn't matter where it is, the point is that the Bishop is here, and we can't allow him to leave us in a temper."

"How about the Marchioness?" shrilled Mrs. Duff-Chubleigh at her end of the 'phone, having first carefully glanced round to see that nobody was within hearing distance of her remarks. "She's just as important to me as the Bishop of Scooter, or wherever it is, is to you. I don't know why he should take such absurd unreasonable offence because Christian missions were unfavourably criticised; anyone might express an opinion on a subject of that sort, even to a Colonial Bishop. It's a very different thing being called to your face a moth-eaten old hen. I hear that she is going to give a hunt ball at Cloudly this winter, and it's quite probable that she'll ask me over there for it. And now you want me to ruin everything and have a most unpleasant contretemps by taking that boy back under my roof. You can't expect it of me. Besides, we can't keep shifting Mr. Chermbacon backwards and forwards as though he was the regulator of an erratic clock. What do you say?"

"The Bishop won't stay another night unless Bobbie goes to-day," came over the phone in hard relentless tones. "I've told Bobbie he must leave the first thing after lunch, and I've ordered the motor to be ready for him. Margaret can follow to-morrow."

Then there followed a pitiless silence at the Pallitson end of the telephone. Vainly Mrs. Duff-Chubleigh rang up again and again, and put the fruitless and despairing question "Are you there?" to the cold emptiness of unresponsive space. The Pallitsons had cut themselves off.

"The telephone is the coward's weapon," muttered Mrs. Duff-Chubleigh furiously; "those heavy blonde women are always a mass of selfishness."

Then she sat down to write a telegram, as a last appeal to Celeste's better feelings.

"Am having carp taken out of fish-pond. I can face drowning, but will not be nibbled.—ELIZABETH."

As a matter of fact Bobbie Chermbacon and the Marchioness travelled up to Town by the same train. He had grasped the fact that his presence was not in request at either of the house-parties, and she was hurriedly summoned to London, where her husband had entered on the illness which, in a few days, made her a widow and a dowager. Bobbie's enthusiasm for chestnut hair and dreamy Madonna eyes did not lead him to repeat his visit to the Duff-Chubleigh household. He spent the winter in Egypt, and some ten months later he married the widowed Marchioness.

The Bystander, October 15, 1913

A Sacrifice to Necessity

Alicia Pevenly sat on a garden seat in the rose-walk at Chopehanger, enjoying the valedictory mildness of a warm October morning, and experiencing that atmosphere of mental complacency that descends on a woman who has breakfasted well, is picturesquely dressed, and has reached forty-two in pleasant insidious stages. The loss of her husband some ten years ago had woven a thread of tender regret into her life-pattern, but for the most part she looked on the world and its ways with placid acquiescent amiability. The income on which she and her seventeen-year-old daughter lived and kept up appearances was small, almost inconveniently small, perhaps, but with due management and a little forethought it sufficed. Contriving and planning gained a certain amount of zest from the fact that there was only such a slender margin of shillings to be manipulated.

"There is all the difference in the world," Mrs. Pevenly would say to herself, "between being badly off and merely having to be careful."

Regarding her own personal affairs with measured tranquillity, she did not let the larger events of the world disturb her peace of mind. She took a warm, but quite impersonal, interest in the marriage of Prince Arthur of Connaught, thereby establishing her claim to be considered a woman with broad sympathies and intelligently in touch with the age in which she lived. On the other hand, she was not greatly stirred by the question whether Ireland should or should not be given Home Rule, and she was absolutely indifferent as to where the southern frontier of Albania should be drawn or whether it should be drawn at all; if there had ever been a combative strain in her nature it had never been developed.

Mrs. Pevenly had finished her breakfast at about half-past nine, by which hour her daughter had not put in an appearance; as the hostess and most of the members of the house-party were equally late, Beryl's slackness could not be regarded as a social sin, but her mother thought it was a pity to lose so much of the fine October morning. Beryl Pevenly had been described by someone as the "Flapper incarnate," and the label summed her up accurately. Her mother already recognised that she was disposed to be a law unto herself; what she did not yet realise was that Beryl was extremely likely to be a law-giver to any weaker character with whom she might come in contact. "She is only a child yet," Mrs. Pevenly would say to herself, forgetting that seventeen and seventy are about the two most despotic ages of human life.

"Ah, finished breakfast at last!" she called out in mock reproof as her daughter came out to join her in the rose-walk; "if you had gone to bed in good time these last two evenings, as I did, you would not be so tired in the mornings. It has been so fresh and charming out here, while all you silly people have been lying in bed. I hope you weren't playing bridge for high stakes, my dear!"

There was a tired defiant look in Beryl's eyes that drew forth the anxious remark.

"Bridge? No, we started with a rubber or two the night before last," said Beryl, "but we switched off to baccarat. Rather a mistake for some of us."

"Beryl, you haven't been losing?" asked Mrs. Pevenly with increased anxiety in her voice.

"I lost quite a lot the first evening," said Beryl, "and as I couldn't possibly pay my losses I simply punted the next evening to try and get them back; I've come to the conclusion that baccarat is not my game. I came a bigger cropper on the second evening than on the first."

"Beryl, this is awful! I'm very angry with you. Tell me quickly, how much have you lost?"

Beryl looked at a slip of paper that she was twisting and untwisting in her hands.

"Three hundred and ten the first night, seven hundred and sixteen the second," she announced.

"Three hundred what?"

"Pounds."

"*Pounds?*" screamed the mother; "Beryl, I don't believe you. Why, that is a thousand pounds!"

"A thousand and twenty-six, to be exact," said Beryl.

Mrs. Pevenly was too frightened to cry.

"Where do you suppose," she asked, "that we could raise a thousand pounds, or anything like a thousand pounds? We are living at the top of our income, we are practising all sorts of economies, we simply couldn't subtract a thousand pounds from our little capital. It would ruin us."

"We should be socially ruined if it got about that we played for stakes that we couldn't or wouldn't pay; no one would ask us anywhere."

"How came you to do such a dreadful thing?" wailed the mother.

"Oh, it's no use asking those sort of questions," said Beryl; "the thing is done. I suppose I inherit a gambling instinct from some of you."

"You certainly don't," exclaimed Mrs. Pevenly hotly; "your father never touched cards or cared anything about horse-racing, and I don't know one game of cards from another."

"These things skip a generation sometimes, and come out all the stronger in the next batch," said Beryl; "how about that uncle of yours who used to get up a sweepstake every Sunday at school as to which of the Books of the Bible the text for the sermon would be taken from? If he wasn't a keen gambler I've never heard of one."

"Don't let's argue," faltered the elder woman, "let's think of what is to be done. How many people do you owe the money to?"

"Luckily it's all due to one person, Ashcombe Gwent,"

said Beryl; "he was doing nearly all the winning on both nights. He's rather a good sort in his way, but unluckily he isn't a bit well off, and one couldn't expect him to overlook the fact that money was owing to him. I fancy he's just as much of an adventurer as we are."

"We are *not* adventurers," protested Mrs. Pevenly.

"People who come to stay at country houses and play for stakes that they've no prospect of paying if they lose, *are* adventurers," said Beryl, who seemed determined to include her mother in any moral censure that might be applied to her own conduct.

"Have you said anything to him about the difficulty you are in?"

"I have. That's what I've come to tell you about. We had a talk this morning in the billiard-room after breakfast. It seems there is just one way out of the tangle. He's inclined to be amorous."

"Amorous!" exclaimed the mother.

"Matrimonially amorous," said the daughter; "in fact, without either of us having guessed it, it appears that he's the victim of an infatuation."

"He has certainly been polite and attentive," said Mrs. Pevenly; "he is not a man who says much, but he listens to what one has to say. And do you mean that he really wants to marry—?"

"That is exactly what he does want," said Beryl. "I don't know that he is the sort of husband that one would rave about, but I gather that he has enough to live on—as much as we're accustomed to, anyhow, and he's quite presentable to look at. The alternative is selling out a big chunk of our little capital; I should have to go and be a governess or typewriter or something, and you would have to do needlework. From just making things do, and paying rounds of visits and having a fairly good time, we should sink suddenly to the unfortunate position of distressed gentlefolk. I don't know what you think, but I'm inclined to consider that the marriage proposition is the least objectionable."

Mrs. Pevenly took out her handkerchief.

"How old is he?" she asked.

"Oh, thirty-seven or thirty-eight; a year or two older perhaps."

"Do you like him?"

Beryl laughed.

"He's not in the *least* my style," she said.

Mrs. Pevenly began to weep.

"What a deplorable situation," she sobbed; "what a sacrifice for the sake of a miserable sum of money and social considerations! To think that such a tragedy should happen in our family. I've often read about such things in books, a girl being forced to marry a man she didn't care about because of some financial disaster—"

"You shouldn't read such trashy books," pronounced Beryl.

"But now it's really happening!" exclaimed the mother; "my own child's life to be sacrificed by marriage to a man years older than herself, whom she doesn't care the least bit about, and because—"

"Look here," interrupted Beryl. "I don't seem to have made this clear. It isn't me that he wants to marry. 'Flappers' don't appeal to him, he told me so. Mature womanhood is his particular line, and it's you that he's infatuated about."

"Me!"

For the second time that morning Mrs. Pevenly's voice rose to a scream.

"Yes, he said you were his ideal, a ripe, sun-warmed peach, delicious and desirable, and a lot of other metaphors that he probably borrowed from Swinburne or Edmund Jones. I told him that under other circumstances I shouldn't have held out much hope of his getting a favourable response from you, but that as we owed him a thousand and twenty-six pounds you would probably consider a matrimonial alliance the most convenient way of discharging the obligation. He's coming out to speak to you himself in a few minutes, but I thought I'd better come and prepare you first."

"But, my dear—"

"Of course, you hardly know the man, but I don't think that matters. You see, you've been married before and a second husband is always something of an anti-climax.

Here is Ashcombe. I think I'd better leave you two together. You must have a lot you want to say to each
other.''

The wedding took place quietly some eight weeks later.
The presents were costly, if not numerous, and consisted
chiefly of a cancelled I.O.U., the gift of the bridegroom
to the bride's daughter.

A Shot in the Dark

Philip Sletherby settled himself down in an almost empty railway carriage, with the pleasant consciousness of being embarked on an agreeable and profitable pilgrimage. He was bound for Brill Manor, the country residence of his newly achieved acquaintance, Mrs. Saltpen-Jago. Honoria Saltpen-Jago was a person of some social importance in London, of considerable importance and influence in the county of Chalkshire. The county of Chalkshire, or, at any rate, the eastern division of it, was of immediate personal interest to Philip Sletherby; it was held for the Government in the present Parliament by a gentleman who did not intend to seek re-election, and Sletherby was under serious consideration by the Party managers as his possible successor. The majority was not a large one, and the seat could not be considered safe for a Ministerial candidate, but there was an efficient local organisation, and with luck the seat might be held. The Saltpen-Jago influence was not an item which could be left out of consideration, and the political aspirant had been delighted at meeting Honoria at a small and friendly luncheon-party, still more gratified when she had asked him down to her country house for the following Friday-to-Tuesday. He was obviously "on approval," and if he could secure the goodwill of his hostess he might count on the nomination as an assured thing. If he failed to find favour in her eyes—well, the local leaders would probably cool off in their embryo enthusiasm for him.

Among the passengers dotted about on the platform, awaiting their respective trains, Sletherby espied a club acquaintance, and beckoned him up to the carriage-window for a chat.

"Oh, you're staying with Mrs. Saltpen-Jago for the week-end, are you? I expect you'll have a good time; she has the reputation of being an excellent hostess. She'll be useful to you, too, if that Parliamentary project—hullo, you're off. Good-bye."

Sletherby waved good-bye to his friend, pulled up the window, and turned his attention to the magazine lying on his lap. He had scarcely glanced at a couple of pages, however, when a smothered curse caused him to glance hastily at the only other occupant of the carriage. His travelling companion was a young man of about two-and-twenty, with dark hair, fresh complexion, and the blend of smartness and disarray that marks the costume of the "nut" who is bound on a rustic holiday. He was engaged in searching furiously and ineffectually for some elusive or non-existent object; from time to time he dug a sixpenny bit out of a waistcoat pocket and stared at it ruefully, then recommenced the futile searching operations. A cigarette-case, matchbox, latchkey, silver pencil case, and railway ticket were turned out on to the seat beside him, but none of these articles seemed to afford him satisfaction; he cursed again, rather louder than before.

The vigorous pantomime did not draw forth any remark from Sletherby, who resumed his scrutiny of the magazine.

"I say!" exclaimed a young voice presently, "didn't I hear you say that you were going down to stay with Mrs. Saltpen-Jago at Brill Manor? What a coincidence! My mater, you know. I'm coming on there on Monday evening, so we shall meet. I'm quite a stranger; haven't seen the mater for six months at least. I was away yachting last time she was in Town. I'm Bertie, the second son, you know. I say, it's an awfully lucky coincidence that I should run across someone who knows the mater just at this particular moment. I've done a damned awkward thing."

"You've lost something, haven't you?" said Sletherby.

"Not lost exactly, but left behind, which is almost as bad; just as inconvenient, anyway. I've come away without my sovereign purse, with four quid in it, all my worldly wealth for the moment. It was in my pocket all right, just before I was starting, and then I wanted to seal a letter, and the sovereign-purse happens to have my crest on it, so I whipped it out to stamp the seal with, and, like a double-distilled idiot, I must have left it on the table. I had some silver loose in my pocket, but after I'd paid for a taxi and my ticket I'd only got this forlorn little sixpence left. I'm stopping at a little country inn near Brondquay for three days' fishing; not a soul knows me there, and my week-end bill, and tips, and cab to and from the station, and my ticket on to Brill, that will mount up to two or three quid, won't it? If you wouldn't mind lending me two pound ten, or three for preference, I shall be awfully obliged. It will pull me out of no end of a hole."

"I think I can manage that," said Sletherby, after a moment's hesitation.

"Thanks awfully. It's jolly good of you. What a lucky thing for me that I should have chanced across one of the mater's friends. It will be a lesson to me not to leave my exchequer lying about anywhere, when it ought to be in my pocket. I suppose the moral of the whole thing is don't try and convert things to purposes for which they weren't intended. Still, when a sovereign-purse has your crest on it—"

"What is your crest, by the way?" asked Sletherby, carelessly.

"Not a very uncommon one," said the youth; "a demi-lion holding a cross-crosslet in its paw."

"When your mother wrote to me, giving me a list of trains, she had, if I remember rightly, a greyhound courant on her notepaper," observed Sletherby. There was a tinge of coldness in his voice.

"That is the Jago crest," responded the youth promptly; "the demi-lion is the Saltpen crest. We have the right to use both, but I always use the demi-lion, because, after all, we are really Saltpens."

There was silence for a moment or two, and the young

man began to collect his fishing tackle and other belongings from the rack.

"My station is the next one," he announced.

"I've never met your mother," said Sletherby suddenly, "though we've corresponded several times. My introduction to her was through political friends. Does she resemble you at all in feature? I should rather like to be able to pick her out if she happened to be on the platform to meet me."

"She's supposed to be like me. She has the same dark brown hair and high colour; it runs in her family. I say, this is where I get out."

"Good-bye," said Sletherby.

"You've forgotten the three quid," said the young man, opening the carriage-door and pitching his suit-case on to the platform.

"I've no intention of lending you three pounds, or three shillings," said Sletherby severely.

"But you said—"

"I know I did. My suspicions hadn't been aroused then, though I hadn't necessarily swallowed your story. The discrepancy about the crests put me on my guard, notwithstanding the really brilliant way in which you accounted for it. Then I laid a trap for you; I told you that I had never met Mrs. Saltpen-Jago. As a matter of fact I met her at lunch on Monday last. She is a pronounced blonde."

The train moved on, leaving the *soi-disant* cadet of the Saltpen-Jago family cursing furiously on the platform.

"Well, he hasn't opened his fishing expedition by catching a flat," chuckled Sletherby. He would have an entertaining story to recount at dinner that evening, and his clever little trap would earn him applause as a man of resource and astuteness. He was still telling his adventure in imagination to an attentive audience of dinner-guests when the train drew up at his destination. On the platform he was greeted sedately by a tall footman, and noisily by Claude People, K.C., who had apparently travelled down by the same train.

"Hullo, Sletherby! You spending the week-end at Brill? Good. Excellent. We'll have a round of golf together to-morrow; I'll give you your revenge for Hoylake. Not a bad course here, as inland courses go. Ah, here we are; here's the car waiting for us, and very nice, too!"

The car which won the K.C.'s approval was a sumptuous-looking vehicle, which seemed to embody the last word in elegance, comfort, and locomotive power. Its graceful lines and symmetrical design masked the fact that it was an enormous wheeled structure, combining the features of an hotel lounge and an engine-room.

"Different sort of vehicle to the post-chaise in which our grandfathers used to travel, eh?" exclaimed the lawyer appreciatively. And for Sletherby's benefit he began running over the chief points of perfection in the fitting and mechanism of the car.

Sletherby heard not a single word, noted not one of the details that were being expounded to him. His eyes were fixed on the door panel, on which were displayed two crests: a greyhound courant and a demi-lion holding in its paw a cross-crosslet.

The K.C. was not the sort of man to notice an absorbed silence on the part of a companion. He had been silent himself for nearly an hour in the train, and his tongue was making up for lost time. Political gossip, personal anecdote, and general observations flowed from him in an uninterrupted stream as the car sped along the country roads; from the inner history of the Dublin labour troubles and the private life of the Prince Designate of Albania he progressed with easy volubility to an account of an alleged happening at the ninth hole at Sandwich, and a verbatim report of a remark made by the Duchess of Pathshire at a Tango tea. Just as the car turned in at the Brill entrance gates the K.C. captured Sletherby's attention by switching his remarks on to the personality of their hostess.

"Brilliant woman, level-headed, a clear thinker, knows exactly when to take up an individual or a cause, exactly when to let him or it drop. Influential woman, but spoils herself and her chances by being too restless. No repose. Good appearance, too, till she made that idiotic change."

"Change?" queried Sletherby, "what change?"

"What change? You don't mean to say— Oh, of course, you've only known her just lately. She used to have beautiful dark brown hair, which went very well with her fresh complexion; then one day, about five weeks ago, she electrified everybody by appearing as a brilliant blonde. Quite ruined her looks. Here we are. I say, what's the matter with you? You look rather ill."

Acknowledgments

Anyone who writes a biography of H. H. Munro will have divided feelings about his sister, Ethel. She set out to destroy all traces of her brother's life that did not accord with the view of him that she chose to present; and since she was as resolute as the aunts who raised her, she did a thorough job. But out of her great love for her brother she also fashioned a splendid account of his youth. On balance, one is greatly in her debt.

Hector's closest surviving relatives have been equally generous in sharing their time and memories but not in the least dogmatic about the direction the biography might take. The book would not have been possible without the warm cooperation of Hector's nieces, Juniper Munro Bryan and Felicia Munro Crawshaw, and Mrs. Bryan's husband, G.A.P. (Pat) Bryan. I also wish to express special appreciation to Mr. Ben Travers, the late playwright, who called up vividly for me scenes with Hector that had taken place nearly seventy years before.

I feel as well deep gratitude for the assistance of Lynn Nesbit at International Creative Management and Deborah Rogers in London; Alice E. Mayhew, Vincent Virga, Roslyn Siegel, and Mary Heathcote at Simon and Schuster; Christopher Sinclair-Stevenson and John Henderson of Hamish Hamilton Ltd. And for the invaluable resources of the British Library, particularly its exhaustive and efficiently staffed newspaper archive at Colindale; the Huntington Library, San Marino, California; the library of the Imperial War Museum, Lambeth; the Kensington Library, London; the North Devon Athenaeum, Barnstaple; Special Collections, The University of Iowa Library; and Doheny Library, University of Southern California.

Then, too, there were individual contributions that I greatly appreciated from the following persons: Rennie Airth, Jon Bradshaw, Eva Maria Brailsford, Dr. Piers

Brendon, George Challis, Charles Cox, Bryan Curle, Dr. Robert Drake, Charles Fleming, C. Grigg, Ida Hemphill, Michael A. Hewson, J. W. Lambert, Doris Langguth, Dr. F. M. Leventhal, Roger Machell, G. A. Morris, Ethel Narvid, A. D. Nightall, Frank Paluka, S. R. Pawley, Christopher Radmall, Max Reinhardt, William Tuohy, Harlan L. Umansky, Roland Whipp and Emlyn Williams.

Notes

KEY TO FREQUENTLY CITED SOURCES

Bryan   Felicia Crawshaw and Juniper Bryan, the daughters of Charles Arthur Munro, and Hector Hugh Munro's nieces, were interviewed several times at Mrs. Bryan's home in Belfast, Northern Ireland, in August 1978 and June 1979. Many papers, notebooks, letters and photographs are in Mrs. Bryan's possession.

Exhibit   An exhibition of material from the 22nd Battalion of the Royal Fusiliers is on file at the Kensington Library, London.

Lambert   Lambert, J.W., Introduction, *The Bodley Head Saki* (London, The Bodley Head, 1963).

Lane   Material from John Lane is on file in the office of Max Reinhardt, The Bodley Head, London.

MP   *Morning Post,* London. On file at the British Library's newspaper collection, Colindale.

Munro   Munro, E.M., "Biography of Saki." Ethel Munro's memoir was first published in *The Square Egg,* a posthumous collection of Saki's work (London, John Lane The Bodley Head, 1924). References in these notes are to the more readily available "Omnibus" edition of Saki, published in two volumes in London by John Lane The Bodley Head and in New York by Viking Press, Inc. Volume I, which included the short stories and Ethel Munro's memoir, was published in 1930; Volume II, the novels and plays, was published three years later.

Reynolds   Reynolds, Rothay, "A Memoir of H. H. Munro," in Saki, *The Toys of Peace* (London, John Lane The Bodley Head, 1919).

Saki   *Rise*   *The Rise of the Russian Empire* (London, Grant Richards, 1900).

Alice	*The Westminster Alice* (London, The Westminster Gazette, 1902).
Reginald	*Reginald* (London, Methuen, 1904).
Russia	*Reginald in Russia* (London, Methuen, 1910).
Clovis	*The Chronicles of Clovis* (London, John Lane, 1911).
Bassington	*The Unbearable Bassington* (London, John Lane, 1912).
William	*When William Came* (London, John Lane, 1913).
Beasts	*Beasts and Super-Beasts* (London, John Lane, 1914).
Toys	*The Toys of Peace* (London, John Lane The Bodley Head, 1919).
Egg	*The Square Egg and Other Sketches* (London, John Lane The Bodley Head, 1924).

In these notes, the first editions are cited. But because of the many later editions of Saki's work, references to the novels are given by chapter. For most of the stories, a second reference in parentheses indicates the periodical in which the story originally appeared and the date. See under Munro for references to "Omnibus" edition of Saki.

Travers   Interviews with Ben Travers, the playwright, London, June, July, 1978.

War Museum   The Imperial War Museum, Lambeth.

WG   *Westminster Gazette,* London. On file at the British Library's newspaper collection, Colindale.

CHAPTER I. THE BACKGROUND (1870–1887)

Page 7
Mother's death. Bryan.
  8
Wills filed at Somerset House, London, provide the following information about the Munro family: Colonel Charles Adolphus Munro,

Saki's grandfather, was born in 1784 and died June 16, 1859, at the age of seventy-five. He married Lucy Eliza Jones, who was born in 1808 and died February 4, 1882. They had five children who survived: Charlotte Maria, Augusta Georgina, Charles Augustus (Saki's father), Wellesley Herbert and Hector Bruce. Hector Bruce Munro married Margaret Bessie Stuart. Saki's father (May 15, 1844–June 27, 1907) married Mary Frances Mercer, who, from records at St. Catherine's House, London, died early in 1872. Their three children were Ethel Mary Munro (April 9, 1868–Feb. 28, 1955); Charles Arthur Munro (July 24, 1869–Feb. 13, 1952); and Hector Hugh Munro (Saki) (Dec. 18, 1870–Nov. 14, 1916). In 1904, Charles Arthur Munro married Inez Mary Muriel Chambers (Nov. 28, 1881–Nov. 4, 1967), and they had two daughters, Felicia (March 30, 1905–) and Juniper (October 4, 1920–). Felicia married the Rev. A. Aitken Crawshaw; Juniper married George Arthur Pollexfen Bryan.

8
Orwell quotation. Eric Blair (1903–1950), *The Road to Wigan Pier,* Chapter 8.

8
"turbulent" Munro, p. 639.

9
Queen Victoria's hostility to Edward. St. Aubyn, Giles, *Edward VII* (New York, Atheneum, 1979).

9
"Tom" from tomboy. Bryan.

9
"Aunts who have never known" "Clovis on Parental Responsibilities," Beasts (WG, May 3, 1913).

10
"The meaning smile" Munro, p. 642.

10
Hostilities between aunts. Munro, p. 639; Bryan.

10
Munro family line. Mackenzie, Alexander, *History of the Munros of Fowlis* (Inverness, A. & W. Mackenzie, 1898).

10
General Munro's son killed by tiger. Lambert, pp. 8–9.

11
Aunts' hatred. Munro, pp. 639–40.

11
"There was something alike terrifying" "The Peace of Mowsle Barton," Clovis (WG, Feb. 18, 1911).

11
Broadgate Villa. Reed, Margaret A., *Pilton* (Barnstaple, The Aycliffe Press, 1977), pp. 162–3; author's observation.

11
"People talk vaguely" "The Innocence of Reginald," Reginald (WG, April 6, 1904).

12
"Choc rot" Munro, p. 638.

12
Hector called "Chickie." Bryan.

12
"Now, my mother never bothered" "Clovis on Parental Responsibilities," see note, p. 4.

12
Charlie reminded Augusta of beau. Bryan.

13
Bedroom board squeaked. Bryan.

13
"I'm God!" Munro, p. 637.

14
"She was one of those people" "Reginald at the Theatre," Reginald (WG, July 17, 1902).

14
"Most of the aunt's remarks" "The Story-Teller," Beasts (MP, Sept. 2, 1913).

14
"A woman of ungovernable temper" Munro, p. 640.

14–15
"It was her habit" "The Lumber-Room," Beasts (MP, October 14, 1913).

16
"Hors d'oeuvres have always had" "Reginald at the Carlton," Reginald (WG, March 24, 1903).

16–17
"Cold beef" Munro, p. 642.

18
"How frightfully embarrassing" "Reginald at the Carlton," see note, p. 13.

18
Books from Major Munro. Bryan.

18
"I will not number" Saki, "Potted Parliament," *Outlook,* August 1, 1914, p. 135.

18
"So good a boy" Munro, p. 638.

18
"horribly good." "The Story-Teller," see note, p. 11.

19
"The art of public life" Bassington, III.

19
"Anything that is worth knowing" "Reginald on Worries," Reginald.

20
Major Munro's promotion. In a shortened version of her memoir for a Penguin edition of Hector's stories, Ethel repeated what she had

originally written (Munro, p. 647), that their father was Inspector General of the Burma Police when he came back to England on leave. In his copy, her brother, Charlie, wrote in the margin, "Not quite correct, he did not officiate as I.G.P. until some time later when he was Lt. Colonel." Charlie's memory on the point is probably the more reliable. His copy is in the possession of Juniper Bryan.

20
"the children are never naughty" Munro, p. 649.

21
"You must take the Roundheads' part" Munro, p. 649.

21
"The Schartz-Metterklume Method," Beasts (WG, October 14, 1911).

22
Hector's possible meningitis. Bryan.

22
"And so I hear, Mrs. Simpson" Munro, p. 650.

23
"After all" Ibid.

23
Lucy Munro's estate. Her will, Somerset House, London.

24
Charlie denied allowance. Bryan.

24
"There was a row." Munro, p. 653.

24
Bedford School. "Our Great Public Schools," *Bystander,* December 15, 1909.

24
Hector stayed four terms at Bedford. The December 20, 1916, edition of the *Ousel,* published by Bedford, showed Hector entering September 1885 and leaving December 1886. Ethel Munro's memoir says Hector was fifteen when he entered Bedford, but he was three months short of that age.

25
"Gaiety and good looks" Bassington, IV.

25
"You can't expect a boy to be vicious" "The Baker's Dozen," Russia (*Journal of the Leinster Regiment*).

25
Egg collection. Librarians at Bideford said in August 1979 that the eggs, which had become very frail, were thrown out when the exhibits were transferred in the early 1970s to a maritime museum at Appledore.

25
"There was a charm, too" William, XVIII.

26–27
Graham Greene–Ethel Munro exchange. *Spectator,* London, June 13, 1952, p. 780; June 20, 1952, p. 811; June 27, 1952, p. 856.

CHAPTER 2. THE FORBIDDEN BUZZARDS (1887–1893)

Page 28
"playmates" Munro, p. 654.

29
Hector's disdain for American materialism. Lane. Letter, Ethel Munro. Replying to an inquiry in 1937 from agents for Robert Montgomery, the American actor, and the Theatre Guild in New York for permission to adapt *The Unbearable Bassington,* Ethel Munro wrote to her late brother's publisher: "Saki had a detestation of that country's commercialism (this is in confidence) and would never have permitted any adaptation for the stage or film unless arranged by himself, and as he did not care for films, no mention of film rights was made in the agreements. So in refusing permission I am doing what he would have done himself. Judging by the vulgarisation of some British authors' works when filmed, I can imagine what a hash would be made of Saki's stories."

29
"twice to Fécamp" "Reginald's Choir Treat," Reginald (WG, June 24, 1902).

29
"One is so dreadfully" "Adrian," Clovis.

30
Ethel horrid to prospective bride. Bryan.

30
A letter in the possession of Juniper Bryan reads in part: "An aunt of mine, my father's sister, Edith Dodd, was engaged very many years ago when I was a child, to a Colonel Munro—the Father I think of Hector, his first wife had died and I always understood that the engagement was broken off because his daughter Ethel Munro was extremely disagreeable! Yours sincerely, Mary Sharp."

30
Schoolgirls and Hohenzollerns. "Reginald on Tariffs," Reginald (WG, November 6, 1903).

31
"They leaned toward the honest" "The Reticence of Lady Anne," Russia.

31
Berlin won with eighteen. Reynolds, p. xiii.

31
"The bravest man's courage" "Karl-Ludwig's Window," Omnibus, vol. ii, p. 357.

32
"the Hen that hatched" Munro, p. 655.

33
"that great curse" Symonds, John Addington, *Essays Speculative and Suggestive* (London, Smith, Elder & Co., 1907), p. 228.

33

The issue of Hector's possible homosexuality caused his family distress at a time when that condition was considered a stigma. Ethel Munro, through an unquenchable honesty or a need to show that she was not ignorant of any aspect of her brother's life, made a rather overt reference to it in her memoir: "In writing all I have cared to tell of Hector's life . . ." (p. 714). In the original version of his perceptive introduction to the Bodley Head's collection of Saki's stories, J. W. Lambert made two references to possible homosexual activity, including, ". . . it is often claimed that he was homosexual." The passages were deleted to spare pain to Muriel Munro, Hector's sister-in-law, who was still living when the preface was published in 1963. In a letter to Lambert, which has not survived, C. William Mercer (who wrote as Dornford Yates) said that there were no obvious signs of deviation in Hector and vehemently denied the truth of the speculation. (Quoted by Robert Drake; see note, p. 168). But Ben Travers, the playwright, who knew Hector through John Lane, says that Hector's homosexuality was known in publishing circles around 1913.

33

Whitman's illegitimate children. Kaplan, Justin, *Telling Lives* (Washington, D.C., New Republic Books/National Portrait Gallery, 1979), p. 53.

34

Nomadic but punctual complexions. "Tobermory," Clovis (WG, Nov. 27, 1909).

34

Smoothed hair dubiously. "Reginald's Christmas Revel," Reginald (WG, December 22, 1903.)

34

Youth suggesting innocence. "The Innocence of Reginald," Reginald (WG, April 6, 1904).

34

"Mrs. Jallatt didn't study cheapness" "The Strategist," Russia (WG, July 3, 1909).

34

"adopted a protective" "Mrs. Packletide's Tiger," Clovis.

35

Rendering of male dog. Munro, sketch, p. 657.

35

Nanny Oram. St. Anne's Museum, Barnstaple.

35

One of his first stories. "The Blood-Feud of Toad-Water," Russia. (WG, January 26, 1901; signed H.H.M.)

36

"Those cherry orchards" "The Guests," Toys (MP, June 30, 1914).

36

"I've been carefully brought up" "Reginald's Christmas Revel," Reginald (WG, Dec. 22, 1903).

37
"a gorgeous hoax" Munro, p. 658.

37
"were so unco' guid" Ibid., p. 659.

CHAPTER 3. A TOUCH OF REALISM (1893–1894)

Page 39
"At the age of eighteen" "Bertie's Christmas Eve," Toys (WG, December 23, 1911).

40
"He would be in some unheard-of" Bassington, XIII.

40
"I'm not going to talk" Ibid.

41
Kipling as precocious. Wilson, Angus, *The Strange Ride of Rudyard Kipling* (London, Secker & Warburg, 1977), p. 58.

41
Crime in Burma and Nga Kyaw. Report on the Police Administration of Burma for 1893 (Rangoon, Government Printing, 1894), p. 48.

41
"wonderfully little real bad crime" Ibid., p. 105.

42
"There are the children" Munro, p. 660.

42
"When I was out of the district" Ibid., p. 667.

42
"Then during the night" Ibid., p. 660.

42
"about sixteen years old" "Quail Seed," Toys (MP, December 26, 1911).

43
"I am agreeably surprised" Munro, p. 660.

43
"My boy continues" Ibid., p. 661.

43
"I hope you will have" Ibid., p. 669.

43
"No martyr" Ibid., p. 663.

43
"The 'Mandalay Herald' " Ibid., p. 666.

44
"Then I am worried to death" Ibid., p. 664.

44
"Tell Mrs. Byrne" Ibid., p. 667.

44
"I was in terror" Ibid., p. 663.

44
"I thought of putting it" Ibid., p. 661.

44-45
"Darwin believed" Ibid., p. 661.

45
"I found the tiger-kitten" Ibid., p. 664.

45
"The kitten throws off the cat" Ibid., p. 665.

45
"The tiger-kitten has had a nice cage" Ibid., p. 666.

45
"An old lady came to the hotel" Ibid., p. 667.

46
"Then I heard" Ibid., p. 668.

46
"I am very interested" Ibid., p. 670.

47
"Aunt Tom's first letter" Ibid., p. 661.

47
"Owl and oaf" Ibid., p. 662.

48
Hector had come home to die. May, J. L., *John Lane and the Nineties* (London, John Lane The Bodley Head, 1936), p. 194.

48
"There's such a deadly sameness" "Reginald on House Parties," Reginald.

48
"There was a Major Somebody" "Reginald's Christmas Revel," Reginald (WG, December 22, 1903).

48
"He is buried" "Clovis on the Alleged Romance of Business," Egg.

CHAPTER 4. THE BLIND SPOT (1894-1900)

Page 50
Fashions in clothing. "Late Victorian Era," Yarwood, Doreen, *English Costume* (London, B. T. Batsford, Ltd., 1952), pp. 239-247.

51
People craved entertainment. Nevill, Lady Dorothy, *Under Five Reigns* (London, Methuen, 1910), p. 312.

51
Men came earlier to drawing rooms. Jeune, Mary (Lady St. Helier), *Memories of Fifty Years* (London, Edward Arnold, 1909), p. 189.

51
Enthusiasm for mauve. Sitwell, Sir Osbert, *Left Hand, Right Hand!* (Boston, Little, Brown & Co., 1944), p. 261.

51
Willie Mercer. Lambert, pp. 34–35.

52
"a very quaint and clever little dwarf." "Dogged," *St. Paul's,* February 18, 1899, p. 206.

52
"Artemus Gibbon" Ibid.

53
"One subject he never wrote on" Spears, George James, *The Satire of Saki* (New York, Exposition Press, 1963), p. 120.

53
"I wish to be buried" Will of Augusta Munro, Somerset House, London.

53
"gave deific being to the sun" Rise, p. 4.

54
"The history of Russia" Ibid., p. 53.

54
"when the head of the Pope's Legate" Ibid., p. 73.

54
"From cathedral, church and roadside" Ibid., p. 92.

54
"The ideal of God" Ibid., p. 307.

54
"All day long" Ibid., p. 219.

55
"The Russians dreamed" Ibid., p. 131.

55
"Grim and dreary" Ibid., p. 251.

55
Advertisements for Hector's book. *Bookman,* May 1900.

55
"An author stands or falls" *Bookman,* July 1900, p. 121.

56
"courageous and intelligent" *Bookman,* August 1900. p. 155.

56
"greatly commend Mr. Munro's volume" *Athenaeum,* March 31, 1900, p. 398.

56
"—and in this connexion" *Athenaeum,* April 14, 1900, p. 466.

57
"A genuine talent for" *Nation,* March 7, 1901, p. 201.

57
"It may be a writer's misfortune" *American Historical Review,* October 1901.

"I've read your book, sir" Munro, p. 675.

CHAPTER 5. A BREAD AND BUTTER MISS (1900–1901)

Page 59
Frank Carruthers Gould. Scott, J. W. Robertson, *"We" and Me* (London, W. H. Allen, 1956), pp. 80–89.
60
"The subject of so many" Ibid., p. 82.
60
Chamberlain objected to being shown as dog. Spender, J. A., *Life, Journalism and Politics* (London, Cassell and Co., 1927) vol. 1, pp. 94–95.
60
"The only daily paper" Scott, p. 27; see note, p. 69.
61
Ethel Munro's books. Juniper Bryan has preserved several volumes.
61
Munro's commonplace book is also in Mrs. Bryan's possession.
62
Saki as a pen name. Some critics have wondered whether Hector was dissuaded from using his own name because of a novel, *Mrs. Emsley,* published by another Hector Munro. That book, however, was not published until 1911. Its final paragraph, on page 422 of the edition published by Constable and Co., London, would persuade the most casual skimmer that it was not the work of Saki: " 'Ah, love!' she stretched out her arms toward him. 'Love too is a wonderful experience. Like death itself, it brings forgiveness—when it has been purified by time and the wider life.' " Lambert (p. 29) notes that the Rev. A. Aitken Crawshaw, who married Hector's niece, Felicia, long after Hector's death, suggested that the name was a contraction of Sakya Muni, one of the names of Buddha. Mrs. Crawshaw does not accept her late husband's theory. In a *Westminster Gazette* obituary on November 24, 1916, the unsigned writer stated, "As our readers are well aware, 'Saki' —a pen name adopted, by the way, from Nagasaki—wrote much of his best work for our columns." The discovery in the Bryans' attic in Belfast of the verses from the *Rubaiyat* copied out in Hector's hand may perhaps put an end to such speculation.
63
"The following recently-discovered Quatrains" WG, March 4, 1901.
63
"An ample note-book" Ibid.
63
Sequel two weeks later. "The Quatrains of Uttar Al Ghibe—II," WG,

March 19, 1901. Twelve years later, Munro returned to Omar for five verses headed "Quatrains from the Rubaiyat of a Disgruntled Diplomat," WG, May 3, 1913. They concluded with a jape about the rulers of what is now part of Yugoslavia: "Two heads are better far than one, 'tis held, / Yet to this observation I'm impelled, / The Montenegrin Eagle wears two heads— / Pray what the profit if both heads are swelled?"

64
Spender's recollection of Hector. Spender, J. A., Foreword, Alice.

64
"Have you ever seen an Ineptitude?" "Alice in Downing Street," Alice (WG, July 25, 1900).

64
Arthur James Balfour. Brandon, Piers, Eminent Edwardians (London, Secker & Warburg, 1979).

65
"Can you tell me" "Alice in Downing Street," Alice (WG, July 25, 1900).

66
"In my Department" "Alice in Pall Mall," Alice (WG, November 5, 1900).

67
Spender on political satire. Spender, Foreword; see note, p. 75.

67
"Of course something must be done" "Alice at Lambeth," (WG, December 12, 1900).

67
" 'If you please—' " "Alice at St. Stephen's," Alice.

68
"Show me your garden" Austin, Alfred, "The Garden That I Love."

68
" 'The Duke and Duchess!' " "Alice in a Fog," Alice (WG, Nov. 11, 1901).

68
"Dwindle, dwindle" "Alice Has Tea at the Hotel Cecil," Alice (WG, Nov. 29, 1901).

69
Demand for Alice in the United States. The best selling of the seven volumes in the Viking edition was The Chronicles of Clovis, at 14,000; the entire collection sold a total of 66,230. Publisher's Weekly, January 10, 1930, pp. 223–224. In a review for the Bookman in November 1927, L. P. Hartley wrote, "The Westminster Alice can and will be read for its own sake."

69
"Deep as first love" and "examine yourself" Hector's commonplace book, Bryan.

69
"Man was a being" and "The evening darkened" Ibid.

70
"Mrs. Saunders, sauntering" "The Blood-Feud of Toad-Water," Russia (WG, January 26, 1901).

70
". . . Hector and I sometimes had plans" Munro, p. 674.

71
Pouring crumpled paper. Bryan.

71
"The duck was a bird" Munro, p. 674.

72
"Aunt Tom came to visit" Ibid.

72
Charlie signed letters "Highlander." Bryan.

72
"Travelling with Aunt Tom" Munro, p. 675.

CHAPTER 6. THE STAMPEDING OF LADY BASTABLE (1901–1902)

Page 75
"I did it" "Reginald," Reginald (WG, September 28, 1901).

76
"Young men of your brilliant attractions" Ibid.

77
"I hate posterity" "Reginald on the Academy," Reginald (WG, June 2, 1902).

77
"No woman should ever be quite accurate." Wilde, Oscar, *The Importance of Being Earnest.*

77
"To have reached thirty" "Reginald on the Academy," Reginald (WG, June 2, 1902).

77
"When a woman marries again" Wilde, Oscar, *The Picture of Dorian Gray.*

77
"No really provident woman" "Reginald on Besetting Sins," Reginald (WG, April 22, 1903).

77
"There is no sin" Wilde, Oscar, *The Critic as Artist.*

77
"Scandal is merely" "Reginald at the Carlton," Reginald (WG, March 24, 1903).

77
"They say when good Americans" Wilde, Oscar, *A Woman of No Importance.*

77
"She believed in the healthy" "Reginald's Choir Treat," Reginald (WG, June 24, 1902).

77
Life is unfair. Among others to make the observation was John F. Kennedy at a news conference, Washington, D.C., March 21, 1962. Cited in *Memorable Quotations of John F. Kennedy*, compiled by Maxwell Meyersohn (New York, Thomas Y. Crowell & Co., 1965).

77
"Life is unfair, for which" Wilde, Oscar, *Epigrams* (New York, Lamb Publishing Co., 1909).

78
"I can resist everything" Wilde, Oscar, *Lady Windermere's Fan.*

78
"Why are women so fond" "Reginald," Reginald (WG, September 28, 1901.)

78
"I wish it to be distinctly" "Reginald on Christmas Presents," Reginald (WG, Dec. 18, 1901).

78
"There is my Aunt Agatha" Ibid.

79
"I am *not* collecting" Ibid.

79
"No boy who had brought himself up" Ibid.

79
"The Political Jungle Book" and the "Not-So Stories." WG, February 11, 1902; May 23, 1902; October 9, 1903; October 15, 1902; November 5, 1902.

80
"The Woman Who Never Should." WG, July 22, 1902.

81
Hector's inscriptions. Bryan.

81
"To be clever" "Reginald on the Academy," Reginald (WG, June 2, 1902).

81
" 'After all,' said the Duchess" "Reginald at the Theatre," Reginald (WG, July 17, 1902).

82
"a frock that's made at home" "Reginald on House-Parties," Reginald.

82
"I told her whole crowds" Ibid.

82
"Beauty is only sin deep" "Reginald's Choir Treat," Reginald (WG, June 24, 1902).

82
"Never be a pioneer." Ibid.

83
"A very pleasant suburb" "Reginald at the Theatre," Reginald; see note, p. 98.
83
"Personally, I think the Jews" "Reginald on Worries," Reginald.
83
One writer who knew Hector. Travers.
84
The *Morning Post*. Hindle, Wilfred, *The Morning Post* (London, George Routledge & Sons, 1937).

CHAPTER 7. THE YARKAND MANNER (1902–1904)

Page 86
Balkans held by Turks. Jelavich, Charles and Barbara, *The Balkans* (Englewood Cliffs, N. J., Prentice-Hall, 1965), p. 67.
87
Miss Stone kidnaped. Mylonas, George E., *The Balkan States,* (St. Louis, Eden Publishing House, 1947), p. 83.
87
"I am within sight" MP, October 2, 1902.
88
Kipling at rifle range. MP, August 4, 1902.
88
"The Kaimakam of this town" MP, October 2, 1902.
88
"The majority of Albanians" Ibid.
88
"I hear that Europe" MP, October 8, 1902.
88
"I asked the news" MP, October 9, 1902.
89
"The 'slava' or family saint's day" MP, November 29, 1912.
90
"the social hub of the local universe." Munro, p. 677.
90
"When his maternal grandmother" "Reginald in Russia," Russia.
90
"Cards are such a waste" "The Stake," Beasts (MP, April 29, 1913).
90
"None of my children" "Clovis on Parental Responsibilities," Beasts (WG, May 3, 1913).
90
"I have voluminous discussions" Munro, p. 677.

91
"On two descending tiers" MP, January 28, 1903.

92
"The frontier monastery of Rilo" MP, February 13, 1903.

92
"Without political bias" MP, March 4, 1903.

93
"As I have previously contended" MP, March 5, 1903.

94
Henry Brailsford. Interview with Eva Maria Brailsford, his widow, London, July 1979.

94
Brailsford and Munro as schoolboys. Lambert, p. 29.

94
"the women are not striking" Brailsford, Henry, Macedonia (London, Methuen, 1906), p. 110.

95
"This is the most delightfully" Munro, p. 677.

95
First byline. MP, April 28, 1903; Munro filed the story from Uskub on April 25.

96
"Under the nose" MP, May 1, 1903.

96
"While traveling from Uskub" MP, May 2, 1903.

96
"The reports which reached Uskub" Munro, p. 679.

98
"There is a 'Young Turk' " Ibid., p. 678.

98
"A highly coloured account" Ibid.

98
"In company with other correspondents" MP, May 8, 1903.

99
"Possibly they possess the virtue" Ibid.

100
H. W. Nevinson. Essays, Poems and Tales of Henry W. Nevinson, edited by H. N. Brailsford (London, Victor Gollancz, 1948).

100
"It is difficult" MP, May 14, 1903.

101
"Since I last wrote" MP, May 15, 1903.

102
"As the earth under the roadway" MP, May 20, 1903.

102
"War between Turkey and Bulgaria" MP, May 22, 1903.

102
"Sofia would simply become" Ibid.

102
"I have telegraphic information" MP, May 23, 1903.

103
"A statement is current" Ibid.

103
"You cannot permanently imprison" Ibid.

104
"Poverty and panic." MP, May 27, 1903.

104
Nevinson's description of guerrilla war. Nevinson, H. W., *More Changes, More Chances* (London, Nisbet & Co., 1925), p. 11.

104
" 'I wonder,' said Reginald" "Reginald at the Theatre." Reginald (WG, July 17, 1902).

105
"the War-at-Any-Price party" MP, May 30, 1903.

105
"The policy of asking for less" MP, June 2, 1903.

106
"I do not invoke" Ibid.

106
Bulgarian envoy's scheme. MP, June 5, 1903.

108
"The buildings are, indeed" MP, June 13, 1903.

109
"Wandering boys from Tzigane" MP, June 20, 1903.

109
"I had seen a King-choosing" Ibid.

109
"The Kingdom of Servia" MP, June 26, 1903.

110
The people of Crete "make more history" "The Jesting of Arlington Stringham," Clovis (WG, August 20, 1910).

110
"The Eastern Balkans" MP, July 13, 1903.

111
Munro's Paula Tanqueray. MP, July 20, 1903.

111
"the peasant, all the world over" MP, July 25, 1903.

111
Macedonians call for revolt. Mylonas, *The Balkan States,* p. 83; see note, p. 105.

112
Two Reginald stories. "Reginald at the Carlton," Reginald (WG, March 24, 1903); "Reginald on Besetting Sins," Reginald (WG, April 22, 1903).

112
"The cook was a good cook" "Reginald on Besetting Sins."

112
"Reginald closed his eyes" "Reginald's Drama," Reginald (WG, September 8, 1903).

112
"Talking about tariffs" "Reginald on Tariffs," Reginald (WG, November 6, 1903).

113
"Spadework Out of Monmouth," MP, November 30, 1903.

113
"The Angel and His Lost Michael," MP, November 16, 1903.

113
St. Nicholas in the Balkans. MP, December 21, 1903.

113
"Mrs. Babwold wears" "Reginald's Christmas Revel," Reginald (WG, December 22, 1903).

CHAPTER 8. THE BYZANTINE OMELETTE (1904–1907)

Page 114
De La Rue's "Fingershape" diary. Lane.

116
"A payment of two dinars" MP, January 26, 1904.

117
Questions in writing. MP, February 6, 1904.

117
"After hanging fire" MP, February 11, 1904.

117
Munro to Vienna. MP, March 5, 1904.

117
"The Innocence of Reginald," Reginald (WG, April 6, 1904).

117
"young (at present)" "The Brilliant Young Man," signed "Digamma," WG, January 16, 1904.

118
"Reginald!" "The Innocence of Reginald"; see note, p. 149.

118
Impressions of Warsaw. MP, April 5, 1904.

119
"It is as though" MP, April 7, 1904.

119
"which gave me a view" MP, May 5, 1904.

120
Ethel Munro's suitor. Bryan.

121

"Omar Khazzam." *Londonderry Sentinel,* copy in possession of Juniper Bryan.

121

Munro swims with schoolboy. Munro, p. 681.

121

"He could not get them" Ibid.

121

"On the most scorching" Ibid.

121

"The amateur valet" Ibid.

121

"Think it over" Ibid., p. 682.

122

"It is not a question" MP, May 10, 1904.

122

Russia's goals. MP, May 18, 1904.

123

"Khunguz." MP, May 24, 1904.

124

"To the Jew in Warsaw" MP, June 3, 1904.

124

Munro leaves Warsaw. Lane, diary.

125

Reynolds' aunt. Interview, Michael A. Hewson, London, August 1979.

125

"They remain a race apart" Reynolds, Rothay, *The Story of Warsaw* (London, Hutchinson & Co., 1916), p. 56.

126

" 'Good Heavens!' " Reynolds, Rothay "The Triumph of Wladislaw," *Bystander,* November 8, 1911, p. 294.

126

"You are Italian" Reynolds, Rothay, *The Gondola* (London, Mills and Boon, 1913), p. 3.

126

"Give me the old days" Ibid., p. 263.

127

"If three-fourths" MP, August 16, 1904.

127

Reynolds' memoir. Reynolds, Rothay, *My Russian Year* (London, Mills and Boon, 1913), pp. 18–19.

127

"The peccadilloes he concealed" Ibid., p. 156.

128

"one of the brightest hands" *Athenaeum,* October 15, 1904, p. 515.

128

"Tubby." Street, G. S., *The Autobiography of a Boy* (London, Elkin Mathews & John Lane, 1894.) Tubby, whose name was Harry, had been expelled from two private and one public schools and sent down from Oxford in his third year. A sample of his language illustrates the difference from Reginald's: "If I pained her now, it was that she might escape a greater pain when her love increased as mine diminished," p. 6.

128
"The *Athenaeum*" Munro, p. 682.

129
"As the crowd is becoming" MP, November 5, 1904.

130
Youths ripe for socialism to propaganda. MP, November 12, 1904.

130
Hector on farming. MP, December 3, 1904.

130
"The cleavage between Russian" MP, January 9, 1905.

131
"There is no force" MP, December 30, 1904.

131
The look in Munro's eyes. Muriel Munro, Charlie's wife, described the look to Professor Robert Drake, now of the University of Tennessee at Knoxville, when he interviewed her in Belfast in 1961. Drake, Robert, *"Saki: Some Problems and a Bibliography," English Fiction in Transition* (Lafayette, Indiana, 1962).

131
Georgy Gapon. Harcave, Sidney, *First Blood* (London, The Bodley Head, 1964), pp. 70–73; Sablinsky, Walter, *The Road to Bloody Sunday* (Princeton, N.J., Princeton University Press, 1976), pp. 34–55.

133
Hector anticipated disappointment. MP, January 23, 1905.

133
Ethel Munro returns to hotel. Munro, pp. 683–684.

134
Munro made a note. MP, January 23, 1905.

135
Munro's insolence. Munro, p. 684.

135
"You cannot beat the Japanese" MP, January 24, 1905.

135
Foraging for food. Munro, p. 684.

135
"with excitement as a sauce." Ibid.

136
Gapon in Paris. MP, February 22, 1905.

136
Trépoff and correspondents. Munro, p. 685.

137
Casualties. Standard reference works, including the Encyclopaedia Britannica.

137
Opera "rule." Reynolds, pp. 48–49. See note, p. 161.
137
Had Voltaire lived now. MP, February 10, 1905.
137
"The *hors-d'oeuvres*" MP, March 1, 1905.
137
"Parisian toilettes." MP, March 24, 1905.
138
"Any relaxation of anti-Jew" MP, May 1, 1905.
138
"A militantly defensive Jewish" MP, May 13, 1905.
138
"Incessantly sipping syrup-sweetened" MP, August 22, 1905.
139
"In British political circles" MP, May 25, 1905.
139
Brailsford's trial. *Daily News,* London, July 27, 1905.
140
"If a good understanding" MP, July 29, 1905.
140
"A young officer" Munro, p. 686.
141
"lithe, athletic specimens" MP, September 15, 1905.
141
"anything savouring of serious" MP, October 30, 1905.
141
"the 'red' Socialists" MP, November 9, 1905.
141
New Year's Eve. Under the Julian calendar of the Tsar, New Year's
Eve fell on what for Hector and the *Morning Post* was January 13, 1906.
141
"Nearly every woman." MP, January 15, 1906.
142
"What particular stage" MP, January 17, 1906.
142
"An individual who is a bully" MP, January 22, 1906.
143
"The police have unlimited" MP, January 24, 1906.
143
Tolstoy interview. MP, February 6, 1906.
143
"devilish" Ibid.
144
"a flowing and elaborate" MP, March 12, 1906.
144
"the scarlet pennons" MP, May 11, 1906.
145
Reuter reports. MP, May 14, 15, 18, 1906.

145
"Of the combined total acreage" MP, June 9, 1906.
145
"Russia is unmistakably" MP, July 5, 1906.
146
"Russia demanded statesmanship." MP, June 23, 1906.
146
Reynolds on St. Petersburg. Reynolds, *My Russian Year,* p. 19; see note, p. 163.

CHAPTER 9. THE UNKINDEST BLOW (1907–1909)

Page 147
"original." Munro, p. 687.
147
"comparatively trifling." MP, January 21, 1907.
148
Munro's influenza. Munro, p. 688.
148
"a dry, burning, consuming passion" MP, February 5, 1907.
148
"The purpose is to present" MP, April 19, 1907.
148
"The first-night audience" MP, March 1, 1907.
149
"they could be found" MP, May 28, 1907.
149
"Madame Liane de Pougy" MP, February 6, 1907.
149
"There are, of course" MP, March 20, 1907.
149
Father's death. Charles Augustus Munro died June 27, 1907; see note, p. 1.
150
"As the ladies rose" Bassington, XIV.
151
"maligned green Muse." MP, July 6, 1907.
151
"It will be most useful" MP, July 15, 1907.
151
"possessed a temperament." Munro, p. 689.
152
Munro as shop clerk. Ibid.
152
Man mistaken for department store clerk. "The Dreamer," Beasts (MP, Jan. 21, 1913).

152
"Quail Seed," Toys (MP, December 26, 1911).
152
"to go directly" Ibid., p. 512.
152
"said horrid things" "The Soul of Laploshka," Russia (WG, May 8, 1909).
153
Munro deprived of father's appreciation. Munro, p. 688.
153
Father's bequest. Will of Charles Augustus Munro. Somerset House, London.
153
"Hawkers did a thriving trade" MP, June 5, 1908.
153
"Indirect taxes" MP, August 17, 1908.
154
"The Macedonian of Bulgar" WG. October 12, 1908.
154
MP's coverage of Wright. MP, August 25, 1908.
154
Munro's sketches. Lane.
154
"A large painting" MP, April 15, 1908.
154
"Georges Rötig has" MP, May 1, 1908.
154
"The marble group" MP, May 7, 1908.
155
"superb" MP, April 4, 1907.
155
"wonderfully well-suited" MP, April 10, 1908.
155
"the magic of her own personality" MP, December 25, 1907.
155
"The playwright's reputation" MP, May 12, 1908.
155
"To understand 'Peter Pan' " MP, June 17, 1908.
156
"Life is largely made up" MP, February 8, 1908.

CHAPTER 10. ON APPROVAL (1909–1911)

Page 157
Cottage for Ethel. In his will, drafted on May 6, 1913, Munro left the cottage to his sister. He described it as "freehold cottage and land

known as 'Warcot' Woodland Way Caterham in the county of Surrey."
He left the royalties on his work divided equally between Charlie and
Ethel. Will, Somerset House, London.

157
Munro liked Lyons Corner Houses. Reynolds, p. xv.

158
Munro wrote as though sketching. Ibid.

158
"The Sex That Doesn't Shop," Russia (WG, March 27, 1909).

158
"Gabriel-Ernest," Russia (WG, May 29, 1909).

160
Ackerley, J. R., *My Father and Myself* (New York, Coward, McCann,
1968).

162
"The Saint and the Goblin," Russia (WG, January 4, 1902).

162
"bitter pill with the coating inside" Quoted in the *Spectator*'s review of
Cabbages and Kings, January 27, 1912.

162
"The Reticence of Lady Anne," Russia.

163
Rents in 1909–1910. The Morning Post of June 25, 1910, advertised a
flat at 35.shillings per week as "suite w/bathroom, lavatory (h and c)
self contained; newly and luxuriously furnished; electric lift;
valeting."

163
History of clubs. Nevill, Ralph, *London Clubs* (London, Chatto and
Windus, 1911).

163
Cocoa Tree. Ibid., pp. 128–132.

164
"the great chair" Ibid., p. 149.

164
"a club is a weapon" Ibid., p. 135.

164
Ethel in London. Munro. p. 690.

164
"Lame dogs" Ibid., p. 715.

164
"Earth is the best thing" Ibid., p. 689.

165
"She had a strong natural bias" "Cross Currents," Russia (WG, September 18, 1909).

165
"spoke of several duchesses" Ibid.

165
"Thank you for your sympathy" "The Baker's Dozen," Russia (*Journal of the Leinster Regiment,* October 1909, p. 33).

165
"The Mouse," Russia (WG, October 23, 1909).

166
"The Baker's Dozen."

166
"The fresh cheque" Lane. Munro copied his answer to a letter in the margins of the original correspondence.

166
"We write to inquire" Ibid.

166
"Thank you very much" Ibid.

167
John Lane's background. May, J. Lewis, *John Lane and the Nineties* (London, John Lane The Bodley Head, 1936). Also, Travers Ben, *Vale of Laughter* (London, Geoffrey Bles, 1957).

167
Corvo's vermin. May.

167
"For behold!" *The Yellow Book, A Selection,* compiled by Norman Denny (London, The Bodley Head, 1949), p. 137.

167
Lane concerned about Beardsley. May, p. 79.

168
"It killed the 'Yellow Book' " Ibid., p. 80.

168
Shelley, an office boy. Croft-Cooke, Rupert, *The Unrecorded Life of Oscar Wilde* (New York, David McKay & Co., Inc., 1972), pp. 128–133. Also, Travers. Other young men in the Lane office called Edward Shelley "Miss Oscar" and "Mrs. Wilde."

168
Contract terms with John Lane. Lane.

169
"Good fellow" Robert Drake. Before the letter was lost, Drake read the account William Mercer supplied for Lambert's introduction to Saki's stories.

169
Ben Travers. Travers.

170
"Tobermory," Clovis (WG, November 27, 1909). A WG copy emended by hand by Hector is in the Lane collection.

170
"was so depraved at seventeen" Ibid.

170
Waugh's criticism. Waugh, Evelyn, "Introduction," *The Unbearable Bassington* (London, Eyre & Spottiswoode, 1947).

171
Highland legends. Wilde, Lady Francesca Speranza, *Ancient Legends, Mystic Charms and Superstitions of Ireland* (London, Chatto & Windus, 1899).

171
Ethel asked that Tommy be killed. Bryan.

173
"Nursed a violent but perfectly respectable" "Cross Currents," Russia (WG, September 18, 1909).

173
Milne's examples. Milne, A. A., "Introduction," *The Chronicles of Clovis* (London, John Lane The Bodley Head, 1937).

173
"apprehensively at the waif's face" "Gabriel Ernest."

174
"The Lumber-Room," Beasts (MP, October 14, 1913); "The Boar-Pig," Beasts (MP, August 20, 1912); "The Penance," Toys (WG, September 24, 1910).

174
"The Treasure-Ship," Beasts (MP, February 20, 1912).

174
"Mrs. Packletide's Tiger," Clovis; "The Recessional," Clovis (WG, July 8, 1911).

176
"Cousin Teresa," Beasts (MP, March 11, 1913).

177
"The Secret Sin of Septimus Brope," Clovis.

177
"Filboid Studge, the Story of a Mouse That Helped," Clovis (*Bystander*, December 7, 1910).

177
"Fate," Toys.

177
"Three weeks later" "Filboid Studge."

179
"How you bore me" "The Secret Sin of Septimus Brope," Clovis.

179
"It's just a couplet." "Cousin Teresa."

179
Beerbohm on Churchill. *Bystander*, May 22, 1912, p. 385.

180
Diaghilev tour. Lifar, Serge, *Diaghilev* (London, Putnam, 1940).

181
"In Russia" Munro, p. 690.

181
"What is it?" Ibid.

181
Mercer's reaction to Munro's friends. Lambert, p. 35.

182
"The wit knows that his place" Leacock, Stephen, *Humour and Humanity* (London, Thornton Buttersworth, 1937), p. 14.

182
Hector not asked to banquet. Travers.

183
Word circulating that Hector was homosexual. Ibid.

183
Duchess of Manchester; Lady Londonderry; Lady de Gray. Benson, E.F., *As We Were* (London, Longmans, Green & Co., 1930), pp. 171–188.

184
Lady St. Helier taken with Munro. Lambert, p. 34.

184
"went in for slumming" "Reginald's Drama," Reginald (WG, September 8, 1903).

184
"One is confronted" Lady St. Helier (Mary Jeune), *Memories of Fifty Years* (London, Edward Arnold, 1909), p. v.

184
"We lived more simply" Ibid., p. 149.

185
Tennyson's letter. Ibid., p. 163.

185
"Once, indeed, I heard a guest," Ibid., p. 186.

185
"Constance—one of those strapping" "Esmé," Clovis (WG, December 17, 1910).

185
Vending machine story. Guthrie, T. A., *A Long Retrospect* (London, Oxford University Press, 1936).

186
Ethel appalled by *Design for Living*. Bryan.

187
"an air of peaceful contentedness" Northcote, Lady Rosalind, *Devon, Its Moorlands, Streams and Coasts* (London, Chatto & Windus, 1908), p. 224.

187
Responsibility for Ethel. Lambert, p. 36.

187
"Mrs. Paly-Paget:" "The Baker's Dozen."

187
Locket from Cyril. Bryan.

188
Ethel's gold tie pin. Ibid.

188
"To the Lynx Kitten" Clovis.

189
The Hoppé photograph appeared in the posthumous collection, *The Toys of Peace*.

189
"To look at, Mr. Munro" The *Bodleian* interview, undated, was supplied to the author by Christopher Radmall, the London bookseller.

CHAPTER 11. THE IMAGE OF THE LOST SOUL (1911—1912)

Page 192
Waugh's analysis.

192
"Mr. Munro, who is a real humorist" *Times Literary Supplement,* November 7, 1912.

193
"tapestry painting." Munro, p. 691.

193
"There is no greater compliment." Introduction to the "Omnibus" edition of Saki. See Munro in Key to Sources.

193
"We will invoke" Munro, p. 690.

194
"Here we go round" Ibid., p. 691.

194
"Foreigners must be puzzled" Ibid.

195
"There was a pleasing serenity" Bassington, I.

195
Flemish painting. Reynolds, p. x.

195
"Francesca herself, if pressed," Bassington, I.

196
"There is one thing," Reynolds, p. x.

196
"Sometimes they sober down." Bassington, I.

197
" 'Nonsense; boys are Nature's' " Ibid., II.

197
"In appearance" Ibid.

198
"Comus drew the desired line" Ibid.

199
Munro insisted on the title. Travers.

200
Scene with Molly McQuade. Bassington, V.

200
Scene with Tom Keriway. Ibid., VIII.

202
" 'Swans were very pleased' " Ibid., VI.

202
" 'Four shillings and fivepence' " IX.

203
"one of those human flies" Ibid., VII.

203
"just receiving due recognition" Ibid., X.

203
" 'The gratitude of those poor" Ibid., XIV.
204
"one of those naturally stagnant" Ibid., VII.
204
" 'such an exquisite rural retreat' " Ibid.
204
"a professed Socialist" Ibid., IV.
204
"gave up the attempt" Ibid., VII.
204
" 'If you had led your highest" Ibid.
205
"Tons of money" Ibid., IV.
205
" 'Whenever I hear his music" Ibid., XIII.
206
" 'And there, dear lady' " Ibid.
206
"I seem fated" Munro, p. 688.
206
"So these people think" Bassington, XV.
206
"She had a devoted husband" Ibid., IX.
207
"Presently two girls" Ibid., XVI.
208
"This story has no moral." Ibid., first page.

CHAPTER 12. SHOCK TACTICS (1912–1913)

Page 209
Family at Carrig Cnoc. Bryan.
210
"What's got Swat?" Osborn, E. B., "The Memory of Saki," *Daily Telegraph,* February 21, 1919.
211
Ethel's dolls. Bryan.
211
"Oh, you mean creature!" Interview, Ida McKay (Mrs. Jimmy Hemphill), Portstewart, Northern Ireland, June 1979.
212
Charlie's rhymes. Bryan.
212
Munro and the fiend. Ibid.

213
Travers chose "Dusk." Travers.

213
" 'To lose an hotel" "Dusk," Beasts (MP, March 12, 1912).

213
"Dusk, to his mind" Ibid.

214
"The Open Window," Beasts (WG, November 18, 1911).

214
"The Unrest-Cure," Clovis.

214
"You may wonder" "The Open Window."

215
" 'Here they are" Ibid.

216
"Romance at short notice" Ibid.

216
"The Lull," Beasts (MP, September 17, 1912).

217
"The Story-Teller," Beasts (MP, September 2, 1913).

217
"The plain person cannot subsist" *Spectator*, July 11, 1914, p. 61.

217
"The smaller girl created" "The Story-Teller."

218
"The first thing that it saw" Ibid.

219
"She's leaving her present house" "Louise," Toys (MP, June 16, 1914).

219
"You're looking nicer" "Esmé."

220
"What an odious" "The Hedgehog," Toys (MP, August 19, 1913).

220
" 'I don't know why" "Wratislav," Clovis.

220
" 'Is your maid called Florence?' " "The Secret Sin of Septimus Brope," Clovis.

221
"Dobrinton was bitten" "Cross Currents," Russia (WG, September 18, 1909).

221
"At that moment" "The Seventh Pullet," Beasts (MP, October 31, 1911).

221
" 'Waldo is one of those people' " "The Feast of Nemesis," Beasts (MP, February 25, 1913).

221
"I was quite disappointed" Munro, p. 663.

222
Mustard on mince pie. Ibid., p. 687.
222
Staged quarrel with Osborn.
222
"I had a hearty supper" Reynolds, p. xv.
222
"The huge antler spikes" "The Music on the Hill," Clovis.
223
"small half-naked gipsy brat" "Esmé."
223
"Sredni Vashtar," Clovis (WG, May 28, 1910).
224
"Sredni Vashtar went forth." Ibid.

CHAPTER 13. THE PENANCE (1913)

Page 225
Ten Cinematographs. Read, Donald, *Edwardian England* (London, Harrap, 1972), p. 66.
225
"Old Tar," WG, October 25, 1913.
225
"The Indians," WG, February 7, 1914.
225–26
September Morn. " 'Matinée de Septembre' by Paul Chabas, a beautiful picture in the Paris salon," *Bystander,* May 12, 1912, p. 390.
226
Saki not representative. George Dangerfield makes the point in *The Strange Death of Liberal England* (London, Macgibbon & Kee, 1966), p. 65–66: "There was talk of wild young people in London, more wild and less witty than you would ever guess from the novels of Saki. . . ."
226
Virginia Woolf recalled the era in *Mr. Bennett and Mrs. Brown* (1924): "In or about December, 1910, human character changed." Quoted in *Lytton Strachey* by Michael Holroyd (London, Heinemann, 1968), vol. ii, p. 3.
226
"people in love" *The Letters of Rupert Brooke,* edited by Geoffrey Keynes (New York, Harcourt, Brace & World, 1968), p. 173.
226
"For a single instant" *Bystander,* April 22, 1914, p. 192.
226
Baroches, bicycles, bulky parcels. Gore, John, *Edwardian Scrapbook* (London, Evans Brothers, 1951).

227
Spires, paneled rooms, and shaven lawns. Ibid.

227
"Since our informal conversation" Lane.

228
" 'War between two such civilized' " William, III.

229
"I am to a great extent" Ibid.

230
" 'I know, I know' " Ibid.

230
"Plarsey had never been able" Ibid., XI.

231
"was a young man" Ibid., I.

232
"He was a bachelor" Ibid., VI.

232
"He had a keen, clever" Ibid., XI.

232
"One thing you may be sure of" Ibid.

233
"The affairs of the county" Ibid., XIII.

234
"And in the pleasant May" Ibid., XIX.

234
"purely classical language" Munro, p. 673.

234
"went through a literary" Ibid.

235
Munro's jotting on a bill. Lane.

235
"To feminine acquaintances" William, XIX.

235
"remarkable *tour de force*" *Times Literary Supplement,* November 20,
1913.

235
"Dear Sir" Bryan.

CHAPTER 14. THE MAPPINED LIFE (1914)

Page 237
"Karl-Ludwig's Window," "The Death Trap," are printed in vol. ii of
the "Omnibus" edition of Saki. See Munro in Key to Notes.

237
Munro took *The Watched Pot* to Harrison. Gillen, Charles H., *Saki*
(New York, Twayne Publishers, 1969), p. 126.

238
"You have written for the theatre?"

238
Ben Travers on Saki as playwright. Travers.

238
Munro and Maude disagreed over plot. "Omnibus" edition, vol. ii, p. 363.

239
"This suit I've got on" The Watched Pot, "Omnibus" edition, vol. ii, p. 384.

239
"Things that are lent to you" Ibid.

239
"Agatha is one of those unaccountable" Ibid., p. 370.

239
"A husband with asthma" Ibid., p. 376.

239
"I dislike the idea of women" Ibid., p. 402.

240
"But if I had a really nice" Ibid., p. 376.

240
"a fatal gift" Ibid., p. 371.

240
"Brevity is the soul" "The Match-Maker," Clovis.

240
Comparisons with Maugham, Coward. Gillen, p. 133.

241
"A suffragette Lobelia was" Ibid., p. 138.

241
Hector at the Trocadero. Ibid., p. 141.

241
Nijinsky and Liberal Whip. Bystander, July 17, 1912, p. 118.

241
"I am not a happy man" Bystander, July 31, 1912, p. 230.

242
" 'You and I have this much in common" Bystander, August 14, 1912, p. 330.

243
"under an impenetrable crust" MP, January 30, 1913.

244
" 'Doubtless there are many' " "Potted Parliament," Outlook, February 21, 1914.

244
"Rather annoying" Ibid., February 28, 1914.

244
"Nothing is more discouraging" The Watched Pot, "Omnibus" edition, vol. ii, p. 413.

244
"with his voice of honey" Outlook, February 21, 1914.

244
"a samovar" Ibid., March 28, 1914.

244
"would really be invaluable" Ibid., June 27, 1914.

244
"armed with his meanness" Ibid., February 21, 1914.

244
"One understands of course that" Ibid., July 4, 1914.

245
"delivered with the gusto" Ibid., March 7, 1914.

245
"intervened in the guise" Ibid.

245
"Russell sat on the Treasury" Ibid., February 28, 1914.

245
"The country had been brought" Ibid.

245
"In making a charge of neglect" Ibid., March 14, 1914.

245
"As Clode has aptly" Ibid., April 11, 1914.

245
"It used to be required" Ibid., May 9, 1914.

246
"If George III. had only" Ibid., July 18, 1914.

246
Munro imitating Bernhardt. Guthrie, p. 332.

246
"Dear Lady Charnwood" Letter in the collection of Harlan L. Umansky, Union City, New Jersey.

247
Saturday night amusements. Munro, p. 708.

247
"For one memorable and uncomfortable" Munro's dispatch is dated Monday, August 3, but appeared in the *Outlook* of August 8, 1914.

248
"Many of them are men" Ibid.

CHAPTER 15. THE QUEST (1914–1916)

Page 250
"Cheese, no butter" Reynolds, p. xvi.

250–51
Munro watched marching youths. Ibid., p. xxi.

251
"And I have always looked forward." Ibid., xvii. On a scrap of paper

that has survived in Mr. Max Reinhardt's collection of Saki memorabilia, Munro either composed or copied out this verse: "Throw out a voice to kingly boys / to call them to t fight / t tt comfortness of unsuccess / that bids to dead goodnight."

251

"Enroled." Bryan.

251

Gossip at John Lane. Travers.

252

Hector sent for life of Jesus. Lane. The book was *Jesus of Nazareth*, published by Harrison and Sons at 5 shillings.

252

Hector reads Flecker. "Letters of Miss Ethel M. Munro," Appendix, Spear, George James, *The Satire of Saki* (New York, Exposition Press, 1963).

252

"Humour" Flecker, James Elroy, *The Best Man* (Oxford, Holywell Press, 1906).

252

"When even lovers" Flecker, James Elroy, *The Golden Journey to Samarkand* (London, Max Goschen, 1913), p. 4.

252

"forgot a few years" Bryan.

252.

King Edward's Horse. *The History of King Edward's Horse*, edited by Lt.-Col. Lionel James (London, Sifton, Praed & Co., 1921).

253

"Dear Lane" Lane.

254

Twenty-second Battalion of Royal Fusiliers. Exhibit. Also, Stone, Christopher, *History of the 22nd Royal Fusiliers* (Privately printed for the Old Comrades Association of the battalion, 1923).

255

Munro teaches German. Munro, p. 700.

255

Munro offered commission. Ibid.

255

Munro distrusted himself as officer. Reynolds, p. xxii.

255

Charnwood took offense. Dated November 26, 1916, Charnwood's letter to the *Westminster Gazette* added, "In his own case, moreover, he discovered a peculiar power to calm the fears and raise the spirit of young and ignorant soldiers, and he was not willing to forgo the opportunities of easy intercourse on equal terms in which he could exercise that power."

256

"The funeral went off all right" Lane.

256

"our cousins." These appear to be the daughters of Hector

Bruce Munro, who are listed in documents at Somerset House, London, as Margaret Bessie Stuart, Helen B. Thomas and Effie Munro.

256–57
Move to Horsham; Munro as orderly. Munro, p. 701.

257
Army menu. For week of April 25, 1915. War Museum.

257
"We have a good deal of fun" Munro, p. 701.

257
"The Toys of Peace," Toys.

258
"An Old Love" MP, April 23, 1915; quoted in full by Reynolds, pp. xviii–xxi.

259
"You may imagine" Munro, p. 701.

259
"One must admit."

260
"never seem too tired" Munro, p. 701.

260
"Diary of the War" and other articles. Exhibit. *22nd Battalion of the Royal Fusiliers' Fortnightly Gazette.*

260
"Sarky." Telephone interview, Roland Whipp, Rickmansworth, England, August 1979.

261
"Many of their comrades of the stage" Exhibit. *Fortnightly Gazette,* May 10, 1915. The article is headed "Pau-Puk-Keewis by 'Saki,' 'A' Company." The title came from Longfellow's "Hiawatha," in which a brave is willing to be called fainthearted and cowardly in return for an exemption from war.

261
"The Soldier's Guide to Cinema," Exhibit. *"Fortnightly Gazette Souvenir Number,"* June 26, 1915.

262
"On Being Company Orderly Corporal," Exhibit. *Fortnightly Gazette,* June 7, 1915. Reprinted, with the stern photograph of Munro, in the *Bystander,* June 23, 1915, and in Munro, pp. 702–704.

263
"Are we downhearted?" Stone, p. 21.

263
Munro pretends to be drunk. Munro, pp. 709–10.

263
"My dear little Wolf" Bryan.

264
Munro tells youth about wolves. Munro, p. 704.

264
Battalion prepares to move. Exhibit. Stone, p. 18.

264
"bean soup" Ibid., p. 26.
264
"Incidentally, anyone" Ibid., p. 25.
264
"After the long months" Munro, p. 704.
265
Channel crossing. Exhibit. Stone, p. 27.
265
"My parting words" Stone, p. 55.
265
"I am writing this" Ibid., p. 28.
266
Munro sent for training. Munro, p. 705.
266
Munro as model soldier. Reynolds, p. xxii.
266
Munro dresses down Spikesman. Munro, p. 710.
266
Munro raised a laugh. Exhibit. *Mufti,* a postwar publication of the Twenty-second Battalion, February 1920.
266
"O death, where is thy sting?" Ibid., Summer 1963.
266
"I had a longish" Munro, p. 705.
267
Christmas Eve 1915. Stone, p. 29.
267
"While Shepherds watched their flocks" Munro, p. 705.
267
"My dear Felicia" Bryan.
268
"We are holding" Munro, p. 706.
268
Details of Munro's near-miss. Munro, p. 711.
269
"In about three years' time" Ibid., p. 706.
269
My Slav Friends (London, Mills and Boon, 1916).
269
"The French have been saying." Munro, p. 706.
269
"What on earth" Reynolds, p. xxii.
270
"I am in very good health." Munro, p. 706.
270
"a perfectly good ear" *Mufti,* June 1951.
270
Creeper's Club. Ibid., Summer 1962.

270
The Back Kitchen Club. Munro, p. 712.

271
Munro on leave in London. Ibid., p. 707.

271
"The dross" Reynolds, p. xxiii.

271
"It would have been" Munro, p. 707.

272
"Kill a good few" Ibid.

272
"I join with" Bryan.

272
"to be the more treasured" Heseltine, Olive, *Guardian,* London, June 3, 1919.

272
"We doubt" *Observer,* London, February 23, 1919.

272
"Is still a lie" *Daily News,* London, February 10, 1919.

273
"Saki will give us" Reynolds, p. ix.

273
Squire on Saki. Charlie Munro pasted this review with others into a scrapbook now in the possession of his daughter, Juniper Bryan.

273
"He had great gifts" *Spectator,* London, March 22, 1919.

CHAPTER 16. "DOWN PENS" (1916)

Page 274
"One, a dear, faithful" Munro, p. 708.

274
"Birds on the Western Front" Egg.

275
"being such a misery." Munro, p. 713.

275
"I keep thinking" Ibid., p. 708.

277
"Put that bloody cigarette out." Munro, p. 714. Stone wrote, p. 40, "Among the dead was Sgt. H. Munro ('Saki') a very gallant gentleman, who brought as much honour to the Battalion as that other self-effacing scholar, L. G. Russel-Davies, who had been killed in the blowing in of a dug-out a month before."

Index

A. J. Langguth was born in Minneapolis
in 1933 and graduated from Harvard
College in 1955. He has worked for several
publications, including the *New York Times*.
Mr. Langguth lives in Los Angeles.

4/82